MILLIONS OF WOMEN ARE WAITING TO MEET YOU

MILLIONS OF WOMEN
ARE WAITING TO MEET YOU

A Story of Life, Love and Internet Dating

SEAN THOMAS

BLOOMSBURY

First published in Great Britain in 2006

Extract from 'Consider Yourself' by Lionel Bart
© 1960 LAKEVIEW MUSIC PUBLISHING CO. LTD
of Suite 2.07, Plaza 535 Kings Road, London SW10 0SZ
International Copyright Secured.
All rights Reserved. Used by Permission

Some names and identifying details have been changed,
to protect friends, partners and acquaintances. All the events
in the book happened to the author as described

Bloomsbury Publishing Plc
36 Soho Square
London W1D 3QY

A CIP catalogue record for this book
is available from the British Library

ISBN-13 9780747582199
ISBN 074758219X

10 9 8 7 6 5 4 3 2

Typeset in Sabon by Palimpsest Book Production Limited
Polmont, Stirlingshire

Printed in Great Britain by Clays Ltd, St Ives plc

Bloomsbury Publishing, London, New York and Berlin

The paper this book is printed on is certified by the © 1996
Forest Stewardship Council A.C. (FSC). It is ancient-forest friendly.
The printer holds FSC chain of custody SGS-COC-2061

FSC
Mixed Sources
Product group from well-managed
forests and other controlled sources

Cert no. SGS-COC-2061
www.fsc.org
© 1996 Forest Stewardship Council

For Lenina

Introduction

How do you propose? I mean, what is the best way to propose? What's the right stage in a relationship to do it? Why, how, who? Where? Hello?

I'm stuck. I have this strange feeling that I want to propose to my girlfriend, Claire, right now, right here, on the roof of my flat as we sip warm Spanish champagne. But the momentousness of it is holding me back. I'm thirty-nine years old and it all seems too remarkable, too unexpected and frightening. Frankly, I'd come to the conclusion that this moment, THE moment, might never arrive; and maybe I never wanted it to arrive, for such a long time. And yet somehow the moment seems to have sidled into my life like a sweet little kid sneaking in the back door of the cinema.

I've been thinking of proposing for a while now. I've even had a few daydreams as to the best place. Last week, I had plans to do it in Venice, in a gondola, under a swooning Adriatic moon. The week before that, I considered taking my girlfriend to Paris, where we could do it walking the Tuileries amidst the lilacs. Then I looked at my bank statement and thought that the local park might be nice, as long as it wasn't drizzling. But here I am sitting on the roof of my flat in London and I have a sudden urge to do it anyway, right now, right here.

My sudden urge to propose, and the consequent scuppering of my Venetian daydreams, is perhaps partly based on the proposal experience of a friend of mine. The other day when I was discussing my plans for popping-the-question, he told me his proposal story.

My friend did it properly. He did this big build-up to The Question and took his girlfriend to a beautiful part of Greece. He set up a lovely dinner with candles and chilled retsina and moonlit views of the twinkling Aegean. Then when he leaned forward across the crisp white tablecloth and took his girlfriend's delicate hand and said, 'I have something to say,' his girlfriend started weirdly trembling and then when he said, 'My God what's wrong?' she said, 'You're going to finish with me, aren't you, that's why you've brought me here! You bastard!' With that she went into a spaz-out, disappeared into the loos for three hours, and had to be slowly coaxed out and told that no, her boyfriend wasn't going to finish with her. My friend finally asked the big question in the back of a scruffy minicab as they returned to their Greek hotel.

So what does this tell me? I think it tells me that portentous build-ups to romantic moments can be somewhat counter-productive. And so that's one of the reasons I am suddenly thinking: Now. Here. Do it. A further thought that is egging me on is that somehow this *is* the right place to propose, in a weird way: in the city I have lived in and loved all my life. Next to the loudly humming air-conditioner of the Pizza Paradiso restaurant, next door.

Setting down my wineglass I go over to Claire and we kiss a little. We kiss some more. It's a good stalling tactic. I can keep this up for a while, as I work up the courage to DO IT. But then Claire starts gasping for air and so I have to let her go.

But the urge is still with me; the blind, groping instinct to ask the fateful question. This urge feels a little weird. It's a bit like knowing you're going to throw up when you are a kid. You want it to happen – and yet you don't. Anyway, here it comes. Stepping back, I open my mouth and . . .

And I close my mouth again. Because Claire is squinting at me oddly. And this has got me thinking that maybe she's a bit squiffy, after three or four glasses of champagne. That's a concern. Should I propose to her when she's had a fair number of drinks? Won't that nullify anything she says? Will her answer be legally binding?

Worse still, will she even remember my question tomorrow?

What, you proposed?! When was that?

The problems in my head are multiplying, I should have come straight out with it a few seconds ago, when I had the queasy urge, the nauseous feeling. Now it comes to it

I can see a host of other complexities. Like: just how should I phrase this telling question?

On reflection, 'Will you marry me?' seems kind of forceful, rather aggressive and blunt. Slightly too close to 'You *will* marry me!' But maybe that's a good thing? How about honesty? Maybe candour and frankness are called for here, not cold calculation? On that basis, perhaps I should run across the roof terrace and fling my arms open and just say, 'Oh marry me!' in a kind of passionate and impetuous outburst.

What am I saying? We're on top of the roof. It's five storeys down to the busy London street, where I can hear the pizza waiters chucking out the prosecco bottles. If I start shouting impetuous stuff as I leap across the asphalt, Claire might topple over the edge in surprise and fall to her death. Which would be a pretty brief engagement.

There's no choice. I've got to build up to it slowly. Start again.

Going over to Claire I smile, and kiss her on the neck. Then I pull back and tuck some stray blonde hair behind her ear, in a vaguely soppy way. I say something in a low whisper. We laugh. I can feel the moment swaying towards me once more, across the disco floor of life. So I take a deep breath and I look at Claire. Her eyes are shiny and languid in the night; the champagne is giving her golden hiccups.

'Claire . . . ?'

I have adopted a profound, wise and loving expression; the look of a man you can trust, in a lifelong kind of way.

Claire squints at me.

'Yep? What is it, babe?'

'. . . Claire, I've been wondering . . .'

Her eyes widen.

'Yes?'

'And, well . . .'

I let the words hang in the air, like the scent of flowers in a warm, moonlit garden. I am aiming to get my timing right. So I pause for a few more seconds and then I think about opening my mouth. It's going to happen. I'm going to say these words for the first – and hopefully the only – time in my life; I am going to say the words that will change our lives, that will commit us, that will ennoble our love and deepen our affection. And so I lean forward and I extend a hand and I open my mouth and Claire says:

'Shall we get pizza?'

I stare. She adds:

'Oh, sorry. You want Thai, right?'

My mouth shuts. I nod and sigh. Then I turn away and walk across the roof terrace and sit on the ledge that over-looks the road. Claire puts a hand to her mouth and says:

'Sorry, darling. You were gonna say something?'

'Oh, no . . .'

'No. You were. What?'

'Oh . . . you know . . . Just thinking . . . maybe we could get a DVD out or something.'

Claire tilts her blonde, pretty, smart, twenty-nine-year-old Scottish head.

'. . . at midnight?'

She is sceptically drinking her champagne, with her arms crossed. I watch her sip that delicately tilted flute. I watch her sigh with contentment in the warm summer air. Then she peers across the Bloomsbury rooftops and with a giggle she says, 'I forgot you can see the British Museum from here!' After that she wanders airily over in her nice sexy dress and she sits down close to me.

There is something odd and superior about Claire's demeanour this evening. It is as if . . . she knows something, senses something. While I listen to the late-night drinkers whooping in my road, I wonder if sweet Claire senses what I am trying to do. Could it be? Maybe it's her female intuition? Or maybe I'm being obvious? We've been going out a year and two months: is that when men always propose? Leaning forward, I stare at the gravel of my primitive 'roof terrace'. Then I get another ardent and surprising urge: to get down on one knee. Perhaps if I did that it would be obvious what I was trying to do and then Claire might help me out by just saying 'yes' before I even have to produce the difficult words, the no-going-back statement. But getting down on one knee seems over-the-top and clichéd. Why is it only one knee, anyway? Why not two? Is that to stop you falling over? If only I had a ring to hand across. That would give me a prop. Yes. Maybe I should have bought a ring. Or maybe I should have got that T-shirt with 'Will You Marry Me?' stencilled across it. Or . . . or maybe I should have got married years ago.

I think that might be the problem. I am thirty-nine. It's an age thing. When you are nineteen and impulsive you can say 'Will You Marry Me?' without a thought because life is nothing but dewy promise and happy prospects. When you are older you see the pitfalls. And the divorces and separations of all your friends. And then it takes more guts to take the risk. Because you know just how big the risk is.

So if it's a courage thing, have I got the guts? I think so. I've done a few brave things in my life. I've spent a Sunday in the Outer Hebrides. I've watched an entire evening of Italian television. I think I have the *cojones* to do this. Let's do it! Then I notice that Claire isn't on the roof terrace. It's possible she has fallen off. But then I would have heard the crunch. Going over to the open hole in the roof, I lean past the rickety ladder that leads down to the landing.

'Sweetheart!'

Her delicate voice floats up:

'Fuck. Have you got any gin that isn't warm?'

'Er . . . no . . . erm . . . Darling??'

Another ethereal reply:

'Bollocks. No ice, either.'

'Could you come up?'

'Just getting some more glasses . . .'

Moments later she re-emerges, her pretty blonde head coming up the ladder, like an albino meerkat scanning the savannah. She periscopes her head, then sees me and laughs. When she is safely on the roof again we sit down

on the ledge side by side together and . . . it just happens.
I ask her.

What I say is this:

'Would you marry me?'

I wait. Claire is staring at me. The streetlight is white across her face. She is smiling. Gratified, I sit back. I've done it. I have committed myself. I have made that commitment I have been fearing all my life, yet wanting all my life. And it feels GOOD.

I notice that Claire is still smiling. Then she says:

'What?'

I am taken aback by this. When you ask a girl to marry you, there is a very small number of possible answers you expect to receive. 'What?' isn't really one of them.

Claire shakes her head, then she clocks my frown and says, 'Sorry, babe – couldn't hear you.' Her head tilts back, indicating the air-conditioning unit, which is loudly buzzing as it goes into overdrive. It must be a hot night down there in the pizza restaurant.

She grins. 'Anyway. Whatcha say again?'

OK. To hell with it. I've done it once. I can do it again.

'Claire . . . what I was saying was . . . was . . . how do you feel . . . you know . . . about . . .' I close my eyes and then I open them again, '. . . about marriage?'

There. Claire looks at me and nods and says:

'Well, I've always wanted to get married. I suppose. But nobody's ever asked me. Ah well!'

She lifts her glass of gin and chinks my glass. And then it strikes me. Oh God. *She hasn't understood.* I've screwed

8

it up again! 'How do you feel about marriage?' What was I thinking of?

Right. Stapling my manhood to the mainsail, or whatever it is Shakespearian heroes do, I decide to have one last attempt. I think I've got one last bash left in me, and if that doesn't work I'm gonna seriously hit my flatmate's lukewarm gin.

'No, Claire, what I mean is: *Would* you marry me?' I pause, and then for emphasis I add: 'What I am saying is: Will you marry me? Will . . . you . . . marry . . . *me?*'

Silence ensues. Even the pizza restaurant air-con seems to go into a respectful hush. Claire is staring into space, ahead of her. Her face is blank.

And then it thumps me. Of all the possibilities I have been entertaining, one, the most likely one, the obvious one, hasn't entered my stupid head. She's going to say 'no'. Of course. Of course she's going to say 'no'. *Natürlich*. Why the hell should she say 'yes'? I might love her dearly, and I believe she loves me, but there are so *many* reasons why she will say 'no'.

Not least, the fact that we met on the Internet. Can you, should you, propose to someone you met via a broadband connection? Can you find true romance in a relationship that was first established through an underground cable? Well, can you?

My heart sinks. I look at Claire. She still hasn't said a word. She looks kind of sad. It's obvious now. She is going to say 'no'. And as she turns her beloved head and gazes at me, I realise I cannot blame her for saying 'no'. I'm ten years older than her. I've had a very chequered lovelife. I'm a man and she's a woman. We're too different. Asking a woman to share her life with a man is like asking a zebra to shack up with a wineglass. What was I thinking?

Suddenly, I'm almost angry. If Claire is going to say 'no', I wish we'd never met. I almost wish I'd never started seeing girls, never become pubescent, got into love. There's just so much pain in romance; so much weirdness and confusion in sex. I could have become a monk, or a lighthouse keeper. So much easier.

Claire is still staring at me. I am thinking of the moment this all began. I am thinking of that meeting nearly two years ago, and everything it led to. I am also thinking about love, and life and sadness and hope. And I am wishing we could just get a Four Seasons pizza.

Welcome to Udate.com!

'I think you should try Internet dating.'

I look at the editor of the magazine I write for, Simon Geller. He is my age, thirty-seven. Unlike me, he is happily married, with a brand-new bouncing baby daughter. And now he's telling me to try Internet dating?

Right. It doesn't take a crack team at MI6 to decode what my smiling but businesslike editor is *really* saying: That I'm a saddo. A no-hoper. A great big terrible loser when it comes to love.

'But . . . Simon . . .' I bluster. 'The kind of people that go Internet dating . . .'

He leans forward. On the wall behind his desk, the last ten covers of *Men's Health* magazine are set in steel frames. All the covers feature black and white pictures of bare-chested hunks.

I press on:

'These people . . . that go Web-dating . . .'

'*Yep?*'

'Well, they are . . . Well let's be honest, they're weirdos, aren't they?'

'Weirdos?'

'Yeah. Muppets. Mingers . . .'

Silence.

'Howler monkeys?'

Quietly, Simon looks at me. Then he says:

'Sean. You're single, right? And you are thirty-seven . . .'

'Yeah . . .

'And you do want to meet someone serious?'

'. . . Suppose . . .'

'So I think it might make an interesting piece if we send you out on a few of these Internet dates . . . See what's out there.'

'Women with sideburns . . . That's what's out there . . .'

Simon shakes his head.

'Let's put it another way: You are a freelancer. You work for us. And this is a commission.' He watches me, then continues: 'So: get put there and see what's going on! Our readers want to meet girls, and they want to fall in love.' He bursts into a chuckle. 'And you're the man to find out if they can do it online!'

It seems I'm on the job. Yet I've still got problems with this whole Net-dating concept. These doubts must show on my face, because Simon looks at me shrewdly and says:

'Of course, we'll pay for your first dozen dates.'

OK, so now I'm interested. As I tilt my head and rethink, Simon starts on other stuff, looking at a notebook, sorting through a drawer for something. A pen to strike out my last expenses claim, maybe. Then he glances up and sees that I haven't yet vacated his glossy office; he looks worryingly surprised to see me still there.

He sighs:

'*Yes*?'

'Uhm . . . Simon . . .'

'What is it?'

'Well . . . I mean . . . I just . . . *dunno* about this . . .' I shake my head. 'I mean, can you really meet someone you love via the Internet? What kind of love would that be?'

He takes a big breath of editorial patience. Then says:

'Ask your brother?'

'Sorry?'

'Didn't you tell me once that your brother found love on the Net?'

Ah yes. Of course. My half-brother, Ross. Staring at Simon's thick black polo-neck jumper, I think about Ross. A year or two ago, my twenty-two-year-old half-brother was a Billy No-Mates who spent most of his time in his bedroom. Then, out of nowhere, he announced he had found a lovely Canadian woman who wanted to be his wife. What's more, he had apparently met her in a Christian online chatroom. Naturally I presumed she would have a serious need for support hosiery; I also presumed she would be bonkers. But when I met her she turned out to be cute, intelligent and sexy. And in love with him.

Intriguing.

Ever since the day my brother flew off to his happy

new life on the prairies, I've been thinking about my single status. In many ways, I still love being single; being able to do precisely what I like, having no one to shout at me for eating scotch eggs from the local garage while playing poker online. At five in the morning. But still. I *am* thirty-seven going on thirty-eight. Maybe it is time to put aside the childish things, the studenty ways. Maybe it's time to admit that the party is over, or at least has run out of champagne and has moved on to cooking sherry.

Moreover, I am running out of peers to party *with*. Most of my friends are now married, many of them with kids. As a result, I've started to hang out in pubs with people ten years younger than me. This is great, but sometimes I feel like the only Swede in a room full of Italians. Kids today are just so *noisy*.

Then there's the fact that, if I am honest, I am getting a tiny bit . . . lonely. I never used to, but just recently something has changed. Despite the fact I have plenty of friends, and even the odd girlfriend, I increasingly find myself alone at night. And as I potter about the place, rearranging my cravats, I sometimes wonder if it wouldn't be nice to do something a bit more social and purposeful, have someone on board to properly share my life – rather than just flat-mates and beer buddies.

Certainly, I could do with some more sensible living arrangements. Right now I live in one room in a minus-cule shared flat in central London – and the only bit of furniture I own is a chair. Just the one, solitary Habitat chair. If two people pop round my place for a nice sit-down, they have to take it in turns.

And then there is the yearning for love. I have been in love before, and I liked it. Most of it anyway, apart from the bit where it ends. So I would really like to fall in love again, and yes I would like to have children with my love-match. But I just don't seem to be meeting the right woman. Or any women. Girls I do occasionally meet. But nice women? Nope.

Why is this? I'm still in my thirties, I'm heterosexual, I've got most of my own hair and teeth – and even a decentish career. And I'm not entirely mad. And yet I'm resolutely single. Why? What's going on? Why am I alone? Where are all the millions of women who must, statistically speaking, be simply bursting with desire to meet someone like me?

Maybe it's the fact I've only got one chair? Or maybe it's because they take one look at me and think, hey, hold on, he's thirty-seven and unmarried, *whassup?*

But if that last reason *is* the real reason, that's pretty chilling. Does that mean I've left it too late? God, I hope not. I don't want to go down the cul-de-sac of terminal bachelorhood, I really don't want to spend the rest of my days eating scotch eggs from Texaco. So maybe it is time to get proactive. To set aside my prejudices, and have a bash at something different, something that worked for my brother. It's time to try Internet dating!

Plus they're going to pay for my dates.

'OK . . .' I say to Simon. 'I'll try it!'

Silence. Then he says:

'I'm *so* pleased . . .'

Striding out of the Rodale Incorporated offices, into the fresh April air of Portland Place, and the agreeable bustle of a London morning, I feel an oddly zestful spring in my step. Almost a relieved glee. I feel like a frustrated soldier who's finally been told which front he's being sent to.

Back in my tiny Bloomsbury flat I stride to my desk, full of purpose. I am going to start by researching this Internet dating thing. Booting up my laptop, I Google the words 'Internet' and 'dating.'

Wow. Seven million hits! Perhaps I should try and narrow it down. But 'Online dating', in quotes, still gets nearly three million hits. And 'Internet romance' gets several hundred thousand. These are impressive totals. I'm obviously about to dip my toe in a very big ocean. Once again I hit Google, this time typing in a more refined search query: 'Internet dating agencies'.

Again, the screen does its thing. Here is a list of the agencies I am going to have to explore, and join. But which ones? There's still a bewildering array. There's Lavalife and Let'sD8 and Udate and Loopylove and MyUKdate and DatingDirect. Not to mention Hi-there, Maxidate, datingpearl, and lovebrowser. And bestcupid. And lovesites. And datingland and Enotalone and oochat and sage-hearts. And, somewhat peculiarly, thisiswiltshire.com.

Some of these sites seem really popular. And I mean

popular. Udate.com, for example, claims to have 4.5 million subscribers. That's a fair old choice, isn't it? In fact it's slightly overwhelming. How do you make a decision which girl to go for when there are two and a quarter million of them? The other day I went to a singles party in north London and because there were *twelve* single women I felt slightly excited and confused. With Udate.com it seems I've got a choice equivalent to the population of Denmark. Which in itself is a bit ominous. So what if I *still* can't find someone, through Internet dating? Where will I try after that? Gay bars? The next life?

Actually, that London singles party was a nightmare. It felt like a kind of special-needs group. Love for slow learners. I felt like someone was saying to us: 'All you lot have got one thing in common: you're completely hopeless at meeting the right person, so we're gonna put a bunch of you in the same room in the vague hope that some of you will cop off.' Charming. In the event I went home when they got out the guitars for the communal singalong session.

Never again. If in the future I ever need convincing that Internet dating isn't such a bad option, I've just got to return to the memory of that ghastly singles party. Indeed, all I will have to do is just think about the gruesome phrase 'singles party'. When exactly does the word 'single', and phrases involving it, become pejorative? When you are twenty-two, 'single' means 'fun, groovy, and welcome-at-parties'. 'Bring lots of singles, they always liven things up.' 'God, I hope she's single!' Then when you are about thirty-three it segues into a very different meaning: 'She's still . . . *single*?' 'Er, just a single glass of the Liebfrau-milch . . .'

Anyway. The Internet dating agencies. Which ones am I going to join? The best thing, I think, is to judge the book by its cover. After all, I didn't get where I am today – in dire need of Internet dating – without being incredibly shallow. So which agencies have the most appealing, or at least non-disturbing, websites?

As I Google through the afternoon I realise there are some agencies I can discard immediately, due to absurdly twee catchphrases. 'The place to meet and mingle if you're single!' (koopid.com). 'The world is your orchard!' (pearmatch.com). Other sites (take a bow, matchnet.co.uk) are tweaking my scepticism because they are free. How good is anything *free*? What kind of strangely bearded women am I going to meet in a *free* site?

Still, other sites look rather too fruity for this early stage: Adultfriendfinder; Teamkinky. Maybe I will move on to these murkier waters in the dark and desperate future but for now I'm happy with the mainstream, thanks very much. And then there are those that seem just a bit too specialist: Meetrussianbrides isn't quite my cup of cocoa. Likewise thailovelink. As for Gaymates.co.uk, that definitely isn't me; similarly bella-online, 'the lesbian friendfinder'. Though I might put a bookmark next to it. Further down the list is Ivorytowers.org, which claims it is the only dedicated Net-dating service for 'intelligent people and graduates'. This, of course, has a definite and self-defeating air of the anorak about it. So I think not. And then finally there's . . . bargain-bucket.com. Duh? I'm sorry, call me Mister Pernickety, but . . . *www.bargain-bucket.com*?

After a couple of hours I finally make a decision. I am going to go for Udate.com, simply because it seems to be so big (4.5 million subscribers!) and Datingdirect because it promises to have the widest choice of UK singles.

Access, it seems, is easy. A few clicks and I've logged on. I can 'browse' some of the women here already (ooh, she's nice!), but to dig a bit deeper I have to pony up. Seeing as *Men's Health* magazine is going to be underwriting my expenses this is a joyously painless process. Anyway, the sites average a mere twenty pounds a month for full membership; which seems a small price to pay for a possible lifetime's happiness.

Now that I'm a member, I have to start building what the websites all seem to call a 'profile'. Essentially it seems I have to sell myself. The first thing to do is to make up an online name. Easy – I'll choose one from my last novel. No one will have heard of that. 'Lyonshall' it is.

Next I have to post a photo of myself online. This appears to be pretty much essential. Already from my brief browsing of the girls ('*Naughtycow69 is thirty-three years old and describes herself as very good-looking*') I can see that, without a photo, an Internet dating profile looks lamentably short on vital information. As I am already beginning to realise, surely the point of Internet dating (as compared to old-fangled personal ads) is that you get to see a photo of the person from the off; meaning you can immediately winnow out the undesirables ('stiff the mingers' as a friend once phrased it to me). If you don't post a photo people will only ask: what have you got to hide?

I've got nothing to hide!

Have I? Searching through my laptop, I can find only two digital photos of me. One is for that not-exactly-best-selling novel I wrote, an author photo. In this snapshot, I have a hand posed in a literary way to my chin and I am obscurely smirking at the camera.

'Smirking'? Maybe not that one then. But the only other photo of me is when I was at a party and I won an award and I got to stand next to Mick Jagger for about a millisecond and someone took a snap. In the photo, Mick and I come across as bosom pals, like we're both having a laugh and enjoying a good old gossip about our mutual friends. I'm also staring at him with a star-struck grin, giving me the demeanour of a Moomintroll on Ecstasy.

But still, I'm standing next to *Mick Jagger*. How bad can that be? Some girls might think I'm a trivial person pathetically pushing the celebrity angle – meet me and I'll introduce you to the stars! – but they'll soon find out I don't actually know any stars. And by then it will hopefully be too late. They'll be hooked!

OK, nearly done. Outside in the Bloomsbury streets, the evening is setting in, the moon is rising in the sky, students are raucously laughing in the pub down the road. I feel like Christopher Columbus on a certain warm night in Cadiz. All is possibility. All is opportunity. Will I discover America, my Newfoundland? Or will I fall off the edge of the world?

Hold on, though. I've still got one thing left to do: fill in the questionnaires. Describe myself. But as I settle down to do this, I pause. Look at all these questions! *How tall are you? Are you introverted? How religious are you? How much do you eam? What kind of woman are you looking for? Are you sexually adventurous?*

What on earth should I answer? Frankly, my life has been . . . a bit different. Fun-filled but crazy. Will any woman want me if she knows the reality that lies beyond these questions? Perhaps I should keep quiet about a few things; or a lot of things. Reticence is, after all, a virtue, as is privacy and decorum and not frightening off potential lovematches. But then again honesty is perhaps even more of a virtue. Isn't that what love is all about?

Gloomily I stare at the Udate screen. Further doubts are kicking in. Once again I am feeling very sceptical about Internet dating. Can you really find love through a machine? Via a screen? With a click of a mouse? Surely any romance born this way would be marred from the start? Surely it would feel manufactured, contrived, artificial, digitised, the Dolly the Sheep of love affairs?

As the pubs start kicking out in the streets below, I stare, blankly, out of the window. A few long seconds pass. Then I remember that I've got a job to do: I've got to get online – and see what's out there. How hard can it be?

The answer is, quite hard. For my first few days of Internet dating I mainly just sit there, quite puzzled.

The main conundrum I am encountering is: why are there so many ultra-pretty twenty-two-year-old blonde girls online? How can they be so bereft of swains as to have to do this Net-dating thing? This confuses me for almost a week. So much so I think about actually emailing some of these women. Just before I do that, though, I notice that many of these girls have Russian or eastern European names. Then I notice that many of them actually live in Russia or eastern Europe.

No harm in that. Russian girls are often quite startlingly pretty, likewise girls from the rest of eastern Europe. One of the most beautiful girls. I have ever seen in my life was a Bulgarian air stewardess on a Malev Air flight to Cairo. It's the only time I have ever stared at the 'if the plane has to make a crash landing' routine with complete and rapturous interest. So I've absolutely no aversion to amazing Slavic cheekbones.

But it still pays to be cautious. Because you can like these Slavic girls just a bit too much. A friend of mine, a fellow journalist, once fell in love with a gorgeous twenty-two-year-old blonde he met in St Petersburg. He was forty and, for all his charm and humour (of which he had lots) he was also quite tubby. A little portly. Put it another way, when he stood next to his petite Russian bride, they looked like Jabba the Hut and Princess Leia. Not an obvious love-match.

Sadly, my dear friend, blinded by love and blondeness, didn't notice this ominous and threatening discrepancy in relative desirability until he moved his bride back to England. And there the inevitable happened. Within five weeks of her moving in, a certain frostiness had developed between the two of them; within another two months she'd maxed his credit cards, stolen his bank details, started an affair with a barman, and moved to France.

Hence my present wariness of the pretty girls from Minsk. I wish God speed, and good luck, and a non-joint bank account, to all that go down that road, but it's not for me, not yet.

But . . . as I sit here now I think: How about some of these other pretty girls? After all, there are lots of them who *don't* live in Belarus and Slovakia. Lots of them seem to live very close to me, in central London. Actually, I am starting to get very excited by the prospect of these girls; I mean, I could just nip around the corner and fall in love, just like that!

Over the next few hours I send out about a dozen emails to a selection of these local beauties, these Sallys down my alley. Within a few minutes, I see the first, the *very* first blinking indicator at the top of my screen. '*Lyonshall*,' it says, '*you have a message waiting for you!*'

Very excited, almost nervous, I click on the Your Messages box. I've actually got *three* messages. The first one reads: '*Thanks for your email. I am available between 16.00 and 04.00. Call this number . . .*'

The second one reads: '*Thanks for your message. You can call me on . . .*' The third: '*Hi. Got your message. If you want to call me between 4 p.m. and . . .*' Not exactly personal. What's going on?

Going back to my search option, I check out the girls' profiles a little closer. Then I notice, perhaps a bit belatedly, that they all say the same thing: versions of 'I really like older men!' and 'I think lesbianism has a lot to offer!'

Now, I know God is a generous chap, but how many hundreds of lovely young girls into both lesbianism and older men can there genuinely be, living in the same postal district in the West End? Ah, *blush*. It seems these aren't the kind of girl my mum will want me to marry, not unless she wants me to start wearing wide fedora hats and using the word 'ho'.

What next? I'm obviously going to have to rule out all the girls who look like they come from east of the old Iron Curtain, and all the girls who seem like they might actually be prostitutes. That, however, still leaves me with 4,435,833 girls to choose from. So things could be worse.

The next day, fully ten days into my Net-dating experience, I start again. This time I'm just going to go for pretty girls outside the West End who don't obviously bang on about their Sapphic tendencies from the off. And these new girls are still quite strikingly young and pretty; surprisingly nice for Internet dating. So why are they online? Dunno. I guess they are just larking about, and keeping their options open; but hey I like larking about too, and likewise I'm keeping my options open. And so I email some of these young and beautiful girls. About a dozen of them. And then I sit back and wait for a couple of days. Then four days. Then seven. And I don't get any replies. Not one, not two. None.

What's going on? Maybe it is my email? The email I am sending these girls is the same: '*Hi. Check out my profile – if you like what you see, do get in touch!*'

Perhaps it lacks a certain personality. If I read that sort of message from a girl, I'd now think she was a sex worker – not the impression I want to give. Maybe what I need is an email that hints at my wit without trying too hard; that is mildly self-deprecating without being wanky, that shows I'm quite interesting without being bizarre. The emails will also need to be carefully phrased and honed, to be tailored and directed to each individual girl, to show that I've closely and properly read their profiles – and that I'm not just hopefully whacking out billions of identical messages to all and sundry.

This is what I come up with: '*Hi. I look like Earl Spencer on a bad hair day* [true]. *I review Lego for amazon.co.uk* [true]. *I live in a fabulously located but pitifully small central London flat* [very true]. *If you would like to chat about Lego, or perhaps talk about* [insert her favourite hobby here], *do get in touch. Lyonshall.*' Then I don't get any replies. Not one, not two. None. Well, I get one. One lovely, horsey girl (ponyclubber24) replies by saying:

'*I've dated a few jockeys in my time! But you are just*

a bit too short!!! Good luck tho, and thanks for the amusing email. P.'

A bit too short? A bit too *short*? Checking back on my profile I go to the *'How tall are you?'* section. There I notice that the measurements are meant to be given in feet and inches. But in my eagerness to get Internet dating I've actually used metrics; this means that, instead of giving my true height of five foot eleven, I'm telling the world that I'm one foot nine.

OK, I can change that. A quick click and I'm back in the saddle – back in the genetic steeplechase. Over the next few days, blessed with a fresh insight into the romantic problems of midgets, I send out my carefully honed but nearly identical email [with her hobby inserted here] to lots more lovely girls aged between twenty-one and twenty-seven. And I wait for another week and I still don't get any replies. What am I doing wrong?

At last, the cold, horrible truth dawns on me: Maybe I am ... *aiming too high*. How many gorgeous, lovely twenty-three-year-old brunettes with Connecticut smiles and long suntanned legs are really going to want to go out with a guy who reviews Lego for amazon.co.uk? Who lives in a very small flat? Who looks like Earl Spencer on a bad hair day? More to the point, perhaps, how many twenty-three-year-olds are going to want to date a thirty-seven-year-old?

It's a bitter truth to swallow. Perhaps I am not quite as magnetic an online prospect as I had hoped. Perhaps I need to direct my messages a bit more sensibly. More soberly. Aim at girls who might be interested in me. Which means girls nearer my age – or even above.

This may be an overreaction. But confidence is swiftly ebbing. The bottom has fallen out of the market; shares in Sean are being traded at a historically low price.

Put it another way: at this stage, I just want someone, anyone, to email back and say, 'You sound nice, how about a drink?' In fact, I just want someone to email *back*. Anyone. Please?

OK. How about this one: kittenlover7? So she's forty-five and she lives in Belfast. She might be interesting, who knows. And after all, I'm nearing forty myself. So I think I'll drop her a line. And what about this district nurse in Plymouth? So she's got five kids? What's so wrong with that? Maybe she's got something to offer as well. I'll email her, too. Likewise Fiona52 and Youngforherage and IremembertheBoerwar.

About six hours later, the messages start flooding in, from all the forty-something divorcees. Some of them seem to be quite, er . . . keen. Indeed a couple seem to be promising an early marriage as long as I'm not actually infirm. What does this mean? What am I doing so *right*?

Of course, a moment's reflection tells me I'm not doing anything terribly right. I've just undersold myself. If I am a brand-new iPod on eBay, I've just offered myself at a startlingly attractive price.

It's a very weird feeling. Internet dating is making me look at myself in a cold, clear and unforgiving light. Net-dating is telling me precisely the kind of people I am likely to appeal to; not just the kind of people I would like to appeal to. It's telling me where I slot, in the marital desirability stakes. And I suppose in that sense it is a salutary experience, if not a terribly romantic one. Even if nothing comes of this I'll have learned something very valuable. Goddammit.

But what am I going to do with these divorcees? If I'm honest I'm not desperate to go and hobnob in Galashiels with forty-six-year-old Hellodolly and her two grown-up sons. Yes, these older women are funny and warm and I am sure they have a lot to offer, but . . . I have to be straight with myself: I would like someone maybe a bit younger than me, or at least no older; I'd also like someone who lives within a hundred miles of London. It would just make things easier.

After a couple more days of over-analysing my reactions, and fifty cups of coffee, I sit down at my laptop and set to it once more. This time is going to be different. This time I am going to get it right. I am going to take things more slowly, and be a little more thoughtful; I am going to contact only genuine women who I honestly find attractive, within a reasonable age range (say twenty-five to forty), and who live within the South East. And I'd prefer it if they weren't hookers.

Catwoman6 looks nice. She's thirty-three, and says she's 'in business'. Her income level is 'high' which I guess is a positive thing. I'm not that materialistic. Well, not much. Sometimes I could really handle owning a brand-new Mercedes. Or just a car. *Anyway* – Catwoman6 has posted three photos. In the first she's on her own and looking wistful, but rather pretty. The second photo shows her being a bit drunk and cleavagey at a party. That's good, as it shows she's got a taste for fun. And nice breasts. The third photo is apparently taken abroad: '*Me! bunjeeing in Oz!*', says the caption (note to self: must remember to caption photo where I'm standing next to Mick Jagger – '*That's me on the right*'). And Catwoman6 has obviously got a good sense of humour because under the heading '*Do you have facial hair?*' she's put: '*Full beard and moustache*'. At least . . . I trust that's a joke. I also quite like the look of Irishlass. In her single photo, taken at some kind of big corporate party I think, she is quite elfin-looking, and she's wearing an amusing hat. But there's also a guy in a dinner-jacket standing next to her – and his face has been blackly scribbled out by a kind of cyber-biro. Photoshop, I guess. But why scribble out the face? Is he a hated ex-husband? A distracting nonentity? Osama bin Laden? Intriguing. Irishlass is in education and she says her income is 'low' so I guess that means she is a teacher. Or she's an adult special-needs person.

Finally, I quite like the sound of Bollweevil. Well, not her name, obviously. But she is in medicine and she says she is Swiss. Right now I like the idea of a Swiss girl. I have no idea why. Maybe it's because they are often sexily French-speaking without being all up themselves; maybe I'm looking forward to skiing holidays with her folks, even though I can barely ski. Or maybe it's the idea of free Toblerone. Fuck knows. I'm going a bit bonkers here.

Four million girls to choose from and all that. Anyway, Bollweevil's photo shows she is a very pretty brunette, not entirely unlike my last girlfriend . . .

This photo is also taken at some party. Which is interesting. She is the third girl this morning to have a photo taken at a party. This must mean either that lots of people like the way they look at parties, all squiffy and smiley and red-cheeked, or that these girls are trying to say something, i.e., 'I am not desperate and alone, I have lots of friends and a great social life.' Actually, I am starting to find these party photos a little transparent, even a tiny bit sad. Then I remember that my own photo was also taken at a party. And I've managed to squeeze in a celebrity. Oh well. It's too late to get angsty. I'm going to email these girls, and a couple of others: Flamehairedchick and Sally72.

Two days later, I have two messages. The first is from Bollweevil and says: '*Is that who I think it is next to you?*' The second is from Catwoman6 and it says: '*Hey – I quite like Earl Spencer.*' This is rather exciting. We start exchanging emails. But then, somehow, these peter out into nothing. Again I seem to be doing something wrong. Then I think: well, maybe I shouldn't keep replying to my incoming messages within fifty seconds. Maybe that feels a bit like I am standing, panting, by my laptop, just waiting. Like a kind of cyberstalker. Yuk.

More painfully still, Irishlass is studiously ignoring me. Naturally, this means she has immediately become the one I *really* want to meet. I send her a couple more emails.

Witty and offhand and self-deprecating and carefully cali-
brated to appeal. I vow to myself that, when she replies,
I will chill out and wait for a day or two, before
sending/composing my own elegant riposte. To show that
I am not desperate.

But she doesn't reply. I email some more. Still no reply.
This is painful. What can I do?

Then I get an email out of the blue.

Bongowoman is thirty-two and describes herself as good-looking

Hmmm. I've read her email and it's pithy, sweet, and not obviously insane. So then I go to her profile, and look at her photo. Bongowoman's photo is a bit strange. It's sort of . . . misty. Grainy, even. Why is it misty and grainy? Perhaps it was taken within the vicinity of the Niagara Falls, or maybe, just maybe, the photo is deliberately obscure, so as to conceal a bit of a nose. Or scrofula.

But then again, my photo makes me look like a total dork pretending he has a celebrity friend. Ahem.

Staring at my laptop, I realise that I'm not actually that fussed by her photo, anyway. No, what is really exciting me here is the fact that Bongowoman's message is *unsolicited*. I have never emailed Bongowoman, I've never come across her profile. I didn't even know she existed. And yet she has found me by searching through the database, and something in my profile has made her write to me. She's made the moves. Amazing.

The amazingness of this is that, of course, as a man,

this just doesn't happen to me very often. Yes, there have been times when women have made the first approach, but they haven't been irritatingly frequent. Moreover, on the few occasions it has occurred, I've often ended up turning the girl down, because I've been so confused by the contrariness of it all, I've presumed my admirer must have made a silly mistake.

I remember a particular example of this with some pain, even now. It was at my university union bar. One boozy evening a very sexy girl, a friend of a friend, asked me if she could *stay at my flat as she couldn't afford a taxi.* As she did this, she *put her hand on my knee.* Now, a normal person, like a woman receiving similar attention from a guy, would regard this as a bit of a come-on. But I was young, male, confused and too horny to believe that a woman could just *offer* sex, so I looked at her and nodded and said, 'Well actually, there are some quite good night buses.' She gave me a glance of pure disgust, and stalked off to get a taxi. It was only about three years later that I woke up alone, in the middle of the night, and with a feeling of cold horror realised that this girl had simply wanted to sleep with me. She had just wanted to get in my pants. And I had sent her off to get . . . a night bus. The N97 night bus. It *is* quite convenient for Tufnell Park.

But I digress. The relevance here is that as a man, and a non-movie-star and non-Premiership-football-player, I am pretty much alien to the notion of a woman being the obvious playmaker. Yet in cyberspace, it seems, things are different. In cyberspace women *do* make the moves. Yay!

33

Once I have stopped dancing around my room singing 'Just a Gigolo', I sit down at my desk once more and start to think about Bongowoman. My admirable suitor. My first discovery is that I rather like her name, Bongowoman. There's just something cool about it. The name has a hint of jungle wildness, a soupçon of self-deprecating wit, and it gives the distinct impression that she has fairly sizeable breasts.

Clicking on the photo, I try to make out if Bongowoman has sizeable breasts. But it's too foggy, no matter how much I enlarge it. Then I notice the caption Bongowoman has appended underneath her photo.

'*Another wedding*', it says. Ah. Listen to that. *Another wedding*. Sitting back at my desk, sipping at my cappuccino, I think about this tell-tale caption, the poignant history of wistfulness it seems to infer. Somewhere in my mind I picture a person who always stands at the back of the wedding party – watching the bouquets fly, listening to the giggles of the bride, smiling bravely as the Roller scrunches away one more time – all the while silently wondering if it will ever be *their* turn.

But that's enough about me. Obviously, this girl feels the same when she attends all her mates' weddings. And I can empathise. But what does the *rest* of the profile say about 'Bongowoman'?

She says she is five foot nine. Works in publishing. Her income is 'moderate'. At the moment she lives in Wandsworth, likes opera and pop, has no children, and is non-vegetarian. Bongowoman is also a Cancer who has

34

green eyes and dark-brown hair. So that's that solved. She also says she would characterise her drinking as 'light'.

This last bit of information makes me pause. Seeing this characterisation in cold black and white, I rather wonder what the point of it is. I mean, how many people, when asked by an Internet dating agency, would deliberately characterise their drinking as anything other than 'light'?

Hi, I'm a Sagittarius, a non-smoker, I live in London and I drink until I get violent. Whatever her true drinking-status, Bongowoman is starting to sound very appealing. Her appeal is underlined when I scroll down to her personal bit, the 'More About Her' bit, the section where it gets loose and chatty, the bit where a disconcerting number of women use emoticons.

Here is what Bongowoman says about herself:

'*Am: sure anything's possible; spirited; multi-faceted; passionate; stylish; cheeky; sensitive; determined; urbane; spontaneous; open-minded; imaginative; true. Am not: constipated; blonde; bitter about not being blonde; reserved; representing Britain in synchronised swimming at the Olympics; stupid; satisfied; two-faced; restrained by logic; insipid; lying. Have an unnatural obsession with: (men in) double-cuff shirts; my duvet; driving fast; biscuits; shoes; cats; cars; cheese; riding pillion; dancing; Sweden; sun; sushi; sake; travel; ads; aesthetics; adventures; lipbalm. Combust on contact with: lorries hogging the middle lane; double-breasted suits; bad manners; coriander; liars; pop-ups; recruitment consultants; washing-up; things that have no point; ineffectuality;*

35

people who don't do things they say they will. Am deeply disturbed by: musicals; caravans; the absence of a Space Hopper in my childhood; people gobbing; tie-clips; lime in G&T; suburbia; getting a bus-lane violation. You: in London, and ready to find out what fascinating adventure we can have togethe . . . Oh, and you should have the vertical capacity for me and my heels . . .'

Cool! Not only is this much wittier and smarter than any other 'More About Her' bit I have so far encountered, it also says much that I can agree with. I strongly dislike musicals; I likewise abhor caravans, double-breasted suits, pop-ups, washing dishes and tie-clips. As for suburbia, I *totally* detest that – mainly because I grew up in it, in a small-town way.

Even better, Bongowoman's *'likes'* get a big thumbs-up, as well. Cheese is a passion of mine. Sushi I adore. I've done more travelling and had more adventures than you can shake a pointy stick at; and I am sure I would like Sweden if I ever went there. In truth, the only tiny fly in this ointment of concord is . . . coriander. I quite like coriander. Not a lot, but in Thai curries and stuff. Could coriander come between us? Should we let a humble herb dictate the course of love?

Hold on, though. Love?? Sitting back, I realise I have been daydreaming completely. The coffee has gone cold and I am staring at my laptop with a big silly smile on my face.

Back to earth. Let's read this email she sent me, one more time. Compared to her profile, it's quite pithy:

'*I think you look a lot better than Mick Jagger. This is a good thing, as he is a halfwit. Get in touch if you feel like a chat about life, or just daytime telly. BW.*'

I still like it. It's nice. Short. Slightly enigmatic. Wry . . . In the same vein I write back:

'*Thanks, Bongowoman. You are right. My job as a travelling herb salesman specialising in coriander means I am much cooler than Mick Jagger. Good luck with the bus lanes, Lyonshall.*'

Then I wonder if this is just too arch and weird. And maybe the third sentence is a bit long and clumsy. But then again, it's only the first email. But then *again* first things are important. First impressions, especially. On the first impression given by this weird email, she might dismiss me as a tosser.

But this is getting out of hand. It's only a four-line email, to one girl, on a website where there are millions of women just *longing* to meet me. Holding my breath, I click on the Send button. Then I stand and stare at the screen. I am waiting, waiting . . . waiting for what? What am I so pensively expecting?

An instant reply, I suppose. And why not? I imagine Bongowoman, right now, opening the email ('*Bongowoman, You Have One Message Waiting*') across London, then rocking back on her chair laughing loudly but girlishly at my email. In her nice, cool, sunny flat in Wandsworth. With art books everywhere. And sexy friends around her chuckling but also saying, 'Oh, he's quite nice,' as they lean over her shoulder to look at my photo on the laptop screen. In fact I can see her thinking for quite a long time about me, sipping her Nescafé this Sunday morning, holding her mug the way that nice girls do with two praying hands either side, then turning to stare dreamily out at the springtime trees . . . Until the moment comes when she finally sits down and opens her laptop and sends me the next mildly suggestive missive.

Two hours later, the website indicates that she hasn't actually opened my message yet. '*Bongowoman Has Not Read Your Message Yet.*'

In a bit of a huff, I go out.

Two days later, I wake up and see the website thingy blinking. '*Congratulations Lyonshall, You Have A Message!*'

It is from Bongowoman. It says:

'*V funny. Actually I hate nutmeg as well, I just didn't want to sound obsessive. Tell me more about yourself . . . over a drink? I hate these email exchanges that go on for weeks. Text me! My number is . . .*'

Wow. She really *is* up front. Almost too keen. Maybe she is a bit desperate. For a few minutes I think about this. Then I remember the wit and intelligence of her profile. Then I remember that we are all a bit desperate, anyway – orem therwise we wouldn't be Internet dating. Picking up my phone, I text her. Her real name is Suzanne; some minutes later, we have a date. This Thursday. Two days' time. We're on.

For the intervening two days I am in a bit of a tizz. What will she really look like? What if she *has* got scrofula? Was I right to suggest my local? – she's only a light drinker, after all. But meeting in a pub seems kind of relaxed, and therefore suitable. A pub's a good place for a first, almost-blind date, it's somewhere neutral where we can meet and make sure we both have the requisite number of limbs. If we like each other, well then we can do the restaurant/theatre/oral sex thing a little later.

Anyway, the time has come; it's my first date with this woman. Suzanne, aka Bongowoman. How should I dress? For a while I loiter by my special and rather unusual velvet suit, but finally I bottle out and opt for a standard, boring, conservative, jeans-with-jumper approach. Of course I also wear expensive shoes because that's what women always notice, or so they constantly tell me. Then I walk down to the pub.

I'm ten minutes early. She's not here. It's crowded with students and people and . . . one rather drunk-looking woman shouting at the slot machine. From the side she looks something like Bongowoman's photo. Instantly a chill suspicion pierces my heart. The woman turns and burps at me, loudly.

God, is that her? If this *is* Suzanne, she has a rather unorthodox approach to dating. The woman is glaring at me, and muttering in a hostile way. But then I come to my senses. This woman is about forty-five, as well as drunk and punchy. I know they can do marvellous things with Photoshop, but hey.

Moving around the pub, I seek out a younger face to match the grainy one in the photo. There are lots of girls in here, lots of students, because there are universities all around this part of London. Girls are drinking, laughing, and generally not looking at me. But then at last I think I see the right face: she's sitting behind a table in a corner.

She looks rather cute. Friendly, happy, vivacious, gorgeous eyes. Not bad! I see her looking slightly askance at my jumper. Damn.

'Sean?' she says.

'Er, Suzanne?'

She nods and smiles, then laughs in a nice way. Good start. I ask her if she'd like a drink. She tilts her head to one side, and says:

'Red wine . . . Big one! Thanks . . .'

Two hours later we're sitting at an intimate little table and chatting and gossiping like we aren't actually having our first semi-blind date at all. There has only been one yawning pause, when I forgot her real name. But I can't help that; 'Bongowoman' just seems to fit her better: curvy, bouncy, funny, forthright. Bongowoman/Suzanne is jolly good company. She is indiscreet about her job, wittily acerbic about past boyfriends, oddly breathless when discussing rugby players. After three glasses of pub wine she actually tells an absolutely filthy joke, and then looks embarrassed – mainly because I am pretending to be appalled. She blushes. Then she screws her eyes up and sighs:

'Ah. You're teasing me. Bastard.'

After this we talk some more and then I tell her I thought

she was the sweary drunk woman by the slot machine and she says:

'Give me ten years. I'm working on it . . .'

My turn to chuckle. We chat away some more. We are getting on famously. So famously, when I go to the loo I feel like congratulating myself loudly as I look in the mirror. I manage to refrain from this. Nonetheless, I am feeling goooood. I'm not sure if it is the wine or the night or the fact that I am hopelessly optimistic when it comes to love and romance, but there is something touching and also sexy about this girl. And there is an endearing shyness to her, too – a demure quality that matches the dimple in her chin.

By the time I get back to the table, I am resolved. I know this is only our first date but I like her and I think she likes me and I am going to try and kiss her.

Trying to kiss a girl for the first time is a momentously tricky process. I am never sure that girls properly appreciate this, when all they have to do is sit there looking cute. I remember once I went to kiss a girl for the first time in her car because I thought she was leaning nearer to me to invite that first kiss, but when I went to kiss her I realised, way too late, that she was just bending down into the gearwell to get something, and so she jerked her head up at the wrong time and I smashed my nose on the top of her head. Our relationship never really recovered from that.

In fact, since that particularly awkward first kiss, I

have sometimes tried jokily to pre-empt First Kiss Embarrassment by saying, 'Would you mind awfully if I kissed you?' in a kind of obviously fake, strangulated, posh English accent. This rigmarole has two benefits: by saying it in a daft accent I get across what I want to say whilst simultaneously indicating that I know that what I am saying is rather stilted. And of course if the girl says 'no' I can laugh it off and pretend I was joking ironically, hence the accent. And if that happens I go home chuckling – and stare desolately out of the kitchen window for a week.

Why is love so hard? So difficult and complex? Why can't girls have big neon signs on their foreheads saying, 'It's OK, you can kiss me now'?

Maybe I *am* just an idiot. Maybe this girl thinks I'm an idiot and has been pretending to laugh at my jokes all night. Maybe she has actually been trying to escape the entire evening, desperately jerking her eyebrows at the barman as if to say, 'Help, Jumper Boy over here thinks he's funny.'

Yikes. Self-confidence is draining out of the bath, I'm getting cold shivers of self-doubt. I need a drink.

Using drink is an appalling way to get the confidence to kiss girls. But I can't help it. Drink just *helps*. Then again, it only helps up to a point. A lot of my life is spent trying to calibrate the right amount of drink – so as to acquire the confidence to chat up girls, without tipping over the edge into boorishness.

I reckon two more drinks should do it. So I go to the

bar and when I come back we drink and chat about Japanese food for a few minutes, before/after which a slight silence settles over us. An expectant silence. A pregnant pause. Is this a signal. Or is Suzanne just suppressing a burp? Whatever, a sudden wave of resolve has come over me. Drumming up the courage I have a strange image of myself as an RAF pilot in the Battle of Britain. *OK chaps, I'm going in. I'm going to do it. I'm going to kiss her. Wish me luck as you wave me goodbye.*

I make my move. For a millisecond I see a wave of panic cross her face as my lips near hers and I have a horrible, prophetic vision of her struggling, fighting me off, and a team of barmen rushing over to pull me away. Charming. But a fraction of a second later her shoulders seem to melt. And then it happens. *There.* We're kissing. How difficult was that? Fortune favours the brave. And the slightly pissed. It was a nice kiss.

The rest of our pub-time is spent in a much more relaxed fashion, as far as I am concerned. My boldness has paid off. Once the first kiss is done, you know you're in and you can chill.

An hour later the pub is about to shut and we look at each other and sigh quite happily and she says:

'Do you . . . ?'

'Yes. Soon as possible.' I say.

And we both laugh. We're going to date again. We're on. This is easy. I *love* Internet dating. And I really like this girl.

It's then that we rise from the table and I realise that she is precisely two inches shorter than me.

Fuck. She's too tall. How could I have missed that? How could I have missed the pretty obvious signals? Like the fact that she says she is five foot nine in her profile? And that, at the end of her 'More About Me' bit, she says that any suitor should 'have the vertical capacity for me and my heels'?

After escorting Suzanne to the Tube, where we kiss again, where I hide my immediate and profound mis-givings quite successfully, I pace back to my flat feeling ultra-deflated. Almost angry. I'm angry at myself. Why do girls have to be shorter than me by about five inches for me to fancy them? Why is sexual desire so tediously basic? I really like this girl. She's fun. Who cares if she's nearly as big as me?

The trouble is: *I* care. I prefer short girls. I just *do*. Short, petite, feminine, sit-on-my-lap girls. Girls I can protect, sling an arm around, be manly with. I do know lots of blokes who love tall girls, who like the lofty elegance, the long thoroughbred limbs, the catwalk grace. But not me. I like 'em titchy. Physically smaller. In need of masculine help. I like those help-me-get-this-box-of-Ariel-down-from-the-top-shelf-in-Tesco's girls. I guess it's evolutionary, or something, or . . .

I'm depressed now.

Loafing around my flat I try to think this through. Why do I like girls of a sort? Why do men and women have types? Where does all this come from? And, if it's a learned thing, can it be unlearned? Can I unlearn my proclivities and get over the short thing, and have a happy life with Bongowoman, or at least anyone over five foot six?

Now my mind is buzzing. I recall the theory of a friend of mine. This friend believes that male sexual propensities are formed the way young geese form an attachment to their parents. (Yeah, I know. *Geese?*) The process the little geese undergo is apparently called 'imprinting': the gosling opens its small gummy eyes and the first living thing it sees becomes the beloved parent. The related idea is that, in the same way, the first thing men have an orgasm over is the thing they will for ever afterwards fixate upon, sexually.

The trouble is that the first thing I had an orgasm over was . . . the cleaning woman.

It happened like this: I was twelve years old. I had been having weird 'stirrings' in my groin for about six months. I knew something was happening; I just didn't know what. Then one day I pulled a sickie and stayed at home from school to loaf about. My dad went off to work to be a lecturer; my mum, once she had satisfied herself that I wasn't actually dying, went off to her job at the local water authority. That left me alone – with the cleaning woman. To cut a bizarre and frankly disturbing story short, when the cleaning woman came into my bedroom to make sure I was OK, I sort of let my pyjamas drop and I exposed myself to her, and she got a bit flustered, and then she went to do some determined hoovering and as soon as she closed the door I felt my groin shake and my insides go funny and it seemed like someone had microwaved a million ice creams in my stomach, and then this kind of stuff came out. Which I wiped away with a Leeds United sock.

Thinking about this now, twenty-five years later, I start to get worried. Am I truly weird? Surely not. But then again, is it normal to have your first orgasm by exposing yourself to the Lady Who Does? The Lady Who Does!!

No, but. Really. In a panic about my possible weirdness, I ring up my friends and have late-night conversations with them about where they had their first orgasm. The first friend laughs at my question, then tells me he had his in the school toilets. At fourteen. He was told by a friend how to do it, 'Roll it like you are making fire with a twig', and he went into the urinals and spent an hour rolling his penis like he was 'making fire with a twig'. My friend chuckles some more, and goes on: 'Then I thought, To hell with this rolling thing, and I started rubbing it up and down and after about ten seconds lots of come suddenly shot out and I thought, Help, I've got the clap!'

This isn't that helpful. So I make another phone call. My next friend tells me he had his first orgasm by pressing his groin against a conveyor belt while on a school trip to a factory. He hasn't visited a factory since, at least not in an amorous way. A third friend tells me his first orgasm occurred when he was eight: he was pushing a girl on a swing and then the swing came back and biffed him in the bollocks but instead of being in pain, he ejaculated. And swings are no longer his thing, sexually speaking.

Finally I ring my friend Joe. Joe is a pre-op transsexual. In fact he's swiftly becoming a Jo. With breasts. Which is quite disconcerting to behold in an old college pal who likes football and snooker. But if anyone will be able to shed some sagacious light on weirdness and sex and orgasms, and men and women, it should be Joe. He has a unique insight.

So I tell him about my inquiry into orgasms. I ask him where, for instance, he had his first orgasm.

He refuses to tell me. Sensing a surprising reluctance in my friend, I decide to put him at his ease by telling him about my first orgasm, my adolescent frisson with the cleaning woman.

My anecdote is followed by silence. A long, silent pause. Then Joe says:

'You exposed yourself to the *cleaning woman*?'

I sigh, and confirm the story. Joe does a low, amazed whistle.

'Jesus, that's weird.'

At my end of the line, I nod. Joe's right. I am weird, terminally peculiar. There's no hope for me. But then I remember something.

'Joe, you're a fucking transsexual.'

'So?'

'You wear bras. And tights. When you're not playing cricket. And you're calling *me* weird?'

Thankfully, Joe chuckles. Then he laughs aloud, for half

a minute or more. Then he assures me that I shouldn't worry about it, that everyone is a bit kinky in some way. *You're telling me, Joe.* After that he rings off because he wants to buy a nice dress from a catalogue.

So it seems I'm not weird at all. Well, not *that* weird. OK, I'm still pretty bloody weird, but sod it. What all these accounts *do* show is that the orgasmic imprinting theory isn't a good theory. After all, I'm not now fixated on cleaning women. I don't get excited by the sound of a distant Hoover, or the first whiff of Windowlene. I just like short girls. Short, sexy, petite, feminine *girls*.

Why?

Actually, I think I do know where this might have come from. The first girl I ever found attractive, the first girl I ever had any sexual and emotional response to, the first girl I ever kissed, was a petite girl called Elizabeth. At my nursery school.

Bear with me.

I only remember this kiss because I wrote about it. Well, when I say 'write', I mean that I recited these words about my new squeeze over the Sunday lunch-table to my family – and they were written down and eventually they got published. Precocious, or what?

Going to my bookshelves I take down the book in which this child poem was published. It's called *Allsorts* 4, and it's a 'collection for children edited by Anthony Thwaite'. I am keen to see this poem again. I am starting to wonder if this childish poem will tell me anything about my self, my sexuality, the reasons I ended up here: thirty-seven, single and full of yearning for short, curvy women with naughty laughs.

Here it is. The right page, very well-thumbed. At the top it says, '*Sean was only four years old when he wrote this poem. Of course he didn't know he was writing a poem; he thought he was just talking.*'

True enough. Then comes the poem itself.

When I kiss Elizabeth
all the clothes dance
and all the boys jump up on the roof
and
do you know what the dinner does?
The dinner comes down from the big school
then it lays itself on the tables
and eats itself up.
Do you know what the plates do?
They gather themselves up
they go to Mrs Herd
they get into the washing basin
and they put themselves back on the shelves and and
    and and . . .
When I kiss Elizabeth
magic stuff comes out of our mouths.

OK, I've shortened the poem – there is quite a bit more – but it essentially follows the same theme. I kiss Elizabeth, and then pianos start playing themselves, and apple trees start growing through the school roof, and light bulbs go to the shops to buy more light bulbs, and so on. And the enigmatic Mrs Herd gets another namecheck.

So what *does* this wistful little poem say to me now? That I was an impossible romantic at the age of four? That we are all romantics from an early age? That I was a bit odd for a pre-schooler? I don't know. I do know I can still remember Elizabeth Mason. She was very pretty (in terms of being four). Dark hair, snub nose, funny, petite (OK she was four, but still). Actually, for a long time after I wrote this four-year-old's poem, I recall that I was actually convinced that Elizabeth Mason and I were destined to be together. But life has a way of teaching you severe lessons. When we were both eight, Elizabeth met someone else. An older man of nine. She was obviously an appalling slut, looking back, but it was a useful lesson in the cruelties of womankind.

The theme continued into my boyhood, when I hit school. My school was a standard co-ed comprehensive: there were lots of noisy boys and lots of contemptuous girls. And there was one particular girl, Sally Ann Long.

Sally Ann Long!

Sally was very pretty in an acne'd adolescent way. She was also coquettish, leading me a merry dance around the playing fields of boydom. She used to tell me if she was wearing white knickers under her blue school skirts. She knew I fancied her like mad. She would promise to kiss me by the Chem block, and then disappear completely. I lusted after her for many, many months, years even, right through my third, fourth and fifth forms. Most of the time she resolutely spurned my clumsy advances, though there was one glorious moment when I put my hand up Sally's school skirt during Geography and felt her thighs. She giggled and carried on writing her notes like nothing was happening. I relived that moment for months. For years. In fact I'm reliving it *now*.

The relevance of this is that Sally used to wear gingham summer dresses and short blue skirts. And to this day I find short skirts and gingham dresses very exciting. I also like girls with bare legs. And, yes, Sally was short. Five foot two or so. Like Elizabeth. Well, Elizabeth was two foot seven, but she *was* at nursery.

What am I trying to say? Well, I think men's fetishistic and psychosexual desires are formed sometime in early adolescence, if not before. Just ask them. I know men who are obsessed with stockings who can date it to one moment in their early teens when they saw a girl doing a handstand in stockings (these are older men). I know men who are into breasts who can date it to one afternoon, aged ten, spent idling through their dad's copy of *Big Ones* magazine. You don't need to have an orgasm, the link isn't that direct, but something does seem to happen in those tender boyhood years that can be very formative.

Or maybe it's just random. I don't know. The fact is I am fighting against it, right now. I really like this girl, Suzanne, and just because she doesn't fit this stupid template in my head, in my groin, seems a very bad reason to not see her any more. So what if every single woman

I have ever fallen properly in love with has been short, petite, and girlish? And looks good in a blue pleated gym skirt? So what if every single time I have tried to fall in love with a taller, longer, more masculine girl it has ended up either humdrum or catastrophic?

The next day, still hiding my doubts, I arrange my second date with Suzanne. We meet in a wine bar. She looks lovely, friendly, sweet, feminine – and I don't fancy her, at least not enough. I just know it. This horrible, cold realisation takes hold from early on in the evening. And I try to hide it but I obviously don't hide it very well because about halfway through the date she looks at me and says:

'You're not very comfortable, are you . . . ?'

I can't say anything. I can't say a cruel and callous 'yes' but I can't honestly say 'no' either. So I just sit there nursing my Tempranillo, feeling guilty and wretched, until she leans across, pecks me on the forehead and gets up, saying:

'Thanks for the wine . . .' And then she is gone.

Back at my flat I go into a tailspin, staring morosely out at the darkness. As if love isn't hard enough, life chucks in types and desires and propensities, and an early exposure to little plaid skirts.

Maybe I should have tried harder with Bongowoman? We got on very well, after all. She made me laugh, I made her laugh. But I know from long and trying experience that you can't argue with neurochemicals. You need that spark. If the apple trees aren't growing through the roof, if the piano isn't playing itself, you may as well give up.

Then I hear a noise. Outside. It's about one a.m. Throwing open my window I lean out and look down: a couple are necking in the shadows, next to the pizza restaurant. The girl giggles, the man puts his hand inside her jacket. Love is in the air.

For a second I wonder whether to hurl a bucket of icy water over them, before calling the police. But then I realise I am probably being a little sour and bitter. Sourness and bitterness are no good. Shutting the window, wishing Necking Couple all the best and a warm alcove, I sit back down at my laptop.

So. What now? The good thing about Internet dating is that you get lots of opportunity. The shop is open 24/7. It always offers a reason for hope.

For a few more days I therefore surf and email, surf and email, working off my disappointment. Then one morning I see that someone called Lizzie has put me in her 'Favourites' file.

I check her profile.

She's five foot four.

Lizziegirl is a member of Udate for 'reasons known only to herself'

She's got a pretty face, dark framing hair, a goofy smile, and she's wearing some kind of white fur coat in the photo. This is probably fake and ironic as she says she reads the *Guardian*. She's 'mixed race': judging by the photo there may be a hint of Spanish, or even Filipino. It's hard to say. But she's palpably exotic and certainly cute. My pulse rate has gone up by about five beats per minute. Maybe ten.

What else? She's a non-smoker. A 'consultant'. She likes Szechuan Chinese food and according to the website she doesn't take drugs. Actually what the website says is, '*I don't take drugs!*' with an exclamation mark. I know this exclamation mark is not her writing, it's just the option given you by the site, but it still looks a little odd. It looks like someone's heard her puffing a crackpipe in the office loos, and she's come out shouting, 'I don't take drugs! I don't take drugs!', while waving away the fumes.

But I'm being irrational. What have I put in my profile?

'*I Don't Take Drugs!*' What else? In the section where the website asks: '*Where will you be three years from now?*' she's put: '*I will be three years older.*' Which is slightly funny. Where it asks: '*Where is a good place to go on a date?*' she's put: '*Not the Mash Bar in Great Portland Street.*' Which shows good taste, I think, as the Mash Bar in Great Portland Street is sucky in the extreme. Indeed, everything is looking fairly good. I don't even mind the fact that she's put 'medium' when asked to describe her build. I am now beginning to understand that, in Internet dating speak, medium probably means curvy-going-on-chubby, but that's OK. Usually I prefer the voluptuous girls.

Cracking on, I email Lizziegirl. '*Thanks for putting me in your "Favourites" file,*' I say. '*Consider me flattered. You don't look half bad yourself. Er, what is it about these dating sites that makes people write rubbish? Do get in touch with me if you fancy a chat.*'

This email may be a bit confused, if not curt, foolish and dim, but I don't care. I'm gaining in confidence. What can go wrong? After all, this girl has subtly come on to me my putting me in her 'Favourites' file. That's the Internet equivalent of a girl sitting across a bar, raising her glass, and smiling. OK, this isn't as fruity as what Bongowoman did – write to me out of the blue (which is presumably the Internet equivalent of the same girl coming around the bar, slinging an arm round my neck, and nibbling my ear). But it's still rather promising.

Two days later, Lizziegirl writes back. '*Nobel Prize eh?*

I like a man with ambition. This is my real email address if you want to avoid this website malarkey . . .' For a second this remark throws me, but then I remember that in the *'Where Will You Be In Three Years?'* section I have indeed put, *'On a dais in Stockholm collecting the Nobel Prize for Literature.'* This was meant ironically, while at the same time betraying a hint of genuine ambition, and it seems to have worked. Hooray! I really am getting the hang of this Net-dating stuff. Maybe I should have tried this sooner. Like fifteen years ago. Would have saved a lot of angst in banging nightclubs, shouting into the ears of young women about my interest in poetry. I never did manage to pick up a girl in a nightclub.

Over the next few days Lizziegirl and I exchange emails of increasing candour and wryness, culminating in her telling me that she likes dancing around in the nude in her flat to heavy metal. I am not sure how to take this, whether to get excited by the nude-dancing bit (OK, I'm excited) or appalled by the taste in music. Who cares? I'm too excited by the nude-dancing bit.

It's time to date. To do it. In another message I suggest we meet somewhere in Hampstead. As she lives in Golders Green, north of Hampstead, this seems fair and equidistant. I'm not sure where we are going to meet but that shouldn't be a problem. Hampstead is full of cool bars.

The evening arrives. I am standing at Hampstead Tube entrance checking my watch. Because she's late. Ten minutes late. Twenty-five minutes late. People coming out of the Tube are brushing past me, kissing their pals, sneering at the loser with no friends, i.e. me. Half an hour late and I start texting my own friends, if only to make out like I have something to do with my evening rather than stand, pathetic and friendless, at the entrance to Tube stations.

Can't believe it. Stood up. Girls! etc.

At precisely 8.57, i.e. fifty-seven minutes after she was meant to be here, three minutes before my absolute definite time-limit for legging it will expire (a time-limit extended from my last, definite, final limit of forty-five minutes when I realised I had nothing else to do this evening (and when I remembered the nude dancing)), Lizziegirl shows up.

Crikey. She's gorgeous. A little bit plump, maybe, but a sweet, winning face, nice skirt, two breasts, four limbs, nice hair, nude dancing, nude dancing, nude dancing. Running up to me (running!) from the ticket gate she makes a massively apologetic face and says, 'Sean? Oh God I'm sorry but my cat went into a thing and my flatmate was away and I had to call the vet I'm so sorry sorry shall we go somewhere then?'

Breathless is, I think, the word. And winning. Nice perfume too. Adopting an understanding but patronising face I say: 'Erm . . .' Then I remember that girls like men to be decisive. Spotting a pub down the High Street that looks suitably busy, well-lit and inviting, I say: 'The pub?'

She laughs and nods. On the way down the hill to the pub she explains why her flatmate is away. And why her cat was ill. And why she likes heavy metal. And why she likes astronomy, Los Angeles, rugby, Provence and monosodium glutamate ('What's wrong with MSG? It makes food taste good!'). She may be a little nervous; or maybe she talks in this breathless and excited way all the time. Either way it's fetching. I actually have the stirrings of tumescence, just by standing next to her.

This happens sometimes. Just standing next to a girl, in a bus queue or something, you can get an erection. Do girls know this? I have a friend who gets erections when he just *thinks* about *phoning* his girlfriend. Then again, I have another friend who gets erections when he talks about dollar/sterling exchange rates. He works in the City.

When I can get a word in edgeways, I tell Lizziegirl a little more about me. Inside the pub I even manage to get her to shut up. She actually shuts up quite a lot in the pub. In fact she shuts up almost completely.

This is odd. One minute we were chatting away, or at least I was listening to her chat away, and we were sipping our drinks and everything was fine. Now she's gone a bit quiet. Have I done something wrong? Said something wrong? We've talked about novels, films and India, her 'seventh favourite country'. We've talked about lots of stuff but none of it too controversial. Staring around the pub I wonder if this is the problem: the location. She went quiet soon after we came in here.

Staring around the pub I try to work out what might have unsettled her. Nothing obvious springs to mind. There's a couple of guys chatting at a table in the corner.

Other guys are gossiping with the barman. Over in the other corner four guys with moustaches and tight jeans are laughing and joking. And on the table next to them two suntanned guys in tight white T-shirts are singing along to Tina Turner while waving their hands in the air like flamboyant Channel 4 presenters.

Fuck. I've brought her to a gay pub.

How bad a choice can you make? A gay pub. A freaking gay pub. What kind of signal am I giving off? What possible signal could she infer from this? That I'm bisexual? Metrosexual? Homosexual but experimenting?

Slumping forward on the pub table I say, staring down morosely:

'I've brought you to a gay pub.'

Silence. Apart from Judy Garland on the jukebox. I look up at Lizziegirl. Her face has creased into a weird shape and I realise she is wordlessly laughing. Laughing a lot. Then finally she stops laughing and she says:

'Well . . . I did wonder. Not something you planned, then?'

'Er . . . Not really . . .'

She laughs out loud now.

'I thought you were being modern. That guy over there fancies you, I think. Shall we go somewhere else?'

Good for her. Good for Lizzie. She's taking it well. I stand up and smile and say:

'Well yeah, of course, if you like? I mean I don't mind gay pubs, I've got gay friends and even a transsexual friend and . . .'

Lizzie is already standing. She takes her arm and slips it through mine and says:

'I know a place that does great cocktails!'

Yes!

Three hours and seven cocktails later, we say goodbye at the Tube. It's a slightly awkward moment which is relieved when Lizzie says to me:

'That was a lie about the cat, you know.'

'I guessed.' I am lying too.

'Did you?' She chuckles. 'Ha. Well, I really had a girly moment. Well, a girly hour. Couldn't work out whether to wear jeans or a skirt. Sorry!'

She is still smiling. Her face is very pretty. I wonder whether to lean forward and kiss her but maybe this is too forward of me. I remember the over-enthusiasm of my first date with Bongowoman. So instead I shake Lizzie's hand in a daft way and wonder what to do next; but then she does a phone-ringing gesture with her hand which says: 'Call me!'

I am about to say, 'But I haven't got your number,' when she thrusts a card into my hand with her number on it and then she pecks me on the cheek and smiles obscurely, and disappears into the Tube station.

When she is gone I think about doing a little dance in front of the station. A kind of cheery cockney leap, with my thumbs tucked in the pocket of my waistcoat. But I'm not wearing a waistcoat. So I go home, where I have to resist picking up the phone and ringing her immediately.

How long do I wait? The next morning I actually pick

up the phone but stop myself in time by having, er, a wank. This may sound gross but I have realised that my judgement is often clouded by sexual desire, and as a wank is the easiest way to get rid of excessive sexual energy, it often helps. After my wank I am notably calmer and I am able to wait until day *two* after seeing her. Which is something of a triumph.

The phone call goes smoothly, very smoothly. This is a warmly positive sign. I always think phone calls can be indicative of how things might be in the sack, i.e. if you've got the conversational rhythm there's a fair chance you'll be good together at the animal thing. Actually I've never thought that before, I just convinced myself of that when I put the phone down after she'd very enthusiastically agreed to a second date.

This time it's a meal and a few beers at a gastropub. Meals can be tricky on dates. That is to say, they were tricky for me once when I took a new girl to a restaurant, ordered some wine, got the bread, stared lovingly over the top of the menu at my first-time dinner date only for her to announce airily she was on a fast and didn't want to eat anything *at all*. She spent the next two hours smoking furiously and staring with resentful hunger at my food. That was our last date.

No such nonsense from Lizziegirl. She eats like a pit pony. Soup, meat, veg, pudding, the works. I like this. It's kinda sexy. I've never agreed with Byron, that women should only consume champagne and lobster salad. Too expensive.

Halfway through her pudding, Lizziegirl tells me more about her family.

'Oh God, we're mongrels. Dad's Italian, Mum's sort of a bit Jewish I think, with Russian, Welsh and, oh God, I don't know, Martian. He deals marble, marble tops and carrara and stuff . . . though . . . though I haven't seem him for about six years.' She looks at me. 'I guess every family has some tragedy and that was ours, my dad and mum used to fight so badly and he had to leave and she tried to turn us against him, but I love her and you know . . .'

'Right. So tell me more about the nude dancing?'

I don't say that really. I want to, though. My urge to get saucy isn't because I am bored with Lizzie's chat – she's funny and candid – it's just that she is wearing a low-cut top and her breasts are sort of *there* in the candle-light, gazing at me in a friendly way, like two fresh-faced presenters on Saturday morning kids' TV.

'Ant and Dec.' I say.

Lizzie looks at me, puzzled. I cough and say:

'That's tough. Your mum and dad. My mum and dad are divorced as well . . .'

'Yes . . .' She is squinting at me, then she is grinning. 'Hey. Are you looking down my top?'

'No,' I say.

'Yes you are.' She smiles.

'Well, yeah,' I say.

We laugh. Lizzie laughs a lot. A crackle of sexual static seems to shoot between us. And something else too. I am getting the first faint feelings of . . .

No, I can't be. Surely not. But I am. No no no. But yes yes yes. It's true. I am sensing something, something like the first intimations of a sensation . . . that could at a push be compared to the beginning of falling in . . .

Come on. Get a grip. Nitwit.

Yet who knows? My insides feel like the butterfly house at Syon Park. I could be falling for this strange, chubby, funny, short, sexy girl. Why shouldn't you fall for a girl on the second date? Because it might go wrong?

At this point in the cinema of my mind the screen goes wobbly. And as Lizziegirl starts on her second pudding (my pudding) I think back to the first girl I ever fell in love with. My first bite of the cherry of love.

Her name was Briony. She was an elfin (of course), rather dark, very pretty, University College London Classics student from Dorset. The first time I saw Briony was when I was on the phone to my mum in the UCL halls of residence where I lived in my first year. I was a gauche, nervous, first-term undergrad with a crap moustache. Briony was a gauche, nervous first-term undergrad too. But she had fantastic legs and was wearing a very short skirt, and she didn't have a crap moustache.

Anyway, I remember when she came tripping down the concrete-and-metal stairwell of that university building, holding one hand in the air as was her wont. I gawped. I thought she was too good for me. Yet a month later I snogged her for the first time at a student hop. Two months later I had my very first ever sex, with her, in her little poster-decked room in the hall of residence; this was the usual clumsy, awful, naff, stumbling first-time sex. And it was glorious.

Briony was the first girl I slept with *and* the first girl I fell in love with. A common enough corollary – and possibly a mistake on my part. Because Briony was also slightly mad. She used to crimp her hair until it burned. She liked to steal shoes and jewellery from her friends. She went self-evidently without knickers in the UCL Student Union bar, sitting on a barstool coyly drinking half-pints of Fosters out of a plastic glass while watching me play Defender, with her demurely golden legs uncrossed and the black fire of her pubes on show to *me*.

Yep, I lapped it all up. Because I *was* falling utterly in love. My heart used to lose it at the thought of Briony. She was mysterious and alluring, elusive and wild, and if sometimes she smelled a bit when she burned her hair, I loved that too. I was full of the rhapsodic anxiety of first love. Plug me into the drip and leave me in Casualty – that was my opinion.

But is that a good description of falling in love? Like an illness? Like being on a morphine drip in Casualty? How do you describe love anyway? Maybe it's easier to picture it. So I'm going to try. The nicest image I have of me and Briony is when I was about nineteen and we were at the peak of our mutual infatuation. Here goes. Picture this:

She is on the back of my Kawasaki 200; we are riding on my teenager's motorbike through the exquisite

Herefordshire countryside. I have brought her back to my family house for a week or two of the long university summer hols. The trees that whizz past us are green cages of gold; the thickset hedgerows are tinged with crimson and dog-rose. Thank you God.

We are on the way to see a favourite little church of mine, tucked away in the remoter part of the county. Despite the warmth of the day, Briony is on the back of the bike in her borrowed crash helmet, shivering slightly as we race down the country roads. She is shivering because she is wearing a very short skirt, one she made herself in her shared London basement flat by scissoring in half a much longer skirt.

'Sean!'

She is shouting, behind me, on the motorbike; I am also wearing a big deafening crash helmet.

'What!?'

'I'm cold!!'

Ah. I can't see my girlfriend, but in my mind I picture her; see her pixie-ish doubting face, the miniature nose, sallow skin, imponderably pouting scowl.

Briony may be cold but I don't want to stop because we are nearly there anyway. To reassure my frozen and, presumably, sulking girlfriend, I reach back and squeeze her bare teenage thigh: it is soft, and extremely cold. And mine. For a minute I sense her resting her head on my back and I get a surge of protectiveness as well as an urge to bite her naked bottom, and then at last – and I feel her relax behind me – we reach our target. I make a solemn turn into a smaller country lane; I trot the bike down past some country gardens; I park the bike in front of an old red sandstone country church.

Getting off the bike Briony half smiles, as if to say, *Now what do we do?* Again I spy that strange, rather shy anxiety in her face. I am blinking. My mind is blackberrying. Then I notice that Briony is staring harder at me; she is looking at me in a sardonic way, probably because I am obviously staring directly at her legs, her little feet in weird, muddy ballet shoes. Briony often wears black ballet shoes. This is because she wants to be the pretty girl from Fleetwood Mac, the ballerina on the album cover of *Rumours*.

But then she laughs, discreetly grins, kisses me briefly; and skips away. In a trice Briony has run laughing up the sunny lane towards the eastern graveyard, towards the ruined Norman castle on the hill behind. I hear girlish laughter through the trees, from the empty graveyard. The laughter is tinged with pity for me, for my helpless maleness. But I laugh too. Fuck it! I run after her and I pass the church wall and there I see Briony giggling in a hide-and-seek way behind a gravestone. I grab Briony, by the hand. She simpers, and tells me stuff about Dorset. I tell her I want to show her the view and she shrugs and says, 'Sure.' Together we walk through the graveyard; I watch her climb over a stile, making her white knickers flash.

Over the other, wilder side of the fence, sheep run away from us. Here, the red sandstone Herefordshire soil is scarred by tractor turns; cottages smoke in the distance. We climb the hill of the castle. The sun is high and glorious.

Somehow, even as it happens, I know this moment is special. Slipping on the red mud, we lift each other through some brambles, over old Norman stones, out on to the top of the ancient rise. At last I stand there and wave my exuberant undergraduate hand at the view: the green and rolling farmland, the churches and Tudor villages, the smoky Welsh mountains.

In the world beyond, Thatcher is imposing fierce monetarist discipline on a frightened country, America is installing cruise missiles across Europe, and China is emerging from the tumult of the Cultural Revolution and the Gang of Four. And here on this sunny English hilltop a nineteen-year-old lad is putting his hand up his girlfriend's skirt.

And with that we grab each other's hands and run down the hill again. Then we sprint through the churchyard, arm in arm, and duck under the porch like a just-married couple in a Merchant Ivory film; we run out on to the road and jump on the bike, and I kick-start the Kawasaki and we zoom away towards the distant hills.

OK, it's not much of a story. Soppy, even. But it kind of sums up the love I felt for Briony, something girlish and elusive in her, something helpless and male in me. A fatal combination.

But is that possibly akin to what I am feeling now, here in the north London gastropub? Is this anything like early love? Or at least the first intimations thereof?

Lizzie has stopped eating. Finally. We pay the bill and

get up, and we walk outside. It's a cool evening, I feel undergraduate and gauche again, but in a good way. The taxis of London are shooting past. Lizzie looks at one and says to me:

'I've got to get up early tomorrow . . .'

'You want a cab?'

'Yeah . . .'

My heart sinks. Second date; and no invite back. What went wrong? How could I get those signals wrong? The comment about staring down her top, the way she giggled when I said stuff. The passionate exchange of heartfelt truths; the fact we didn't stop talking for three hours. Except when she was busy eating, of course. Surely that meant . . . Surely that means . . . ?

Lizzie is on the pavement, scanning the street for an empty cab. One looms into view, orange light aglow. She really is going. But just as the cab parks up and I'm feeling lower than low . . . then Lizzie turns, and looks at me, and walks towards me, and she says:

'I had the most wonderful evening,' and her big eyes seem to go kind of melty and I can smell her gorgeous perfume and then; then we are kissing.

It's a proper kiss. The sort of kiss they did in Paris in August '44. It's a delicious kiss. The butterflies are wild in my heart. Feeling unsteady I open the cab door and Lizzie climbs in, and as the cab zips off I see her sweet face in the window and she is waving like the Queen at me, sarcastically, but nicely too.

I can't help it now. I'm off on one. Hope springs eternal,

especially when it is sharing a bottling plant with desire. For two or three minutes I just stand there, beaming. Then I go home and I don't remember much of the walk except that the homeless people get some serious money from me.

The mood continues for several hours. A day, a day and a half. Halfway through this dreamy reverie I text my friends about Lizzie. *'This could be the one,'* I say. *'This could be the one!'*

And then, on the second day, I open my email box and I see the message.

'I'm sorry, but I don't think it's quite right. Sorry. Lizzie.'

I stare at the email. Then I laugh, dryly. And oddly. Very slowly I read the message again, and then once more. Then inexplicably I shut down the email – and actually reboot my computer, in something of a daze. What do I think has happened, some kind of software glitch? But when the computer is up and running and I open the message box, there it is again.

'I'm sorry, but I don't think it's quite right. Sorry. Lizzie.'

Now I analyse the sentence. What wasn't quite 'right'? What's 'right'? Why is she 'sorry'? Twice? Is it because she actually liked me and it's a shame? But if she liked me, why trash us so prematurely, when it all seemed so promising?

I am quite upset. I have a stinging sensation somewhere near my spleen, and a kind of heavy feeling in my head. Thwarted libido is part of it, for sure, but it's also, I think, a very very small kind of heartbreak. Just as, halfway through that gastropub dinner, I felt some strange, early, minor intimation of love, so now I am enduring a kind of miniaturised heartbreak. The new Heartbreakman by Sony.

I know this is mini-heartbreak because I know what bigtime heartbreak is like, very well.

Briony broke my heart. Badly. Of course I should have seen it coming. There were plenty of signals. Falling in love with Briony turned out to be a *less* than brilliant decision. She was quite mad, scatty, funny, wilful, and seriously smart and cracked. And sexy. And mad. And I was too young, too naïve and gauche and laddish and keen, to know how to handle her. When she was nasty to me I was nice in return; when she was obviously flirting with other men I ignored it, and bought her flowers. And this just made her crazier, and more prone to getting drunk, and ignoring me. She was just too much for me, a gauche, moustached nineteen-year-old. Being in love with Briony Smith-Addison was like being given a vintage Ferrari to drive, on your eighteenth birthday: she was a complex and dangerous machine capable of exhilarating me madly, and capable of hurting me badly. *And* I didn't know which fucking buttons to push. Sometimes I would sit there, in the union bar, dazed, watching Briony dancing with other guys, and think: Are all women like this?

Over time – too late maybe – I worked out where Briony's excitingly frightening nature came from. The realisation happened when I went to visit her family for the first time. It was in deep darkest Dorset: an army base. Her stepfather turned out to be an abrupt Scottish colonel; her Italian mother turned out to be a woman who was kissed by Mussolini as a baby, a woman giving to wearing no knickers under her skirts.

What made the whole thing bizarre was when I realised the real family set-up. After some fairly insensitive questioning from me, it turned out that Briony's real father, a publisher, was now married to the stepmother *who was previously married to Briony's stepfather*. The two families had done an official wife-swap. Crazy enough, I thought, but then I discovered that – even madder, madder still – all of the combinations of sixties parents had had children. The result: three different sets of variously inter-related kids who shared a number of things in common, chiefly deep neurosis.

At first, at the time, I thought this made Briony and me even more alike. My own parents were divorcing; my own parents had once had their own version of seventies 'open marriage' type stuff. But Briony was way ahead of me. Different league.

So that's why Briony was a bit barmy. But she still had great legs. And I still loved her, ardently.

In November of that year, back at college, Briony left a message for me one day, on my answerphone, asking to meet me in a church near our university in London.

I replayed the message. A dull feeling entered my lungs. I ignored it, and went to meet her.

The sky was blank white and oppressive; a cold, late-autumn day. And I had a crap moustache, dyed blond hair, and something approaching a mullet hairstyle. Perhaps I should have seen what was coming.

When I pressed the door to the cold, silent church, I saw Briony. Standing by the font. Slowly I went up to her, sensing something was wrong, swallowing the tension. She regarded me flatly. She was wearing blue jeans and a strange purple top. I had a crap moustache.

'Hey . . .'

'Yeah . . .' I said.

By now I kinda knew what she was going to say.

'Yeah, well . . .' she said.

'What?'

'I'm sorry . . .'

And that was it. Silence surrounded us. Cold air. I looked at her. She was beautiful. I drank in her beauty: her overdone pout; her stupid ballerina shoes; her lank, over-crimped hair; her tiny, pathetic hands that couldn't open a marmalade jar, so I had to do it for her. At that moment I loved all of it with a painful anguish. Briony shrugged again. Then she sighed and she just walked past me towards the church door; as she did I smelt her perfume and I felt like hitting her, but I didn't. Instead, I called out to her disappearing figure:

'OK, who is it then? Briony? Briony? You can't do this to me. Briony? Who the fuck is it??'

All she did was raise a delicate hand on one side; then as she turned left to leave the church I could see in profile that she was actually *half laughing*. Laughing? *Laughing?*

Not only was Briony chucking me, she was chucking me with derisive contempt!

I did not react well. Over the following weeks I went into a minor breakdown. Without realising, I had built my whole student life around Briony; my self-image was comprised largely of 'me and Briony, the lovely girlfriend'; certainly my way of escape from the lonelier troubles of teenagerdom had been Briony. And now she'd ripped that away from underneath me. Consequently, I went apeshit, spazmo, doo-lally tap. For weeks I was inconsolable. Most nights I didn't sleep properly. Most weekends I went to student parties in Earls Court bedsits with cheap wine and bad punch and lots of Moroccan hashish, and I would find myself wandering the streets outside, because I was unable to talk to girls, girls who weren't Briony.

I also plagued my poor but long-suffering friends with questions: Why did she do it? What did I do wrong? How could she leave me when I was so nice to her? At one point, I rang my mum up from a payphone and actually burst into tears (for the first time since I was about thirteen).

Then I tried to win Briony back. I sent her poems and flowers; I left letters in her pigeon-hole with amusing but, I hoped, poignant notes. She wrote notes back to me saying, 'Please go away.' One day I got the bus miles up the Camden Road to Briony's basement flat and sat in the council library opposite her building for the entire afternoon, waiting for her to turn up so I could tell her how much I loved her.

When she did turn up – about eight hours later – it had got dark and the library had shut, and I was standing in the cold, absolutely shivering, and when I saw her I just let her go into the flat without even calling her name and then I got back on the bus and went all the way home.

Pathetic, I think you will agree. But why so pathetic? Part of it was just the suddenness with which the sexual tap had been turned off. When you have spent six pubescent years craving sex and then suddenly you get sex; and then suddenly you don't get sex any more, the pain is substantial.

Not that Briony and I had an amazing sex life. It was good, mildly orgasmic for her, I think; wonderfully exciting for me just because we were having SEX. About as kinky as it ever got was a near-threesome Briony and I and her flatmate Katherine had; but anyway it wasn't really a threesome because it was just me having sex with Briony while Katherine lay in bed looking at us somewhat oddly. Then it got too intense and Briony and I went into Briony's room to finish up.

So. Where was I? Heartbroken. Yes. But why was I so pathetic and heartbroken? Because I'm a man? I think maybe that's true. I could fill books and books (slightly boring books, maybe) with the stones of my friends' sad, dippy behaviour at the end of relationships. So why do men get so crap and dippy when relationships end? I'm not entirely sure, but the contrast with women is stark. Women are – in my experience – much more efficient and ruthless *at the end* of relationships. It's like, once a woman has made a decision it's over, *it's really over, dude*. Men, by contrast, will be complacent, careless and blasé in a relationship for years, then when it not unexpectedly goes wrong they get all romantic and yearning and desperate to win the woman back. And so you get the endless silly letters and foolish text messages; embarrassing and fumbling attempts to retrieve an irretrievable situation. Poetry left in pigeon-holes.

I think this discrepancy is maybe because women have that biological clock, a clock that ticks louder than a man's. Women have to move on; find the right guy; cut the schmuck out of their lives; sort out the situation before they've wasted too much time. Women *have* to find the guy with the right genes, the right stuff, and soon. Or maybe women are actually just harder than men, emotionally, and just pretend to be nice on the surface. And maybe men are just noodles.

My own heartbreak over Briony came to a pitch when I decided that a fake 'suicide bid' was the way to win her back. Clever boy.

I was staying at a friend's flat. He'd been listening to my whisky-sodden lament about Briony and we'd fallen asleep on the floor, and when I woke up he'd gone. Can't blame him. Lying on that floor with a hangover and an ashtray by my nose I felt the bleak Briony-less-ness of my life come roaring back.

So I sensibly fixed on the 'suicide' idea. If I faked a suicide Briony would see how in love I was, how true, how noble, and she would come to her right mind and return. Naturally.

Determined, I went into the bathroom to find a razor. Trouble was, there weren't any real razors. So I snapped open a Bic razor and started making a few scratches on my arm with this mangled bit of plastic and steel.

It hurt. So I stopped. Then I realised that one single scratch wasn't exactly going to impress Briony enough to win her back, so I did a few more scratches until the first beads of blood appeared and I got all dizzy and stopped.

There, I thought, staring at the mildly impressive scratches. Yes, that'll do. She'll have to come back to me now. Wrapping tissues around my slightly bleeding wrist I went outside into the wintry grey cold, climbed on a bus and, ignoring the stares, I went into town, towards college. But instead of going to uni I went to the hospital over the road. University College Hospital. There I waited in Casualty for a sweet nurse to be shocked by my tissue-bandaged wrist. But when the nurse had wiped the small amount of dried blood from my 'wound' she looked at me and softly said:

'It's not that bad actually.'

'What do you mean?' I was outraged. All that work!

'Well . . .' She was sweet, mid-twenties, a bit older than me, quite cute. I gazed at her as she bent over my wrist, as she lifted her face and looked at me in a kind way and said:

'I mean, it doesn't need stitches or anything, it'll heal itself.'

Uh-*huh*. This wasn't what I wanted to hear at all. Glumly, I looked down at the evidence of my attempted 'suicide'.

Silence. We both paused. The nurse pouted, thought-fully, as if working something out. Then she said:

'Tell you what: I'll put a bandage on it if you like?'

I looked up again.

'Could you? Really?'

The next day, my wrist dramatically bandaged, I waited in the chilly classical quadrangle of University College London for Briony to turn up. I knew that this day, Wednesday, she had tutorials in one of the weird, tiny observatory-like buildings that sit either side of the UCL quad. This meant that, to reach her tutorial, Briony would have to cross the quad at about noon, after alighting from her Camden bus.

At noon, a small, dark, half-frowning, winter-coated, very elfin Briony appeared round the corner of Gower Street and UCL. She looked sexy in the middle of the big quadrangle. I thought about her bare legs in wellington boots. Briony was carrying books and hurrying like a good girl student. I had placed myself theatrically on the central steps of UCL portico, with my bandaged wrist to the fore.

Briony did not see me, so I called out her name. Briony looked up. She saw me and made a weird, blank expres-sion. Then she smiled. I did not know why she was smiling, but I was encouraged. So I got up and went down the stairs, feeling nobly agonised. The sleeve of my coat was rolled up to the elbow, even though it was a very cold

February day, just so Briony would be able to see the bandage, the evidence of my love for her, my attempted suicide, the clinching factor in Briony's return to me.

Briony looked me in the eye. I gazed at her, expressing all my love, all my pain and despair. As I did, I slightly lifted my wrist up so she could *see*.

She was still looking at me. Then she said:

'Oh for fuck's sake leave me alone. Wanker.'

With that she turned on a trainered heel and walked towards the observatory. For a moment I stood there, looking down at my bandaged arm. Then I peeled back the bandage and stared at the slight white scratches on my wrist. They were healing already; in a few days they would be gone.

Walking towards the UCL gates, I ripped off the bandage and dumped it in a bin.

And that, in a way, was where I began to stop being heart-broken. The most intense period of the heartbreak had lasted about three months. I am told this is about average for an eighteen-month relationship. Of course, I kept on being sad and wistful about Briony for a lot longer, and I was overwrought in many other ways for months and months, but it never got that bad again. Six months later I shaved my moustache off.

And now? With Lizzie? The heartbreak lasts about four hours. By teatime I am feeling a lot better. It's time to go back to Internet dating. And this time I am going to be a little more ruthless.

Chinalady5 is 'also available in colour'

Over the next few weeks I have a series of dates with unsuitable girls. There's the slender English thirty-something architect who meets me in a Korean restaurant in Primrose Hill and starts off by telling me that she is really happy . . . because she met her perfect man just two days before this date that she had already arranged with me. I ask the girl why we are meeting, then. She tells me she thought she 'should still come along'. I'm not sure quite what she means by this – because she spends half the evening exchanging giggly text messages with her new man before looking up and blushing in embarrassment.

We split the bill.

Then there's a smart, attractive Iranian girl, from Qom via Cambridge University. I take her to a pub, where she tells me that she dislikes men because they are lying and weak. She graciously allows me to buy all the drinks. After two hours of her misanthropic riff she then says, 'I presume you want my number.' For a moment I am about to say 'yes' (she *is* rather pretty in an imperious way), but then I get a sudden rush of righteous outrage on behalf of my slighted gender – I know we can be pretty crap, but we do deal with bath-spiders – and I actually say 'no'. At this, she stares at me with disdainful surprise and stalks off in a huff. Sigh.

The third date on this accident-prone love-slalom is with a Russian girl who has been in the country about two years and barely speaks English. She tells me she was living in Smolensk when she was contacted by a rich businessman in Nottingham – who found her on a Russianbrides website. So she moved to England, but she didn't like his friends. Or his house. Or his car. Or, in the end, him. So she moved out.

I quite like this blonde, curvy Russian girl. There is something touching about her naïvety. We meet in Kensington and as we walk down the summery streets she marvels at everything: the cars, the bins, the pavements. 'It is all so clean!' she says. 'Not like Smolensk!' It strikes me this could be a good motto for Kensington Tourism. *Not Like Smolensk!* But then when we go to a pub and have a couple of drinks she starts getting maudlin, and after three more vodka-tonics she actually starts crying and saying she misses her parents and the way they would all sit in their flat with the carpets on the wall in the winter, living in the same room, too poor to wash, with no hot water, eating pickles. 'It's not like here. Everyone is rich here. But maybe we were happier. I do not know. *Dos vedonya.*'

We clink glasses, and then she starts on the weeping jag again. I'm really not sure how to react to this weird Russian chiquita. Her life seems slightly tragic and she appears to be a little mixed up, but she's got . . . a Pulitzer Prize-winning bottom. I am aware that this is shallow, but I can't help it. This girl is confusing me. She is bonkers. She's weeping again. But what about that arse!?

What can you do? After bidding the girl a sweet goodbye, I go home and wonder whether to email. But I eventually decide I can't cope with the tears, no matter how lovely-bottomed she is. And, to be honest, I'm not totally convinced she was that into me anyway.

Two days later she emails me and tells me she is moving back to Smolensk. I wish her well.

Am I disheartened by this litany of failure? Surprisingly, perhaps, no. It's been sorta fun. I may be lacking in success – and any sexual contact whatsoever – but at the very least I am meeting some interesting new kinds of people, and getting a new insight into the weirder recesses of the female mind. I have also learned that the people of Smolensk put carpets on the wall in the winter.

Yet I would be lying if I said it was all cheery good fun. There is a hidden but melancholy downside, too. The downside is finding out just how many solitary, yearning people there are out there, in the big bad city. Before I started this Internet dating thing I was vaguely aware of the truism that cities are full of lonely people. Sure. Natch. Uh-huh. I may even be one of them, at least for the moment. But the scale of loneliness that I am uncovering is spectacular. A trawl through the websites shows this. There are, literally, tens of thousands of Londoners online, all looking, all yearning. I am discovering that London is the Kuwait of loneliness: it sits on vast reserves of the stuff.

Which makes, I suppose, Internet-dating agencies the oil rigs. Whence, er, this loneliness gushes.

The weekend after my Smolensk-carpet woman experience, I spy a sweet-looking Chinese girl on DatingDirect.co.uk. She is called Chinalady. Having always had a penchant for Oriental women (which my ex-girlfriends have told me is because I am immature and need submissive women (to which I have always replied, yes that's true, but at least Oriental girls will do the washing-up)) I drop the twenty-nine-year-old Chinalady a line. Within a few hours she emails back. She misspells quite a lot of words, but she looks sweet in her slightly formal and stilted photo – with feline eyes, an agreeable nose and long, dark, lustrous hair. Her profile is also fun. Under one photo she has put: '*Yes, this is me! This is Chinalady!*' Which has a fetchingly funny candour about it. And under her other, black and white photo, she has put: '*Also available in colour.*'

That makes me actually laugh. But then I wonder if it was meant as a joke. Maybe she is just very naïve and ingenuous? I have to find out.

We meet at the entrance to Goodge Street station, near my flat. It is a dulcet summer night and people are happily ambling for the Tube, ferrying winebottles and bouquets of flowers to their beloveds. There is an agreeable air of expectation.

And there she is: Chinalady. She is wearing a cheongsam, one of those long, tight Chinese dresses that slits to the thigh – in her case a very lissom and attractive thigh. She is also carrying a posy of flowers. I have never seen a girl do this on a date before; it's rather touching. I get a little choked when I see it. All the effort she has gone to. Bless.

So far so good – so far so *very* good. Yet the date itself does not pan out so smoothly. Chinalady is chatty and companionable, but her spoken English is as shot as her written. When we go for pasta, at one point she seems to say 'hot penis'. This throws me. Why would she say 'hot penis'? It's a weird thing to say on a first date, especially when you have just been discussing the spaghetti. But then again I wouldn't wholly put it past Chinalady (who tells me her real name is Jun) to say 'hot penis' at the wrong moment; Jun seems mischievous and rather amusing, when I can understand her. The difficulty is I can only understand about a third of what she says. I think.

At the end of the date, when we are both pretty drunk, something unexpected happens. Jun leans over the tiramisu and tells me I look like 'Jem Bon', and she kisses me on the cheek. I have never been compared to James Bond before and even though I know it is a somewhat hyperbolic comparison, it's kinda flattering. In fact it's very flattering. As is the little kiss. And so as I escort Jun to the Tube, her arm through mine like you're meant to do on nice warm evenings, I get an optimistic surge. I am starting to think I could get used to this. I could get used to being with this strange, feminine, cheongsam-wearing, perfumed, posy-carrying, oddly forward Chinagirl – who thinks I look like Jem Bon.

Two days later, I email Jun once more. A day after that, she emails back and agrees to a second date, but this time near the caff where she's a waitress. After some thought on my part, we end up meeting in a Notting Hill bar with beers from Estonia and Slovenia and louche types in baggy jeans trying to find out who's got the most obscure mobile phone. This turns out to be a good choice. The bar is so loud I can ask Jun to repeat things – without appearing rude about her broken English.

At the end of the date – a fun and agreeable date, with not too many pauses – we stroll outside. It's a warm evening. It gets warmer when Jun squeezes up to me and says:

'Where are we go now?'

I look at her. We are in a little lane off the Portobello Road. Cars the colour of summer fruits are arrayed along the road, sparkling expensively in the leafy streetlights. Jun is looking up at me like an orphan child who's just stolen your wallet. Vulnerable but mischievous. What the hell! Leaning forward I kiss Jun fully on her hot-penis-saying lips – and she kisses me back. Then my hand goes to her jeans and her hand goes to mine and we are suddenly in quite a serious clinch.

Quite a few moments later, we disengage.

'My place?'

The Tube journey home is a steamy affair. At Lancaster Gate we start snogging again. At Oxford Circus, I have to stop myself undoing her bra. When we finally reach the flat we have been reduced to a state of wordless lust. I chuck on some music. I pull off her jeans. With a sensual sigh she switches off the light and now it's dark and the windows are open and the moon is beaming over the rooftops of Bloomsbury and all is going fanTAStically well; until . . .

Until we are about to have sex. Until we are about to actually do it. Then, at the very moment, Jun backs off. She physically backs up the bed. She looks embarrassed, shy, worried, and unhappy. What's worse: she won't tell me what it is, what's amiss. She just . . . wants to cuddle. So we just cuddle. Maybe it will be all right in the morning?

It isn't. This concerns me. But then I decide not to worry. Maybe we rushed it. Maybe things might be better and less nervous on the third date. So we arrange a third date. But things aren't better on the third date: on this date, Jun actually seems much less keen than before to go near sex. This is weird as she was hot to trot last week. Is something really wrong? I want to ask Jun – but whenever I hint that I am going anywhere near the subject she lets off distress flairs, and starts telling me about the moped her parents share in Guangdong.

By the fourth date we are just . . . kissing. Then, on the fifth date, even the kissing seems to get less frequent. The way the relationship is going soon we will just be waving to each other from passing buses.

Hm. It doesn't take Carl Jung on caffeine pills to work out that something is awry. Jun, I suspect, has some kind of psychological barrier vis-à-vis sex, some deep and reflexive 'no' about her person. If she has such a problem, she has my eternal sympathy.

Ever since Briony dumped me, I have suffered from temporary bouts of impotence. This sporadic and depressing impotence of mine has been ameliorated hugely (indeed almost completely) by the advent of Viagra in the late nineties. But back in the eighties, in the days of the miners' strike and the fall of the Berlin Wall and the protests against the Pershing Missile and the campaign to right the Leaning Tower of Pisa, there was no Viagra and my impotence was a living nightmare.

What made this impotence worse was the fact that, post Briony, having shaved off my ludicrous moustache and done something cool (ish) with my stupid hair, I had, it seemed, become more attractive to women. For example: it was in this post-Briony renaissance that Tufnell Park Night-bus Woman came on to me. And there were others. Not droves. But some. A smattering. Suddenly, I seemed to be magnetic. Well, at least not repellent. Yet when I got these women back to whatever dingy London flat I was sharing with my laddish friends, the same terrible frightening stupid idiotic thing would happen, again and again.

Everything would be going well. We'd have our clothes off. The bedsheets would be agreeably tousled. But then when I went to actually penetrate, I'd remember what happened the last time, and my erection would wilt like an ice-sculpture in Egypt. And then I would get hugely anxious about it, about my ability to penetrate, making any further attempts to penetrate pointless. Even counter-productive. Cuddling was always an option.

Where did this impotence start? I'm not sure. Perhaps I failed once when I was drunk and from there the doubt set in. What's for certain is that this ongoing disaster must have happened seven or eight times – with seven or eight different young attractive women – in the year after Briony. And I didn't know what to do about it. The situation got so bad, I ended up actively avoiding sex, avoiding the whole issue. I would meet a girl and chat to her and then when she showed the slightest tremor of interest in me I would say to myself, 'But she's not like Briony, I can't fancy her,' and that would give me an excuse to back off, to forget about it, when in reality I was very keen on the girl but very scared of encountering that moment again, that block, the anxiety spiral, the embarrassed excuses, the 'Can we just cuddle?' Yuk.

I was mixed up, I was confused, I was – just occasion-ally – miserable and annoyed. So I tried to read around the subject. I discovered in Freud that this 'performance anxiety', the inability to achieve penetration by men other-wise healthy and sexually capable, was often encountered in highly sexed men, paradoxically enough. This was reassuring for a while: 'Hey, I can't have sex because I'm highly sexed.' But I still wasn't having sex. Which is a nasty state of affairs when you are twenty-one and women are making eyes at you. It felt like God was saying to me: 'These Are Your Shagging Years, Make the Most of Them,' but He had forgotten to put some gel in my hair. So I couldn't make the most of my opportunities. I was wasting all my chances. I was a spendthrift, a squanderbug, a wanker.

This situation might have gone on for years, for the rest of my life, if my life hadn't taken a sudden turn. Twenty long months after Briony, I finally, unexpectedly, wonderfully, and catastrophically, fell in love again: this time with my true love, or at least the girl I have most loved in a sexual and passionate way, to date.

This love was very different. Whereas my love for Briony had been romantic, boyish, adoring, the next one was deeply eroticised, obsessional, adult. Perhaps I should have expected this. Indeed I think the Russian writer Pushkin once said that 'first love is sentimental, second, voluptuous'. Trouble was, I hadn't read that at the time: I was keener on boozing with my mates in scruffy pubs than looking out prescient warnings in Russian literature.

Her name was Eleanor. Despite the English name she was half Swiss, half Jewish. She was also very posh. Viola lessons. Au pairs. Modern art. You know. My first encounter with Eleanor, Ellie, El, was when a friend of mine who shared my flat brought her back to our squalid, beercan-strewn, noisy Camden home. Sitting there amidst our pizza boxes and snooker cues, the blonde, manicured, cultured, trilingual, richly rich Eleanor looked a bit out of place. Like a unicorn amongst trolls, like a peacock in a flock of starlings, like a rich girl slumming with the bad boys. Which isn't surprising maybe: that's precisely what she was. I was twenty-two and leading a feral, aimless, enjoyable, thinking-of-freelancing post-university life; Ellie was seventeen and as smart as she was rich: she was already at university.

Bizarrely enough, when we first met, I didn't really fancy her. I didn't even notice her, much. I was too busy getting drunk and partying on down. (Months later Ellie told me it was this that got her into me. She was used to men fawning over her. I was too careless to notice her, and that's what drove her mad. Women!)

But then, on the second or third time she came round to our flat, Ellie invited me on holiday with some of her friends. Just like that. To her parents' villa in Provence. And I suddenly realised what had been staring at me all along: this slender young thing was very attractive indeed. And she was rich. And smart. And blonde. And inviting me to her parents' house in Provence.

In Provence we fell for each other. Helplessly. I'd like to say this happened in a very romantic way; I'd like to say it happened as we talked about Cézanne over the tapenade or watched shooting stars from the lavender fields. But it didn't. For me, the clinching moment was when Eleanor became the first girl to give me head successfully. It happened on the last night of that idyllic French holiday.

Until then I had never managed to orgasm that way. Indeed I had only ever managed to orgasm during sex by having sex with Briony (as she was the only girl I'd had sex with). But Ellie, like the experienced London girl she was, led me into the warm, cicada-y, midnight garden of the villa and she took me in hand and sorted that particular problem out. I can see and feel that moment now: her soft blonde hair across my twitching stomach. Me staring out across the cypress trees. A Van Gogh moon in the sky.

I was in love.

Not only was I in love, I was deeply in love, puzzlingly in love. Ellie was, in so many ways, the kind of girl I had never encountered before. And I was fascinated by her curious personality: the mixture of compassion and thoughtlessness, the serious cleverness mixed with notable immaturity, the way she (was this an eighties thing?) often went without knickers. She was also very good at poker (acting like a dippy girl and then winning all the money).

And she was appallingly scruffy – but even that was somehow curious to me; she was scruffy and messy because she was rich, leaving clothes around for servants to pick up. A bit like Prince Charles, but with breasts. I was the impressed provincial lad, despite myself.

And of course she gave great head. Yet Ellie had not solved all my sexual problems. As the holiday proved, I still couldn't manage to penetrate. This was particularly vexatious to me as I SOOOOO wanted to penetrate Eleanor. To make her mine. To make me hers. To be properly in love.

Back in London, and five weeks into our already passionate and giddying relationship – like two people falling out of the sky, holding on to the same parachute – I decided to fess up. I told Eleanor my problem. And . . . she, well, she understood. She was just happy I'd told her. She had been wondering what was wrong. She'd even changed her perfume just in case that was putting me off. Bless her little Mercedes sports.

And, yes, her tolerance and understanding worked. A few weeks later it all came right. One night, one blessed night, Eleanor's patience, and a quart of whisky, finally combined to relax me enough – enough so that I slid things into place. God, I was happy. I think I might have almost cried, afterwards. I was a man again.

Can I apply any of this to me and Jun? I'd like to think so. But first I have to know what is wrong with her. I really haven't got a clue, though. And so I ask my ex-girlfriends. These consultations are mildly productive (the diagnoses range from 'frigidity', to 'vaginismus' to 'she thinks you've got a stupid willy') but they don't get me very far in terms of talking about it to Jun. For that, Jun is going to have to talk to me. The trouble is, she won't even *begin* to talk about it. And what's worse, her behaviour is getting more eccentric.

One day Jun arrives at my flat – unannounced. I try to tell her that, even though I am pleased to see her, nonetheless I would like a bit of warning before we meet; but she just chatters away as if I haven't said anything. The next day she sends me a loving note. Hmm. The day after that she sends me . . . a birthday card. It's not even my birthday.

Staring at the birthday card, I start to get a cold, sweaty feeing. This is getting too much. Consequently, I decide it would be best if . . . we take a breather. I don't want to end it totally; not yet. I don't want to trash it completely. But Jun and I need to think. And so I sit at my laptop and send Jun an email, an email very sensitively phrased – I hope – very delicately designed – I believe – in which I subtly indicate that perhaps we should just cool it for a little while, see how we both feel, have a think about how things are going, and get back in touch within a fortnight or so.

The next day, she sends me another card, some flowers, and a small piece of Chinese linen in a frame.

The conclusion is inescapable: I'm being stalked. She has fallen obsessively in love with me. And is stalking me with linen.

Inwardly, I groan at this. Outwardly, I groan too. Because I know how dangerous obsessive love can be. Ellie and I had an obsessive affair, and it turned out to be very dangerous.

The problem with Ellie and me was that, despite our disparate backgrounds, we were too alike. Too similarly foolish. Too identically reckless. It was like we were separated at birth and we were making up for lost time . . . Put it another way: personality-wise, we were twins. We both wanted to try everything, and this unfortunate conformity of appetites was most apparent in our sexual relationship.

As I have indicated, Ellie was, sexually speaking, much more experienced than me (not that that was a particularly hard thing). Whereas I had only had sweet, soft, vanilla-y sex (apart from the pseudo-threesome with Katherine), Ellie had had some very un-vanilla sex. Within a few weeks of our sexual relationship kicking off, it became obvious she was au fait with sexy things that I had only imagined. Things like oral sex with ice. Things like sex involving fruit. Things like sex on a boat with a vibrator and furs.

Moreover, the one place where she *really* knew about weird sex turned out to be a place I was quite keen to explore myself.

One day I was having sex with Ellie in one of the many bedrooms in her temporarily parent-less Hampstead house, when she looked up at me with a frank and shrewd and I've-solved-it expression, like a tennis coach who has worked out what's wrong with your serve. Except she was naked apart from some black leather boots. Anyway, flopping back on the Conran pillowcase, Ellie looked at me and nodded to herself and wiped some sweat from her forehead and she said:

'I think it's time you tied me up.'

At first, I confess I was a bit thrown by this. It made me stop and pause, and think. Did I really want to do this? Did I really want to go down this experimental road, the road that leads who knows where? About five seconds later I said, 'You betcha!', skipped into El's bedroom and, following her instructions, retrieved some silk scarves from a drawer in her bedroom. The scarves were in the same drawer as a vibrator and some lubricating gel, as if waiting to be used together. I didn't notice this at the time.

Two hours later, Ellie had two of the most panting orgasms of our three-month affair, and I was struggling to unknot the scarves around her wrists.

This tying-up session swiftly turned to other stuff. It turned out that Ellie liked to be spanked. Vigorously. And to be handcuffed. She wasn't afraid of a belt, either. Or a gag. She also liked to have sex in broom cupboards where we might be discovered. And in royal parks right across London. And on the verge of a motorway with juggernauts racing past and honking. She even liked the idea, at least, of hiring a prostitute to join us in a three-some (though in the end we bottled out and went for a pizza).

But perhaps I am being a little self-serving in making Ellie responsible for all of this. The truth is, looking back, much of this kinky stuff might have been my idea just as much as El's. OK, Ellie had started the whole thing off, she'd, er, shown me the ropes; but I took to this new departure in my sex life with gusto. I definitely wanted to try it all out. I absolutely wanted to know what it was like. I was very much up for it. Ellie and I had uncovered an interest in the wilder kinds of sex in each other: it was *folie à deux*, as the French so wisely say.

It was also perhaps like some gay male sex. There was an exact symmetry in our sexual interests; we shared the same aggressive sexual abandon; and we also liked doing it in toilets. Put it differently: in our relationship the male libidinous principle – *Right, I want sex now!* – operated on both sides. There was therefore no restraining female influence, no coyness, no shyly different appetite, no traditional coquetry to slow things down. I'm not saying Ellie wasn't feminine – she was, very (not least in her mood swings, her capriciousness, and her ownership of seventy-five pairs of shoes she only looked at) – but when it came to sex, Ellie thought like a man. A gay man. A promiscuous gay man on Hampstead Heath. And I was up for a bit of cottaging too. You do the math.

What made this even *more* dangerous – and claustrophobic – was that El and I had no breathing space. Because we were so suited, personality wise, we spent all of our time together. And I mean all – not just the torrid nights. When I wasn't tying Ellie up with her girl-guide outfit, or making her walk around London in just a winter coat (the memory burns me now), she and I would drink together, laugh together, spend whole nights talking endlessly and satisfyingly about politics, sex, philosophy, and what was the most farcical kind of disco dancing (the Hustle, we decided). And when we weren't talking we would play those endless games of backgammon together, through the night, just me and her, laughing softly.

In fact, I think if there is an image of me and Ellie in love it isn't actually an image of her and me coupling in the props cupboard of a theatre, or shagging in Richmond Park with a deer watching over us; it's actually a much more humble image: of her and me, happily playing backgammon, alone, late at night. As I remember, she always won. Perhaps because she often played topless.

Naturally, it had to end. Ellie and I were burning the fuel of love at a heck of a rate. There was one three-month period when we didn't spend more than six hours apart at any one time. This obsessive togetherness, allied to our newly discovered mutual interest in fruity sex, meant that to keep the rush going, to keep things exciting and weird and heady, we had to keep upping the sexual ante very frequently. And so we ended up heading for some very strange places indeed: one time I tied Ellie up and put her outside the Hampstead house, naked and trussed, for a laugh. She came, she told me, but it was scary. Another time we tried to make each other bleed.

And then it ended. Just like that. This wasn't the slow, melancholy falling out of love you normally get. It was dramatic and explosive. We just started fighting, from nothing. One afternoon she tried to push me out of her car – while she was driving. Another time, I threw a whole Christmas tree at her. She ducked. Why were we suddenly fighting? It was almost a kind of sibling thing. We were so close we felt able to hurt each other. But then the hurting got serious. Or maybe it was another way to keep the relationship spicy, maybe it was yet another game that we started for a laugh – that this time went wrong. I don't know, maybe it was just the built-in obsolescence of love, the way it's designed to go wrong after eighteen months, like a mobile phone – so you have to get a new one. I *do* know that Ellie and I let the sex obscure the other good things in our relationship, the laughter and the backgammon, the food fights and the country walks. We'd forgotten how to do anything but fuck. And so when we weren't fucking we just lay there, staring at each other, two strangers, wordless. With a broken Christmas tree lying forlornly by the bed.

It sounds like madness. Maybe it was. I think at its most devouring and impassioned, as with me and Ellie, young love can be close to lunacy. In fact this kind of obsessive love is one of the few things that make me doubt the evolutionary explanation for human behaviour. Passionate love just seems, I don't know, excessive somehow – it's too much, too good and too bad at the same time. And you don't sleep. And that, in the end, is why it can't go on. As Byron said, you can't be helplessly in love all the time – 'because when would you shave?'

And so it ended. Not with a whimper, but a bang. After one session of particularly furious arguing/sex, I moved out. Just like that.

Actually, it wasn't just like that. I had the nail-scratches on my back from that last love-making session for nearly a fortnight. And even when they had healed, the deeper wounds lived on. Big time. In my bruised and conquered heart I still loved Ellie more than I had loved anyone before. But I also hated Ellie more than I had hated anyone before. I hated her, particularly, for making me miss her so much, miss her hair, her thighs, the way she played backgammon topless. For months I masturbated about Ellie three times a day; and when I wasn't masturbating

I would walk the streets where we used to live, looking for women who looked like her, looking for her. And then I would get palpitations when I thought it was her. Weirdly enough, though, it never was *her*. Over the following weeks, the following months, I managed to avoid bumping into Ellie. Or perhaps she managed to avoid bumping into me. Either way, I didn't meet El again for many years, even though we lived not far from each other for much of that time. Perhaps God was looking after us, keeping us apart, saving us from more loved-up lunacy, the love that could only damage us more.

All in all, it took me, at a guess, two years to get over Ellie; perhaps in some ways I never have. Second love is the deepest, as Pushkin nearly said. But I am still glad I experienced that depth of despairing love; I am fairly sure I never want to experience it again. It's seriously fucked up.

Anyway. Where was I? Jun? Yes. So is obsessive love what Jun is experiencing now? Surely not. I'm flattering myself if I think so, and we haven't had anywhere near the time or the intimacy to get that crazy about each other. But I know there is *some* kind of obsession going on.

Because she's started hanging out by the bins. One morning I wake up, lift the blinds on the window of my flat, gaze out into the London street – and there she is: standing by the bin bags. Looking up at my flat. Perhaps she has got a job with the Camden Refuse Department, but I somehow doubt it. Closing the blinds again I get on with my work, and try and forget about her. Surely she will soon go away?

A week later, there she is again. Binwoman. This time I see she is staring up at my flat and using her mobile. Then my mobile rings. I pick it up. It's her. I am almost angry, but I am also pitying. I know I have to do something. Now.

So I gird my loins, and I go down the stairs, and I cross the street to where the bin bags are kept, where Jun has started hanging out. Standing in her sweet little denim jacket, Jun looks ludicrously and painfully pleased to see me, like she thinks it's all going to be all right now. It isn't. Shifting a bin bag out of the way, I say to her: Jun, it's over. I'm sorry, but it's over. You've got to stop doing things like this, Jun. Please?

How will she react? I'd prefer it if she was angry and unreasonable, then I wouldn't feel so guilty about what I've done. She could even hit me, that would be good, and absolve me of responsibility. But instead Jun just weeps a little, and turns away to hide her tears. Then she says a mumbled 'goodbye Jem Bon' – and she walks slowly off down the busy London street.

And that's the end of it. I feel awful, and empty, but it seems to be over. Indeed, it is over. The only contact I have from Jun in the following weeks is just one touching card. A birthday card. The weird thing about this is that it actually arrives on my birthday. How did she know? Oh crikey.

Apart from my conscience-stricken guiltiness, the main

result of this sorry and startling episode is that I am rapidly going off Internet dating, indeed I feel like giving up dating altogether. It's such a lot of . . . hassle. And it's so easy to . . . hurt people. Sitting over my laptop one day, a few weeks later, the first scents of autumn blowing through the window, I think about what I am doing as I look at the dating websites. I haven't sent an email for yonks. I haven't scanned a gallery for ages. And I don't care. I've had enough, I think. But just as I am about to click on the Unsubscribe button, I get a phone call from my editor, Simon.

'How's it going, Sean?'

'What?'

'Hello? The Internet dating?'

'Oh . . .' I say. 'Oh . . .' Well, what can I tell him? I think about lying, and saying it's all good – but then I decide to tell him the truth. 'Well, I met a girl I liked who dumped me; I've been stalked by a Chinese woman; I had to chuck a real sweetheart 'cause she was three inches too tall; and I've met a nice girl who moved to Russia after our first date.'

There is a pause at the other end of the line. Then he says:

'Sounds like great copy! Keep it up.'

The phone goes dead. Then the phone rings again. It's Simon again.

'By the way, we're thinking of making it a cover story.'

I think on this. And then, for some reason, I start laughing. I've just noticed I've got a '*Message Waiting*' for me.

How HOT do you want things to get?

'Hey, I think my flat might be smaller than yours. If that doesn't put you off, drop me a line when you get a chance, Bumps.'

She is thirty-one years old. Short (I guess you figured that already), blonde, very cute, looks a little like Robin Hood as played by a girl in a pantomime. She says she works in the movie biz. She says she was also a dancer, but she got injured – *'but I can still do the splits big time'*.

I compose a message to return to her. *'A flat smaller than mine would be, technically, a kennel. Can't believe you live in such inhumane circumstances.'* Then I look again at this message. What a load of toss. 'Inhumane circumstances'? I bin the message. Then I have a think. I try again, veering off the already weary theme of small-ness of flats.

'Hello Bumps,' I say. *'I used to go out with a dancer. She had muscles everywhere and when she . . .'*

I bin that, too. What the hell am I banging on about?

This one is going to sound weird or brazen or both. I don't want that. But I want to say something wry, witty and slightly seductive, without going over thirty words, as I suspect that long first messages are off-putting. So I go back to Bumps's profile. There's not much in her profile to go on. Her profile is quite opaque and evasive. So I decide to throw caution to the breeze, and this time I message her a simple but slightly forward:

'Bumps, eh? Are you boasting? I'd love to meet for a drink if you have the time . . .' In my so-far quite limited experience of Net-dating, this is pretty risky – to be so pushy and fruity. But I'm feeling bored of the angsty, long email exchanges, and I'm also horny.

Two days later, I get a message back.

'I normally wait at least a couple of weeks before I agree to that! But hey, at least you can spell. You'd be amazed at the number of guys on these sites who can't spell. Sure, let's have a date.'

Yes!

We arrange to have our first date in a mildewy but intimate little basement bar off the Charing Cross Road. When I get there I'm slightly nervous, but only slightly. Becoming something of an old hand at this. Then she walks down the stairs, smiling and waving. My heart does not skip a beat, but neither does it sink. Truth be told, she is not quite as pretty as she looked in the photo, but then again I'm not standing next to Mick Jagger. So we're quite well matched. I'm happy with this. I actually quite like the way Bumps is not devastatingly beautiful. Because right now I don't want devastatingly beautiful (that's a lie, but you know what I mean). I haven't got the time nor the patience for one of those complexly beautiful girls, one of those dauntingly difficult stunners. Right now I don't want to get hung up, strung out, moonstruck, wiped. What I want is: a bunk-up.

Bumps's real name is Lula. To be honest, I'm not totally sure that *is* her real name at all, no more than Bumps is – she seems to be pretending about things generally. But then again, so am I. After an hour or two, I am getting the feeling we are both pretending here; both pretending we want a relationship, when actually all we want is some fun and a cuddle. At least to start with.

I could be deluding myself, convincing myself that we are on the same promiscuous and casual wavelength. But I think I am allowed to make this hopeful presumption, because there's simply no way of telling otherwise without totally mucking things up. I mean, if I lean across this candlewaxy table and say, 'By the way, I just want to get laid, how about you?' I don't think it will go down very well. Even if Lula is up for it, up for promptly casual sex, she will not admit it, nor should she be expected to. The essence of promiscuity, of casual sex, is, to my mind, partly in denying that it is quick and casual sex, or at least in not explicitly spelling it out. And that's as it should be. Casual sex should be wordless, sudden, unvoiced, spontaneous. Casual 'loveless' sex should be a sudden and wonderful recognition of each other's pressing and identical needs. I'm talking clothes thrown over the stairs. Knickers lassoed over winebottles. Broken zips. Remember?

Before everyone points out that I must be talking through my flipping hat because I have (judging by what I have told you so far) had a very limited sexual experience, I should say that I know something about this because, after a slow start to my sexual life (two women by the age of twenty-three!) I turned things around somewhat, and had some periods of quite profound promiscuity.

The first one of these periods came a year or two after my shattering experience with Eleanor. It happened like this: When I finally emerged from my heartbreak and delirium, my post-romantic stress disorder, I sat down and looked at myself, my woman-bruised heart, and I decided a few things. I decided I was going to become a lot more ruthless and cynical in future; more self-sufficient, less dippy, tougher, a man. Bluntly – I was going to get *laid*.

That might have been my intention, but it didn't work out like that at first. The weird thing about trying to get laid *ex nihilo*, if you are man, is that the obvious fact that you are trying to get laid is the one thing absolutely guaranteed to make sure that you won't get laid. To put it another way, for a sex-seeking man, success breeds success, and failure feeds off failure. Indeed I think this is what Jesus's Parable of the Talents is about: the more shagging you do, the more shagging you will do.

But why? The reason for this stark and unhappy truth

is that women like a man who knows what he's doing, a man who has a self-assured air with women, which means in essence a man *who has had sex recently*. Whether it's intuition or evolution, women can sniff the confidence on a man, the piercing scent of an alpha male, and they respond to that perfume with their own yielding cologne.

It sounds far-fetched, but this perfume thing may be a literal truth. I have a friend who, whenever he has casual sex, never washes for a few days. He swears that women start sidling up to him on the Tube when he does this. Supposedly they want to sniff some of that alpha-male body-scent. Gross, I know, but plausible, perhaps.

Equally, I think women can spot the panicky whiff of a male sexual failure from a mile off. I have another friend, rather handsome actually, who in his mid-twenties didn't have sex for *three whole years*. Three whole years is a shatteringly long time for a young man to go without, and it nearly sent my chum bonkers. His hair started growing in strange directions. He started knitting. He learned Welsh. Like I say, he nearly went mad.

It was a cruel sight: watching my chum in action, during his biblical stint in the sexual desert. One minute he would be in a pub, chatting away with the rest of us – relaxed, humorous, charming – then, God help us, he would see a woman making eyes at him. As he was attractive (despite the hair; despite even the Welsh) this would happen to him quite frequently. So he would wander over and begin talking to the smiling girl. And then it invariably went wrong. I don't know exactly what it was he said to these girls, but within a few minutes they'd have stopped smiling, then they'd start rolling their eyes and backing away nervously. A few minutes later they'd be flinging dry-roasted peanuts at him in a desperate bid to escape.

It was awful to witness. The poor guy just exuded failure and lack-of-confidence, and it seemed the girls could always spot this; he came across as so desperate and needy they soon decided that, no matter how good-looking he was, he was either mad or secretly deformed in some way. And so he failed. And so his confidence got worse. A cruel and vicious spiral. I should add that eventually he did meet a girl, a lovely girl, who was arguably more eccentric than him, and that got him back in the saddle. But the scars remain. He can still speak Welsh. At the time, and ever since, I had serious sympathies with my friend. Because sexual droughts like this happen to every man. As I have intimated, they certainly happened to me.

For about a year after Ellie, I wandered around in a state of total sexual famine, desperate to have sex, but failing to have sex. This unslaked thirst, this Dickensian street-urchin hunger, naturally made me even more obsessed about sex than normal (and I, like many men, am normally very obsessed with sex anyway). And this obsession got pretty bad. Here's a couple of pointers (you may skip the rest of this paragraph if you are of a queasy disposition). Once, during my schlep across the Sinai of celibacy, I caught myself looking at a 'naked' mannequin in a shop window. With *lust*. Another time, I was researching a journalistic piece on diseases (I was a proper journalist by now; I was growing up) and I caught myself glancing for quite a long time at a picture of a young woman with polio in the medical textbook. The disease was awful, but the woman was also . . . naked.

It was at this point that I realised I had to do *something*, but what? As I said at the beginning of this passage, it's hard to bootstrap yourself into sexual successland, to conjure the Genie of Boomboom from the Dull Brass Lamp of Too Much Wanking.

That said, there are various ways of addressing the problem: I know a man who likes to visit prostitutes when he has a sexual drought. He claims that having sex with a prostitute gives him the confidence that he can actually do it, that he still remembers what a vagina *is* and what to put *in it* (it is amazing what doubts will pass through a man's mind in these wilderness times).

Other men have different techniques. Some men I know like to reintroduce themselves to sex by going for a woman they would normally consider beneath them. Once they've proved to themselves that they are still attractive to women as a species, once they've dipped a toe in the shallow end of the gene pool, then they can be more ambitious, because emboldened.

It has to be said that neither of these methods are morally beautiful. In fact, they could be construed as nasty and disturbing. I'm just telling you what happens. As for *my* case, I was mercifully saved from stooping to such moral depths during my Carnal Famine, the Great Potato Blight of Love, by the precise fact I *was* so overwrought and angsty. I was twenty-three. I'd had sex with two women. I was still hung up on one of them a lot; maybe both. I was also looking at mannequins in a libidinous way. In other words, I was way too horny to think straight, let alone adopt any dubious 'techniques'.

So I didn't. And yet, funnily enough, one day the rains came anyway. One minute, it just happened. And the reason it happened, I think, is that a few weeks before the blessed release, I stopped worrying about not getting sex. This was because some other stuff suddenly happened in my life, a family drama that was far more important and urgent than not having had sex for a year. This new anxiety made me unhappy, but it had the side-effect of making me less anxious about my lack of sex. All of which had the curious result that, once I stopped caring about whether I got laid or not, I got laid.

Having said all this, I'm not quite sure what my experience teaches us. It's not the most practical advice: if you are a young man and you haven't had sex for a year, try and get your house firebombed, or your family kidnapped in the Sudan, so you will be so anxious about other stuff that you won't worry about women so much and then women will come on to you because you seem attractively nonchalant. Mm.

But anyway: one day, out of the blue, I got laid. Just like that. After a year of fretful and unwonted celibacy, a Welsh girl sat on my lap, at a party, and a few days later we did it. It was great.

Then a week later I did it . . . again. With a different

girl. I repeat, *with a different girl*. She was an English student, friend of a friend, with breasts like two young labrador puppies leaping up at a pet-shop window. *Cool*. And then, glory be, about three weeks later, it happened once again. With another girl. Also different. This was, to me, remarkable. Without warning I had turned from a Loser in the Lottery of Love to Mister Moneybags. I had gone from timidity and despair with girls, to walking into bars (or parties, or editorial meetings, or train stations) with an actual swagger: I was now the kind of guy who slept with women, and so women slept with me.

For the initial few weeks of this bonanza, I was suspicious of my own luck. Surely it couldn't go on. Yet, incredibly, it did. It turned out the first of my purple patches wasn't a momentary thing. It actually went on for some time. Quite a long time; years even. It was heaven.

Why was it heaven? Let's try and break down the appeal of promiscuity. I think it's interesting and more complex than it appears.

One pleasing aspect – for me – was and is the very namelessness of the act. To my own surprise, it turned out that for all the romantic yearnings and monogamous certainty of my early youth, I liked the blind, anonymous, to hell with it, what's-your-name-again casualness of casual sex. For instance, there was one girl I met on a trip to Rome. There were just the two of us – two journalists on this trip – and a PR woman. By the end of the first night, the lady journalist and me were doing the creaturely thing in my posh Roman hotel room. I particularly remember this night because it was the day Clinton was first elected. We had CNN on in the room. So every time I did something to this girl, it would be punctuated by an announcement from the TV. 'And Clinton's taken Arkansas!' Twang. 'And Ohio's gone Democrat!' Squelch.

Yet despite these vivid memories, I cannot remember the girl's name, to this day. Indeed I reckon I never noted it in the first place, properly. I do recall that she possibly worked for the *Daily Express*. Hey, maybe she is still there. If she is, I hope she doesn't write to me reminding me of her name, because the fact I can't remember her name somehow adds to the memory of our blind and ardent coupling. It wasn't love, it wasn't romance, it wasn't even particularly affectionate. It was just SEX. Sudden, glorious, filthy, unexpected sex. And Clinton's taken South Virginia!

One other thing I remember from this event was the girl's attempt to talk dirty. When I took down my trousers, with the Spanish Steps glinting in the moonlight through our bedroom window, she said: 'Are you going to put your big willy inside me?'

'Are you going to put your big willy inside me?' Where did *that* come from? As soon as I heard the girl say this I wanted to know what thought processes went through her head to make her come up with a statement like that. Did she think she was 'talking dirty'? If she did, then surely she would have been better advised to use the word 'cock'. No? Or was she too shy to use a really dirty word? If so, why talk dirty at all? To please me? Who knows?

Maybe she had her own secret garden, some secret construct of eroticism that revolved around the word 'willy', and this statement was to please herself? Curiouser and curiouser. As it happens, I found this statement of hers absurdly arousing, anyway, because of its mixture of embarrassed coquetry and fumbling hussiness. And, of course, I was flattered.

This statement points up another alluring aspect of promiscuity. Having casual sex is a very direct, incisive and immediate way to get to know a person, to swiftly map the sea floor of their selves, to see what naughty word they use for 'penis'. Humans just seem to be more honest in bed, more revelatory, than they are anywhere else. Maybe it's something to do with lying down that makes people fess up to stuff. That's why Freud put his patients on couches, as I understand. Or maybe it's because, once you have exposed your private parts to another person, showing other stuff, like a hatred for garden peas or your mother, is less traumatic.

During my shagging years I certainly discovered lots of amazing and curious things about girls – things it might have taken me weeks or months to discover any other way – merely by having penetrative intercourse with them.

There was a feminist I met at a wedding. She was pretty serious: earnest, *Guardian*-reading, hardcore, radical, disdainful, smart, cool. But after five minutes in a borrowed bed she was saying things like 'call me your little kitten' and after another five minutes she intimated that she wanted to be taken from behind with some vigour while I forced her head into the pillow. And then she radically orgasmed when I grabbed a fistful of her hair and pulled it back extremely hard. This told me more about this girl than many semesters of discussion on the sexist semiology of car repair.

Then there was the charity PR girl. She was beautiful in a sad way and had once had cancer, and she liked to hit me on the back when she came like I was a pair of bongoes. Poignant. I also recall an intellectual English girl, a writer on Russia, who asked to be mildly choked within fifteen minutes of our kicking off. I'm not sure how this connected to her love for Dostoevsky but it seemed of a piece. There was also a girl with tiny ears who was as white as an albino dolphin, who liked to fight before sex; physically fight. Wrestling. I think her dad had left her when she was young and there was a lot of anger. There was also a black air hostess in Trinidad who was fascinated by having sex with a white man: she kept putting her arm next to mine and saying 'Look!'

And then there were the others. Girls who hid their breasts and girls who cried when they came. Girls who refused to take their glasses off, and girls who just lay there like they wanted to play dead. Girls with red hair, girls with no hair, girls with silvery wisps of hair. Even Canadian girls.

All this was great fun, the greatest fun. Those years of wildness and debauchery were a glorious time. And the biggest hoot of all was the girl I met on the stairs. She was, maybe, nineteen. One afternoon I heard a knock on the door of my flat. Opening it, I discovered this tall, pretty English girl. She looked at me and said she wanted to borrow a pencil, to leave a note for a friend of hers who lived in the flat upstairs. For some reason we got chatting, for some unfathomable reason I asked her if she fancied a drink while waiting for her friend; she nodded; we had a couple of afternoon shandies – and then we came back to my flat and had vigorous sex. After that she left without giving me her number. It was still only six p.m. The whole thing had taken about three hours; I barely knew her name, I had no idea where she was from, or what she did, apart from borrow pencils.

In its briefness, its 'purity', its spontaneity and sudden-ness, this encounter was a highpoint in my promiscuity. It may not be impressive to everyone – I have a friend who claims to have met a Norwegian girl in Hyde Park and actually asked her back to his flat for sex, directly, to which she acceded, the whole thing taking about fifty minutes – but to me it was still remarkable and spiffing.

It also made me cocky. After my fantastic pencil encounter, I got the feeling that this was what life was always going to be like: from now on I would be able to have sex at will. All I had to do was talk to a girl, and maybe lend her a biro, and she'd be doffing her panties within hours. But of course in reaching this height of pride I was sowing the seeds of my downfall.

Because just as suddenly as it started, something happened to bring my halcyon days to an end. I started getting blasé, and bored, even a little callous. There was one time, a few weeks after Pencilwoman, when I met three girls at a party and I think (I may have been wrong but I got this feeling) that I could have slept with any of them. Being so horribly full of myself, I decided it would be very amusing to sleep with the (sorry about this) ugliest one, a rather chubby girl. I did. Then, when I left her flat the next day, after the hunt for the second sock, I had my normal chuffed and self-approving feeling. (Hey, I did it again! Another notch! Where the fuck am I?) But then halfway to the Tube this feeling disappeared and something else took over. Instead of gloating, I was thinking: Er, what about *her*? How did *she* feel about this? Was it a nice thing to use a girl like this? It was the first pin-prickle of conscience.

I ignored it, and went whistling to the Tube.

Nonetheless, the warning signs continued to pile up. By now I was getting girls into bed and doing kinky stuff with them simply so I could retell the story afterwards to my friends in the pub in an amusing way. I was also using the same lines again and again because they had always worked, saying the right words mechanically, by rote, without thinking about the girl herself. Not good. Another symptom of increasing callousness was that I was becoming very keen to have sex with two different girls on consecutive evenings (I succeeded) to see if the second girl noticed (she didn't).

I was, in short, a wanker.

And one day the wankiness really hit home. I was with a girl, a very beautiful Iranian girl. I'd met her in a bar.

I used my normal lines on her. She invited me to walk her back to her flat. On the way there we linked arms. I told a joke I had told many other girls; she laughed and squeezed my arm. Everything, in other words, was going well. But then, as we strolled past Green Park Tube station, I suddenly felt this strange revulsion about what I was doing, the way it had become mechanical, the harsh utilitarianism of it, the pointlessness. I even felt slightly nauseous. I didn't know what to do. So we walked on, still chatting. I was trying to hide my feelings. I didn't understand my feelings.

When we reached the door to the girl's block of flats I could see her waiting for me to kiss her, and follow her upstairs. But instead I kissed her on the cheek and wordlessly turned – and I got on a bus and went home to my lonely bed. I felt queer and empty. I couldn't sleep that night. I just stared at the ceiling for hours and hours, until the blue fist of dawn started punching the curtains.

And that's where it ended. Something good, bad or weird had happened to me. From that moment on I was never quite as promiscuous again.

Not for want of trying, though. Six months later, after I had actually been out with a girl – in a vain attempt to find love, to get off the treadmill of casual sex – I decided I had made a grave mistake in giving up my philandering ways. I also decided I had made a grave mistake with the Iranian girl. So I tried to go back – to grab back what I had so carelessly thrown away.

I arranged to meet her in a bar. But this time, after a couple of beers, she looked at me – and shook her head. Firmly. And then she got off her barstool and walked out, with a rather contemptuous chuckle. And that was that. I was bereft. I had lost it. Whatever magic I had had in that three-year period of womanising had disappeared, or at least dwindled. I drank my drink alone.

But why? Why had I suddenly reverted to type? Why was I back to my usual faltering, nervous, often-unsuccessful self with women, when I had recently been the opposite? It was hard to say. I hadn't put on weight, I hadn't started learning Welsh. But something had left me: the confidence. The absolute self-assuredness. The nerveless self-belief that I would have sex tonight, and that if I didn't it didn't matter because I would have sex tomorrow. Also, I seemed to have developed, at least in embryonic form, a debilitating hint of a conscience. Conscience and concupiscence do not mix so well. Conscience doth make cowards of us all, at least when it comes to the lithe commerce of limbs. I wanted a conscience-ectomy. But no deal.

So that's how my promiscuity ended, almost. But what does that teach me about Bumps? Can I learn from my experiences? Can I tell if she and I are on the same wave-length? Between the main course and the pudding, I fret about this; but then, as we pick up two spoons to share our tiramisu, she suddenly and unexpectedly reveals that she is Australian. She hasn't got much of an accent;

she's been in England quite a few years; but her upbringing was in *Perth*.

Stone the crows, what was I worrying about? She's an Aussie! Now I can relax, because in my experience Australian girls are not only feisty, relaxing, spunky, fun – they are also quite easy to sleep with.

I know, I know. But before I get lots of hate mail from Melbourne, please understand that this is not *my* opinion, it's my doctor's. He told me all about Aussie girls, right at the end of my first and most promiscuous period. Here's how.

I was sitting at a café table, when I suddenly noticed that I was itching 'down below'. The itching was quite constant, and rather irritating. But it wasn't debilitating, so I had a good scratch and thought nothing of it.

Then, over the next few days, the itching got worse. Then it got worse and worse. And worse: until other people started noticing. I can't blame other people for this; by now I was shoving my hand down my trousers with alarming frequency. In cafés and pubs. In libraries. I don't normally do this, not even in libraries.

The crisis reached a peak when I was on a bus and this infernal itching started up again. The bus was too crowded, and too public a space, for me to shove my hands down my shorts and have a good rummage. So I decided to relieve the itching by moving my pelvis a lot, writhing my hips and clenching my buttocks, and at the same time probably grimacing. Then I noticed that I had cleared the bus quite quickly, and we hadn't even stopped.

Enough. I had to find out what was wrong. What the hell was up in my salad? Did I have an allergy? Maybe my latest girlfriend and I were having some unfortunate pheromonal reaction to each other?

That evening, in the privacy of my bathroom, I pulled down my shorts and investigated.

Oh . . . Jesus. I hadn't expected *that*. Goodness me. This wasn't an allergy or a skin reaction. This wasn't a humble little rash. Oh no. No. Not at all. There were . . . *bugs* in my pubic hair. Small white moving creatures, like fleas, but more hi-tech and determined-looking. What's worse, some of them seemed to be . . . laying eggs.

Snapping my shorts back, I leant for support against the sink because I was feeling dizzy. I didn't know where to put myself. The truth was too painful to acknowledge: animals? In my pubic hair? Grazing on my privates? This was not good. This was pretty bad. A few moments later I started leaping around the room, cavorting and gambolling like a new-born lamb in a ballet class. I still don't know why I did that.

Then I got a grip on myself – and had three baths in a row, hoping the 'bugs' would go away. Had they? Standing in the steamy bathroom I gazed tentatively down at my self, and parted the hair. No joy. 'They' were still there. Still very much alive. Indeed, they seemed some-what refreshed by my bathing. A couple of them were affably climbing my pubic hairs like they were on a hill-walking holiday.

Then I noticed something even more fiendish: one of

'my' crabs had decided to make a break for it, and was heading up across my stomach for my chest hair. What the fuck was he trying to do? Start a new colony in my eyebrows? Caramba! Flicking this Oklahoma Pioneer of lice, this Johnny Appleseed of pubic crabs, from my wincing stomach, I sat down on the toilet in a slump and rested my hand over my pallid face like a consumptive Victorian poetess.

The next morning found me banging on the door of my doctor's surgery. At eight-thirty a.m. I was very keen to get this sorted, whatever it took. But when I sat down and my doctor asked me what was wrong, the words just wouldn't come.

'Yes well, what is it?' he said.

'Er . . .' I said, 'uh . . . I've got these . . .'

'Yes?'

'These . . .'

'Yes??'

I was now looking down at the floor. I was finding it very hard to say. How do you say: I've got lice? It's not exactly easy. Eventually I managed to squeeze some words out:

'I've got these . . . things . . .'

'You've got . . . *things*?'

'Yes.'

'Where exactly?'

He was leaning forward now. I carried on stammering:

'. . . in my groin . . . but you see they're . . . they're . . . they're alive . . .'

'Ah!' His face had lit up. 'You've got pubic crabs!'

His whoop of diagnostic joy was unwonted. Nonetheless, the shameful truth was out, which was probably a good thing. So I nodded my head – and shivered. And then I looked at the floor for a while longer. When I next glanced up again I saw that my doctor was trying not to smile (he was a bit of a card, my doctor).

'Tell me . . .' he said. 'Was she Australian?'

I blinked in surprise. What was he talking about? How did he know this?

'Well actually she is,' I replied. 'Yes. My new girlfriend's from Brisbane.'

He did a curt nod.

'Whenever I get men with this sort of thing, the girls are always Australian.' A pause, then he smiled. 'Filthy sluts the lot of them.'

Come again? I opened my mouth. And closed it. And opened it again. What? I couldn't believe what my GP had just said. This was a vile attack on an entire nation of pleasant, sportingly gifted people. I was outraged. But I also couldn't deny the facts. It was true, in a narrow way. She *was* Australian. He was right. But what did this mean? Dumbed into silence, I watched my doctor write out my prescription. Then I slowly walked home, armed with a bottle of special blue shampoo, a brand-new metal comb – and an insight into the sexual mores of Antipodean women as seen by cynical London doctors.

Incidentally, if you are offended by this, please don't write to me. Write instead to my doctor, Alan Johnson, at the Holborn Medical Centre, 64 Lamb's Conduit Street, London WC1. I'm sure he will welcome your enquiries.

So where does this leave me and Bumps, twelve years down the line from that particular episode? Actually, it leaves us in bed, as I had so fondly hoped. After our nice Italian meal we go back to her flat, and there we have more wine and then we move to the bed and have sex by candlelight and she turns out to have agreeably big breasts. Hence the 'Bumps'.

The next morning, without exchanging numbers, I leave her chuckling over breakfast in her flat, and I walk out of the door with that old-fashioned stud-muffin feeling, literally zipping my flies as I walk to the Tube station.

And then? Well, it's good to have that old laddish feeling back, if only for a fleeting moment. It's also good to have had sex for the first time in a few months. But I don't want to go back to my utterly ruthless womanising ways, at least probably not. Well not for long. OK, I do. It would be fantastic. If I could only manage it without making a fool of myself, or getting stricken with guilt, or catching something, or failing. But I also know that my heart is seeking something a little more serious. What I want, I guess, is love. Yet I'm not having much luck. And then, the very next morning, I get an email which is *most* unexpected.

Is that who I think it is?

Yep, it's her again. Irishlass. The girl who messaged me about four months ago. After I sent all those emails and made all that effort, she has suddenly gotten back to me, out of the bluest blue.

This is sweet. It's nice to rekindle an old flame, even if the old flame was just a five-day-long exchange of emails back in the spring. I know people say you should never retread an old relationship, that you should never return to the fizzled-out firework of love, but frankly in the circumstances I am willing to overlook The Rules. Besides, I think I may be on a roll now, after my quickie with Bumps.

The new girl emails me this:

'Hi, I'm sorry I didn't get back to you, I've been in Shanghai. Hope that doesn't sound too boastful or anything! Cheers, Irishlass.'

I write an email in return:

'Don't worry, I'm not impressed by Shanghai, I've

recently been to Belgium myself. Cheers, Lyonshall . . .'

Then I wonder if Irishlass will understand the sarcasm in this message, that I don't actually think Belgium is a particularly impressive place to visit. Maybe I should have put a little note at the end of the message to say this: I don't think Belgium is a particularly impressive place to visit. Bit stilted, though. What can I do?

Maybe instead I should have used an emoticon? This is not the first time I've thought this; as I trot along with this Net-dating project, I am beginning to see why some people use emoticons in their emails. A winking face, or a smiley face, or all that other stuff, allows you to nuance your messages, to be ironic or sarcastic or double entendre-ish, while ensuring that everyone notices how witty or ironic you are. But then again, emoticons are wank. I send the message.

Next day, Irishlass messages back. It's quite a long message with stuff about her cats and her favourite kinds of luggage, and it includes this bit:

'Don't knock Antwerp, I met my ex-husband there. He works in TV.'

I'm not quite sure what that last bit means. 'Works in TV.' Why is she telling me the profession of her ex-husband? Do I know him? Am I meant to know him? Returning to Irishlass's profile I see again that she is the one with the photo of herself at a party, with the man next to her scrubbed out somehow. Maybe that's her husband. But why scrub him out in the photo and then mention him in a message?

At this point I think: Do I frigging care?

Well, I do, slightly. And even if I didn't care, this girl is markedly cute in her photo. So I send another message, agreeing with her about luggage and asking about her husband. She then pings me back with more info: apparently he is a well-known TV personality.

Perhaps this should set off warning klaxons in my mind, but it doesn't. I've still got the scent of Bumps's body lotion on me, and I am keen to capitalise on my new-found confidence. So Irishlass and I arrange to meet in a swank Knightsbridge sushi bar, at her suggestion.

The bar is eccentric. You have to order your tempura and tuna belly at a counter downstairs, make your way past the throngs of young Italian men in brand-new tweed jackets, and then you sit down and wait for the Lithuanian waitress to bring your fiddly but delicious Japanese food on a kind of cake-stand. The food, like I say, is delicious, but the service deeply confusing.

What is less confusing is Irishlass. She is twenty-eight, very slim, quite pretty, dark-haired; you can imagine her as a kind of stunt double for a Corr. She is also, I reckon, something of a star-fucker. This becomes obvious ten minutes into our date, when we are sharing our third saucer of Californian sushi-roll, because she says:

'So how do you know Mick Jagger, then?'

Her big green Connemara eyes are wide and expectant; the yawning chasm of imminent disappointment is even wider. When I say: 'Well, I don't actually . . . he just gave me an award and we chatted for a bit,' she looks visibly let-down, as if I have popped her favourite balloon at the fair.

'Not at all?'

I shake my head. Then I decide to make a joke of it.

'Well he did keep ringing me up afterwards, but I had to let him down gently.'

'. . . Sorry?'

I'm not sure she understands. I try again:

'The bastard kept ringing me all the time – "Sean, come on, let's go for a pizza, anything" – so I had to tell him: "Sorry Mick, I'm busy, I'll let you know when I've got a free moment."'

Irishlass looks at me.

'Ah. You're joking.'

I feel like saying, 'Duh, yeah', but instead I move the chat on to luggage, which seems to be a safe area for both of us. But inside I am appalled and fascinated by the obvious star-fuckiness of this girl. She wanted to date me 'cause she thought I knew famous people, I think. Is that bad? Yes and no. Yes, it's bad 'cause it doesn't really turn me on. No, it's not so bad because I kind of understand the syndrome. Because I've seen it all before. I've had my brushes with star-fuckers. I may be one myself.

To explain: I think I've had at least two encounters with the star-fucking impulse from below, as it were. The first came towards the end of my rampantly happy but sadly finite period of promiscuous success with girls, when I slept with a young, dark-haired Texan model for a few weeks. This girl wasn't a supermodel, but she was moderately well-known and did work in mags and news-papers and stuff. This was a buzz, a real rush. Yet my giddy fling also had a cost. There is a dark downside to star-fucking, that became apparent after the event.

Two years after my liaison with the model, when my promiscuous golden age was fading into legend, at a time when I hadn't had a date, let alone sex, for about four months, I was sharing a room with a friend on a spartan trip abroad. This trip was so austere, we had to sleep in bunk-beds. One morning I woke to find the bunk-beds shaking. 'What the fuck are you *doing*?' I called from the top bunk; 'Oh, having a tug,' my friend replied. He was masturbating. 'Sorry,' he added. The bunk continued shaking, then it stopped. At that point, having finished the job, my friend chucked up to me the visual stimula-tion he had been using. It was an old copy of the *Daily Mirror*. 'Get a load of that,' he said.

I opened the paper and immediately felt a surge of heart-burn, of emotional loss and sexual yearning. It was, naturally, my old girlfriend, posing in lingerie. The girl I had casually screwed and deserted back in my balmy days, thinking that my life would be full of stars and models from here on in.

'Hey,' I said, heart thumping, 'I used to go out with her.' Silence from below. Then derisive and disbelieving laughter. To say my friend didn't believe me would be understating the case, in the same way that calling the Queen 'a tad fond of bling' is understating the case.

Poignant, no? Perhaps more poignant was my relationship with Amelie Nilsson. That, of course, isn't her real name – but lawyers can be touchy about revealing the real names of celebs. And Amelie was just that: a real, genuine, copper-bottomed British TV star, a funny, ski-jump nosed, pan-European media beauty . . . *who went out with ME!*

The first time I saw Amelie was at the making of a TV show, a pilot for a pop programme. It was about a decade or so ago. A friend, aware that I was a little bored and lonely, had invited me down to the making of this new, youth-oriented, pop-music-themed telly programme in Brixton, which was being shot in an old cinema.

It turned out to be quite a dull evening, with lots of milling around in the stalls for us audience nobodies, while the presenters did tedious and repetitive stuff on the stage, between the bands. The only highlight of this evening, for me, was the sight of one of those presenters: Amelie Nilsson. She was really rather beautiful, quite strikingly lovely. Nice figure, too. And witty, judging by her presenting chat.

Towards the end of the evening, I drifted to the back of the yawning hall just to watch Amelie's presenting as it was relayed on the TV screens dotted around the cavernous old cinema hall. She looked great on TV too. She was, in a word, mint. But so what? What gives? I was just a punter; just a nobody. I may have briefly dated a minor model – once – but that glorious era was over and I was back to my default mode of fumbling uncertainty with women. What chance did I have? I went home wondering what kind of guy got to have sex with someone like Amelie.

Kind of guy like me, as it turned out. Six months later a friend asked me to come along to a charity do he was organising in a London hotel. The knees-up was in aid of the Arvon Foundation, a literary organisation that sponsors and subsidises poets and poetry. Not terribly glam, but my friend had corralled a number of celebs and well-known writers to the cause.

Amongst them was Amelie Nilsson, and she was sitting next to me. Now, normally such a close proximity would induce in me a spasm of nerves. Normally, the presence right next to me of a beautiful (and famous!) young woman would reduce me to gibbering idiocy. Not this time. Instead, I was suddenly filled with articulate charm, and also a notable surge of self-belief.

Why was this? I confess, I don't know. I'm never sure what mental process it is that flips me from failure to success with women, that turns my normal shy anxiety into those brief but wonderful upsurges of sunny confidence. I think copious amounts of free champagne often have something to do with it.

Whatever the reason, something good sure happened that night. When I next sat down at my table Amelie and I immediately started talking, and joking, and laughing – making her smile. And then I shoved my hand up her skirt.

Yes, I shoved my hand up her skirt. This may seem shocking. It shocks me now – because it's not something

I normally do, especially with well-known women, especially within an hour of being introduced. One might, moreover, expect it to be a fairly disastrous tactic. But not this time. Instead of wincing or slapping me, Amelie just carried on eating her prosciutto and chatting with everyone else – as I carried on fondling her lovely thighs under the table. God, it was fun. It was verging on being splendid. It was like being back at school with Sally Ann Long at the back of the Geography class.

Couldn't last, of course. Hours later the party broke up and that was it, Amelie left. She didn't even give me her number, even though we'd chatted all night, and I'd stroked her underwear. Subsequently, as I wended my wobbly way home, I concluded that I'd never see her again. Oh well. I put the whole thing down to luck, something to tell my grandchildren – 'Hey kids, gramps once fondled a star!' – and prepared to treat it as just an amusing story-ette.

I was wrong. A week later Amelie got in touch with me. God knows why. Perhaps Amelie, being a very attractive and rather well-known woman, found that most men were too inhibited to approach her; and so my unusually robust method, of whipping my hand up her dress at a formal charity function, paid off. It is possible she simply fancied me, I suppose. Either way, a week later Amelie and I started having a relationship.

It lasted all of six months, until she decided I was way too much of an immature nitwit to continue going out with (she was right). But even if it didn't turn into lifelong love, I still had a whale of a time going out with her, with a TV celeb, for several reasons.

One of the main upsides of dating a star, as I discovered, was the envy of other men. Sometimes during that six-month period I'd be sitting in a room with a bunch of lads I didn't know very well, and Amelie would come on the telly, doing some movie review or pop-show presenting. At this point all the guys in the room would go 'phwoooar', 'get that', 'she's hot', before making lots of ribald remarks about the voluptuousness of her lips and their possible role in a remake of the film *Deep Throat*.

Around this time I would lob my conversational grenade. Sitting back, with a nonchalant sigh, I'd let slip the casual words: 'Oh, yeah, I'm shagging her actually.'

Cue stunned silence, followed by disbelieving catcalls. Then the horrible truth would sink in, and they'd start swearing viciously at the unfairness of it all, or hurling cushions at my head. Finally a kind of dumb, sullen respect would settle over the group. I have to say, I liked dumb, sullen respect most of all. Dumb, sullen respect is great. It's what you want from your peers. It's almost better than friendship.

But if the reverence of my peers was an agreeable aspect of dating Miss Nilsson, so was the sexual 'stable' I joined thereby. And it was quite a stable. In the years before me Amelie had been linked with other famous men (I mean other men who were famous, not that I'm famous); after me, she would go on to be linked with even more famous men (pop stars, TV comedians, George Clooney, etc.). Now I was a guy like them. In going out with Amelie I was temporarily elevated to that same order of male status; for six months I was the kind of guy that escorted Amelie Nilsson; put it another way, the kind of guy that escorted Amelie Nilsson was typified by people like *me*.

Indeed, in my fondest dreams I still imagine people saying things like, 'Oh, so you think you've got a chance with Amelie Nilsson? Sorry mate, she's way out of your league – she only goes for people like George Clooney, or Sean Thomas, the guy who reviews Lego for amazon.'

OK, I know people are not actually going to say that, but even the hint of it is very pleasant.

Another good thing about dating Amelie was the song. When I was with her, she received a tape from a fan in the north of England. He was a member of a band and the band had written a tribute to her, a kind of skiffling ballad. It wasn't overly inspired in the lyrics department; I don't think Noël Coward would have lost sleep over it, given that the chorus went, 'Amelie Nilsson, Amelie Nilsson, Amelie Nilsson.' But I have to admit it *was* a rush to think there were musicians I had never met in Macclesfield who were busily writing songs about the woman who lay naked beside me most nights.

And finally there was the greatest accolade of all: when *my bird* appeared, in cartoon form, in the adult comic *Viz* – as the epitome of fanciable blonde celeb beauty. She was, the magazine thought, someone to whom you could dedicate a Palm Sunday (for those that don't read *Viz*, that means, in their inimitable argot, someone you would use as material for a whole relaxed Sunday of masturbation). When I read this, I threw down the magazine and smiled a broad smile of satisfaction. I'd made it. I was dating an A-lister, or at least a B-plus-lister. Fantabulous, darling.

It was at that moment that my star-boffing cocksureness got the better of me. I actually started wondering if Amelie was good enough for *me*. Maybe she wasn't quite pretty enough. Maybe she wasn't quite sexy enough. Most especially, maybe she wasn't famous enough. Perhaps next time I should date Catherine Zeta Jones, or the latest French starlet, or a couple of supermodels at the same time.

A week later Amelie chucked me – for a more famous bloke. Not exactly hard. And of course I haven't been out with anyone famous since. Indeed, when I now look at pictures of Amelie, at the height of her retroussé-nosed cuteness, I get a strange stabbing sense of loss, as if I've been mugged by regret in the dark alleyway of my stupidity.

Like I said, it's a poignant story. At least, it is if you are me. But more importantly, the story also proves that I really *have* experienced star-fucking from below. And I have witnessed the phenomenon from other angles, too. A couple of years ago I went, courtesy of a Californian friend of mine, to a post-Oscars party in Hollywood. This, I should immediately say, is not something I normally get to do. My idea of a top night out, wherever I am, is a few beers in the boozer. But this visit of mine to LA coincided with the Oscars and somehow my friend wangled these precious invites to this major beano. We were on.

The security for the shindig was eye-poppingly tight. It started down on Sunset Boulevard. Only once you had proved your correct bloodtype were you allowed in a minivan with blacked-out windows and then ferried through the streets to a modernist palace way up in the Hollywood Hills. There everyone was frisked and quizzed, and finally allowed into the inner sanctum, where the stars and their acolytes were sipping daiquiris as they stared out over the lights of LA. I'd like to report that I was blasé and unimpressed by this show of glamour. But, nah. I was overjoyed and overawed. This party was AMAZING. Cameron Diaz was there (she handed me a beer from the fridge! She is exceptionally pretty but has acne!) and I also spotted Jennifer Lopez, Ben Affleck, Nicole Kidman, plus a host of famous film directors, agents and producers – and approximately three-dozen top models flown in from agencies across the USA. It was big-time celebrity stuff, a fabulous bash; and I was wearing a £25 shirt from Next.

Halfway through this remarkable, once-in-a-lifetime party, I noticed Adrien Brody. He was being treated like the absolute acme of celebrityness, even in that glamorous crowd, because he had, that very evening, five hours earlier, won the Best Actor Oscar for his performance in *The Pianist*. He was actually carrying the Oscar with him, in an endearingly modest way. He seemed like a nice guy; he even let me touch his Oscar when he brushed past me.

Later that evening I star-spotted Adrien Brody again. This time he was standing in a corner of the party. He was now talking to a very pretty girl. But just behind the girl was another girl, also notably pretty. She was actually lined up behind the first girl. Then behind that girl was another girl, and another, and then another. There was a whole line of them, about a dozen strong. It was very weird. It looked like a queue; because these girls weren't talking to anyone else, they were just lining up, patiently, occasionally checking their watches, waiting to have a chat with Adrien Brody.

I asked one guy, something of a Hollywood insider, what was going on with Brody and Co.

'That's a fuck queue,' he said.

I gulped.

'A what?'

'A fuck queue. The girls are waiting to talk to Adrien Brody, in the hope that he will take them home and fuck 'em. Maybe he's going to choose someone from the queue, and maybe not.' My informant shrugged. 'But the girls live in hope.'

To be fair to Adrien Brody, he looked mildly embarrassed and apparently discomfited by the whole thing. I looked at him in sympathy (well, sort of). Then I looked again. Could this be true? For a moment a wave of disbelief hit me: maybe my informant was winding me up, and the girls just wanted to discuss Adrien's deft and sensitive portrayal of Jewish survival amidst Holocaust-torn Warsaw. But no. Judging by the way the girls were adjusting their hair and twirling their eyes, this was no line-up of movie critics. This was indeed a 'fuck queue'. Ben Affleck looked very jealous. Weird.

Before I reach my conclusions as to what this tells us about star-fucking, I've got just one more relevant story: the single time I was star-fucked myself. It happened, yes, when I was winning that award, and I got to meet Mick Jagger (who was very pleasant, by the way. Indeed he was just how you imagine him to be: mid-Atlantic cockney accent, quite sharp, obviously clever, mildly friendly in a detached way, somewhat wizened). I was totally in awe of him, just as everyone at the party was in awe of him.

And then it happened. Somehow, Mick Jagger's intense charisma rubbed off on me. After I had stood next to Mick, talking on live radio, chatting to TV cameras, making a little speech, a girl approached me. She was young, funny, Superdrug-blonde, a journalist. Before I had even had a chance to chat her up, she kissed me. Later that night we went back to her place, and had some fun. Later in the week we had even more fun.

This was, somehow, too easy. I was mildly suspicious. My suspicions were justified. After about a fortnight, it became very obvious the girl and I weren't going to get married. And then it was, as we were having our break-up conversation, that the girl confessed: she admitted to me that she had been attracted to me mainly because I had been up there on the stage; I had been the man with Mick. In other words, I had had my Fifteen Minutes, and that was enough to stir her hormones. I wasn't flattered, but then again I was.

And there you have it. That's how sexually powerful fame is – even if it lasts less than an hour, and is essentially reflected from someone else, some major popstar who in real life looks like a superannuated stick insect – it is enough to get the juices flowing.

So what *does* all this prove about celebs and sex, about star-shagging? To my mind, having encountered the behaviour from all angles, above, beneath, and sideways, I have come to this conclusion: I think star-fucking must be something to do with genes.

I believe that, self-evidently, we are all programmed by our DNA to try and sleep with the alpha male and the alpha female, with the genetic celebrities of our species. In the past that meant screwing the big-chested caveman who brought home the heftiest springbok, or the woman with the best moss-gathering skills and the widest pelvis. We were programmed this way because sleeping with these people meant we had a chance at getting the best genes into our potential kids.

Then we moved out of the caves, and developed social hierarchies. As springboks and lichen loomed less large in our table of desires, we now wanted to pass on money and status to our kids, as well as good looks and health. And so we desired people at the top of society: kings and dukes, heiresses and princesses. That era lasted a long time. But then it ended. Now the aristocratic age has come to an end, and the celebrity era has begun, and so it's media stars who have the fame and wealth, the status we crave, perhaps subconsciously for our potential children, and it's TV stars and weather girls who are the apples of our sexual eyes.

If this sounds depressingly deterministic, it needn't. It's just one aspect of the human condition, after all – and a temporary aspect at that. By our mid-twenties most of us have largely grown out of the mentality, and have accepted that happiness is probably not to be found giving oral sex to drunken bass guitarists in the backs of limos, or sending lurid fan mail to Scarlett Johansson asking for a pair of her most recent pants. We move on. We grow up.

Well, we largely grow up. I'm still sitting here in this fashionable London restaurant with Irishlass, and I've just noticed that a film actress of some repute has walked in. She's a bit shorter than I expected; and her hair is slightly unkempt.

'Who are you staring at?' says Irishlass. I've obviously lost the plot of our conversation. What do I do now? I decide to confess. I don't think Irishlass and I are going anywhere, I don't think we're madly keen on each other, but she is a lot of fun and I seem to be not boring her. Might as well have a laugh.

Doing that don't-look-now, sophisticated Londoners' star-spotting semi-nod, I somehow indicate to Irishlass that she should subtly check out the area of the restaurant at seven o'clock to our table. Irishlass nods at me.

Then, pretending to be checking the state of the coat-rack, Irishlass turns and stares discreetly. Then she chirrups.

'Gosh. Is that who I think it is?!'

'I reckon so.'

'Jesus.' Irishlass does a low, amused whistle. 'She's about two foot three.'

I agree. Then I say:

'Nice hips though.'

Simply seeking frolic . . . lol!

'Hi Joe'.

It's my pre-op transsexual friend, Joe, on the phone. We've been talking a lot of late: I'm trying to persuade him to give Internet dating a go, just as I'm attempting to persuade all of my single friends, and a good few of my ex-girlfriends. For some reason, possibly because I have been having a lot of fun (stalkers aside), I have become something of an evangelist for the process, for Internet dating. Well, I say to them, what have you got to lose?

So Joe and I have our usual chat: he asks me about work, I ask him how big his breasts are now ('Oh not bad, the hormones are kicking in'). Then we move on to football, and scrotal depilation, and politics. Then I mention how much time I am spending online, doing my work, researching and stuff. He does a verbal nod, and then says, mysteriously:

'Watch out for all that porno though, they say you can get addicted.'

'What?'

'Uhuh. Friend of mine at work, he got into some porn websites. They sacked him when they found seventy-two thousand images on his company laptop.'

'That's quite a lot of images.'

'Nearly crashed the office network. Anyway – watch it . . .'

I think about this. Then I dismiss it. It's a cold, fresh October morning and the idea of being addicted to images of middle-aged German men in mullets having sex with ageing hookers is, frankly, risible. I tell Joe this. He demurs. 'I'm serious, Sean: You should be careful, Net porn isn't like ordinary porn. It's totally different . . .'

With that we move on to other topics, not least the high price of a decent wig. And then we ring off and I forget about our chat. Later that day though, when I am checking to see if I have any messages at Udate ('*You have no messages at Udate*'), my mind moved back the topic of our discussion. How can Net porn be that different? So what if it is different? And what does different mean?

I can't believe that Net porn is really any better or more alluring than ordinary porn. And if it is like ordinary porn, I'm safe, because I've never really liked porn. That may seem surprising – it surprises me sometimes – but it's true. Despite the odd copy of *Fiesta* under my bed, I have generally found serious and hardcore pornography quite dispiriting; not to mention tedious, bleak, sad and repetitive. And the Estonian guys with bad haircuts don't help.

So, *can* the Net be any different? Sitting down at my laptop I close down my Net-dating sites, and I Google the words 'girls' and 'panties'. I guess I am looking for something soft, something fluffy. Nothing too disturbing. Just cute girls in their birthday suits, that'll do me. See how we go. See what's out there.

Wow. In front of me the screen has instantly flooded with suggested websites – hundreds of thousands of them. Millions, maybe. This *is* impressive. Even more impressive, some of these porn websites seem to be free. Dare I have a look? Oh, I think so. Clicking on a website called The Hun, I do a smug you-can't-touch-me nod, and I put a finger to my chin, awaiting.

The Hun turns out to be a website with a simple roster of various different kinds of small pornographic images, arranged in 'galleries'. Each gallery has been given a basic description, e.g. 'Two lesbians in a Jacuzzi'; 'Japanese coed loses her knickers'. Mulling my options, I click on one of the lesbian picture-galleries and sit back again. Quickly my laptop screen fills with about a dozen small photos of the aforementioned lesbians. The images are pretty small – but with a click they can be enlarged into something quite sizeable.

I have never seen pictures of naked lesbians in a hot tub before; somewhat to my surprise, I find the images pretty arousing. And so, after a few minutes' scrutiny, I go back to the main page of The Hun, and I keep looking. For the next hour or two I look at more pictures of lesbians; after that I check out the Japanese co-ed, and a woman in the shower with her boyfriend, and then sixty-three galleries of more Japanese co-eds.

Then I sit back and wonder if what I am doing is right or proper. Perhaps instead I should message that sweet-looking girl on match.com. A few seconds later I look at several hundred more hardcore images, some pictures of group sex, a few billion pics of naked celebs, and finally something called 'bukkake' – this seems to involve men ejaculating over submissive Asian women.

Yuk. The latter is not at *all* my thing. However, there are enough things that *are* more my thing to drag me back for more images the very next day. Something has changed. Over the next few days, whenever I have a spare few minutes – better still, half an hour – I find myself logging off Udate or Datingdirect or Loopylove, and instead hungrily checking out Net porn. I soon discover there are lots of websites which are much better and more comprehensive than The Hun; sites with tens of thousands of categorised images, of everything under the sexual sun. It turns out the Net is something of an erotic cornucopia, and it seems to be available 24/7, mostly for free. Indeed there is even a site called Pornucopia.

At this stage, four or five days into my exploration, I don't, however, think I am hooked – despite what Joe said. I may be finding cyberporn seriously intriguing and very diverting, but it's not actively addictive. I'm still concentrating some of my energies on composing an email to Sandre7 on Udate.

But that soon changes. One day I am surfing away

merrily, and I happen across a site that has 'spanking images'. The thought of this appeals. Quite a lot. I'm surprised by how much. Of course, I have long known that I have a vague interest in spanking – no doubt as a result of my experience with Eleanor. But hitherto I have always ignored this side of my sexuality – or at least, have never felt a serious desire to explore it properly.

Yet here's a site that promises me 'excellent images of ladies being spanked by their husbands'. So, what the hell, let's do it. When I click on, the screen flashes up what was promised; *more* than what was promised. In front of me is a series of clear images of a very cute twenty-something brunette being undressed, and then bent over a desk to be robustly spanked by a spectacled Russian-looking bloke. The series of images is so enjoyable I am actually left *panting*.

This intense sexual reaction confuses and, I confess, excites me. What the hell is going on? I had not the slightest idea I was *that* into 'spanking images', but now the Net has taught me that I am. Amazing!

The next day, at about 6.30 a.m., I go right back on to Google and start searching out more spanking-rich websites. It ain't too hard. Bernie's Spanking Pages. BDSM Cafe. The Spanking College. Spanking-spanking-spanking.net. There are, I discover, dozens of websites devoted to my new-found kink, and most of them are unexpectedly enjoyable.

And that's not all. After paging through the tumultuous

archives of www.overtheknee.net, a thought suddenly strikes me. As I head off to Tesco's to buy some more Kleenex, perhaps two boxes, I ask myself: If I'm that into spanking, what *else* do I like? Just what *other* kinks am I harbouring? What other secret and rewarding corners lurk in my sexuality that I am now able to investigate in the privacy of my own flat?

Plenty of corners. Soon I am haring off in dozens of different sexual directions, clicking on things that I would never have considered clicking on before. And to my unbounded surprise I discover that my newly discovered spanking thingy is just one of a number of proclivities I have lurking within me. Put it another way: whereas before I have thought myself fairly mainstream in my sexual tastes, it now turns out that I have a serious yen for lots of very wacky stuff – up-skirt photos taken in church; netball players having interracial sex; drunk Russian secretaries exposing themselves to their bosses; unsuspecting Italian nymphets on suburban sunbeds; and extremely convoluted scenarios where submissive Danish actresses are intimately shaved by their dominant female doctors. In the shower.

So what's going on? What's happening to me? Who cares? I am now surfing for porn twice or three times an evening, and totally neglecting my Net-dating project. I have even joined a few pornographic sites that cost money. (What the hell – I'll put it on my expenses. 'Sorry Simon, I had to take one girl to the opera. Yes. That's right. In Vienna.')

And then I discover the even *more* fascinating world of adult dating sites. It happens one day when I am doing some particularly intense research into the girls at japanesebeauties.net who like to parade around in their very diaphanous kimonos. Right at the top there's a little panel which allows me to click into another website. It says, mysteriously: '*Make new adult friends in Harlow!*' I'm not sure why I am being tempted to make friends in Harlow; I've never really considered making a friend in Harlow. I'm not quite sure what I'd do with an adult friend in Harlow.

Nonetheless, I click on.

It turns out that this is a website devoted to people who want to make contacts; to swingers, etc. And not only that; it is full of people advertising precisely what they want out of their encounters. '*Bi-curious girl in Leicester wants to meet mature white female.*' '*Well-hung guy in London into mixed-race groups.*' '*Older lady has husband who wants to watch her with randy stallion.*' Etc. Of course I've seen contact ads before, in old-fashioned mags that friends would leave lying around (honest!), but somehow these Net ads have a lot more impact – because you can see, for instance, the bi-curious girl in a series of graphic images when she divests herself of her panties and then grins like a loon. She's also rather cute.

Here's another clickable link. I click, it links. I have now been directed to a different site which is dedicated to 'dogging'. I think this means having sex in public places. Am I right? Yup. This site is *very* informative. It tells me that if I go to a car park in Crawley I can watch couples having sex in their cars. As it happens, that's a little far, Crawley – to go and watch steamed-up Toyota windows. So maybe not there, then. But the site also tells me that there is a grille over a Tube-station platform in Baker Street where women – apparently – come to stand and expose their knickerless privates to the men standing below. I'm not sure what to think about this. Really not sure at all.

Still another site, accessible by a single click, is offering me members' webcams. What on earth are these? I've no idea, but the mind certainly boggles. A few minutes of research shows me that these webcams are providing live coverage of various people sitting at their computers around the world. The webcams also come with a visitor counter. This is fascinating. As of this moment, it seems that 456 people around the world are watching a middle-aged woman in Merseyside. Why? I click on the webcam and then I see – the woman is sitting at her computer, and she is naked as a newborn, and she is masturbating with a vibrator.

For a few minutes I watch this, fascinated and appalled. Mainly appalled. But also fascinated. The good women of Liverpool! Really! Then I click off this image, and join the 5,989 people around the world who are watching a live relay of a young couple in Melbourne Australia. Mike and Jane are their names, and Jane has got a cute and flashing smile, judging by their profile photo. They say on their profile that they are a young, fun couple, 'up for a laugh and a gas'. This could mean many different things – but as the webcam shows, what it actually means is that they are up for having very bouncy sex in front of the entire globe. When they are finished, Jane winks at the camera.

Any others? Plenty. 2,978 people worldwide are at this second having a good look at thirty-six-year-old Vancouvergirl2 ('Simply seeking frolic . . . lol!'). Clicking on the site, I wait for the webcam image to clear. What can be attracting so many punters? Ah. Vancouvergirl2 is a voluptuous and rather pretty thirty-something woman in a flimsy green nightie. And sitting next to her, in Surrey, British Columbia, right now (I check the time in BC, it's five a.m.; don't these people sleep?) is a man in a dressing gown. As I watch, the dressing-gowned man takes off Vancouvergirl2's negligée and assiduously kneads her ample buttocks. Then she goes down on him, sucking his erection in between drags on her cigarette. Nice touch.

That said, not everyone is quite so popular. Such as the husband and wife team that comprise sexyduo999 in Cleveland, Tennessee. When I click on their webcam, I see that the forty-five-year-old husband is going to the trouble of screwing his wife with a dildo, while wearing a leather jumpsuit. And a measly six people are watching. Six! That's appalling. More people actually bought my last novel, and I didn't write that in a gimp mask while fisting the missus on global TV. Sitting here, I actually find myself feeling sorry for them, and so for ten minutes

147

I stay and diligently watch sexyduo999, out of sympathy rather than desire. I just want to boost their numbers, the poor dears. I sometimes go into failing restaurants for the same reason, just to cheer up the waiters and make them feel less lonely.

At the end of my webcam frenzy (after a quick glimpse at Flavia6, a girl in Milan who is answering her emails in a thong) I sit back and try and grasp what I have seen. It's fairly hard. The sheer scale of this hidden universe is awesome. If, three months ago, I was initially surprised at the number of dating sites on the web, now I am gob-smacked at the enormous number and size of these contact sites, overtly sexual websites devoted to swinging and contact-making.

For example: Adultfriendfinder, the largest webcam contact site, claims to have eighteen million members dotted around the world. Eighteen million. *Eighteen million!* I have my doubts about this figure, as it is about one per cent of all the sexually active people around the globe; but still, even if this number is in *any* way accurate, it's a momentously huge statistic. And there are plenty of other contact sites, with large numbers of people doing just the same thing.

To my own astonishment, I'm actually shocked, in a moral way, by all this. Shock of the prurient variety is not something I am used to. I am also slightly suspicious. I keep looking out for the catch. For instance, why are these people doing this stuff on live webcams? Are they getting paid? Where's the credit card demand? I am waiting for one of those time-limit shutdowns ('If you want to see more, type in your Visa number', you know).

But this doesn't happen. Much as I keep examining the websites (and I examine them hard), it seems the first impression is correct: these people, Mike and Jane in Melbourne, Vancouvergirl2 in British Columbia, many of the good housewives of Liverpool, are having vigorous sex/getting their tops off/having their buttocks palped, solely for the benefit of the rest of us; and also, I guess, to satisfy some exhibitionistic urge in themselves.

That is to say they are doing it for a laugh, for the fun, for kicks, for me and you and the whole damn world, and to repay the debt to pleasure. And, I reiterate, it seems there are *thousands* of other people doing this, and tens of thousands of people participating around the world, and millions of people who have some involvement, if only to have a look. (Where have I been all this time? Shopping?)

But enough already. I'm done. Done and dusted and more than a little knackered. Sitting back in my chair, I check the time. Nine hours have passed. I've spent a whole 'working' day exploring this strange, cybernetic *demi-monde*. Nine hours – and it felt like six minutes.

Joe was right. This is compelling stuff. So compelling, I think I'm going to do exactly the same tomorrow. And maybe the day after that I'll do the same. And the day after that. And the week after that. Indeed the next time I do this, I might stay up for twenty-four hours at a stretch; after all, who needs sleep, when there are people having live group sex in Toronto, Ontario? When you can down-stream a movie of breasty Italian sixth-formers playing ping-pong in the buff?

Not me.

In the event, my next move is not to download some porn videos – it is to join one of these adult friendfinder websites. I am trying to turn my new-found obsession into copy, into something I can put in my article (I am, in essence, trying to excuse my bad behaviour) and so I have decided that I need to interact with people: to get in the chatrooms, to send messages, to make contact. But to do this I have to join. So I do.

First thing is to give myself a codename: mamba6. I don't know why I call myself mamba6; mamba6??? After a quick self-deprecatory chuckle, I change my name to something much more sensible: Marmaduke Skewes. That, let it be known, is my 'official' porn name (i.e. the name of my favourite pet allied with my mother's maiden name). And it certainly seems to fit me better. Hey you lucky ladies, its the Duke!

Now for the profile. As I have no intention of actually meeting anyone for a serious relationship via these adult dating lists, I opt to have some fun with my profile when it comes to describing myself. On the vital statistics, I knock a couple of years off my age, add a couple of inches to my height, and to, er, my endowment. ('I am excep-tionally well-hung.') I tell everyone that my salary is very high and I live in Boston, Paris, Albania and Gloucestershire. I also say that I am keen on meeting women, couples, groups and transsexuals, which covers most of the bases, I think. Animals are out. Probably.

My profile complete, I sit back and wait for the offers of sexual interest to flood in from the two or three adult contact sites I have joined. They don't. Although, for instance, adultfriendfinder says it has 1,789,345 UK members (again a figure I doubt, but don't quote me on that (but what if it's true!!??)) not one single member even visits my profile, not one single contactee puts me on their official 'hot list'. This is harsh. Indeed it's quite depressing: I am in effect being ignored by 1,789,345 people, many of whom are self-confessed sex-addicts willing to have intimate chat and even actual coitus with just about anyone. Apart from me.

On the second day, I get a note from a girl, Gemini. Gemini's profile shows her to be a very cute-looking twenty-something from Essex. Yay! But before I can read the actual note, I have to pay the website some cash. So I pay the cash, and then get to read the note. It says: *'Hi, I was just browsing . . . thought I'd drop you a line.'* This is not exactly *The Story of O*, but then I remember it's just my first adult message. So, swallowing my disappointment, I email a little note back, something very slightly fruitier. *'Hi Gem, where are you? What are you wearing?'* etc. etc. Then I wait for a quick reply, as this must surely be the essence of erotic chat, as promised by the website. Won't be that erotic if I have to wait several weeks between messages.

But: no dice. Nothing. I wait for a couple of days . . . and still nothing. Then it dawns on me: the message was assuredly generated by computer when I joined; it was designed to get me to cough up cash. Clever.

For a few minutes I feel like signing off the sites, so annoyed am I at being suckered. But I don't. Instead I persevere, telling myself that this is my job, something I am being paid for (dark and lonely work, but someone's got to do it. Eventually, I decide it's time to join one of the chatrooms. I am going to tell people that I am writing an article, see what reaction I get. I feel the need to be honest. Who knows what will happen? My brother did this in a Christian chatroom and he met his wife.

But the flavour of this chatroom is different to the one my brother entered, I guess.

Elliebunny (F): Hey room anyone want to suk my pussy!?

Sinty (M): Sure thing Ellie where u?

Elliebunny (F): Me in Cambridge

Thebigman (M): Sexy student eh? . . .

Elliebunny (F): akshly I fancy two men with Big Cox!

MarmadukeSkewes (M) has entered the room . . .

MarmadukeSkewes (M): Hi. I'm writing an article about all this for *Men's Health* magazine..

Stifle262 (M): ooooh oooh ooooh you wanna squeeeeez my big DICK EL?

Totaltease (F) has entered the room . . .

SeraphicStranger (F): hey it's the Teezer!

Totaltease (F): Hey room I got idea – I gonna make an aerosol for womens parts, for their fannys

Beanzy57 (M): . . . ouch!

MarmadukeSkewes (M): It's just a short article.

Pussylover271 (M): what the name of your vaginal aresol Teaser??!

Totaltease (F): Sprunt!

MarmadukeSkewes (M): It's all above board

Beanzy57 (M): Sprunt! ROFLMAO!

MarmadukeSkewes (M): It's an article on the Net, on sex and stuff . . . anyone want to chat?

CLASSYLADE (M): Ellie you do wan sum spit roastin girl!

MarmadukeSkewes (M) *has left the room . . .*

Not a huge success, so I decide to try again. This time I am not going to tell anyone about my true journalistic intentions. This time I am just going to hang out and use a lot of chatroom slang like ROFLMAO and Damn Skippy and w00t.

It works. Within an hour or so I am having a one-on-one chat with a sparky young woman of thirty-two from Cheshire who says she is bored at home and would like me to 'spank her v ruffly' and 'shuv my Big Damn Thing' up her. The photo of her shows a rather petite girl with a lovely smile and her pale breasts hanging out of a school-girl's blouse. I suspect I may actually be talking to a forty-five-year-old transvestite van-driver in Milwaukee, but so what. Good copy, as Simon says.

Then I go one-on-one with a number of other girls/disguised men. Again it is compulsive stuff. I'm not sure

153

why. It's not actually physically arousing exchanging emails and messages with girls you never meet – at least not at the time – but there is a strongly addictive quality to the process. Just as Joe said. Just as Joe so clearly predicted.

And so it is: I have become addicted. I've now tipped over an edge, taken a step too far, I'm gone. Even though I now want to stop, I can't. I can't stop surfing and chatting, chatting and ogling, compulsively watching Mike and Jane in their bedroom, palely loitering in the precincts of Osakababes.net, desperately asking pussygirl to send me 'a foto of her v kisable buttcheeks'.

I am now, in fact, regularly spending eight or nine hours a day staring wild-eyed at my laptop, usually in the early hours when everyone else is in bed. Which means I am getting about three hours of sleep at night.

Not surprisingly, the other people who live in my flat are at last beginning to notice the change in my lifestyle, the hard yakka I am putting in, perhaps even the spiritual degradation, or at least the bags under my eyes. One day, my oldest female flatmate stops me on the stairs and asks: 'Sean, why do you look so tired?' I shrug, and pretend not to hear properly, but she persists: 'Hey wow, have you finally met someone on the Net?! Are you seeing someone at last?!' She is standing there, grinning cheerfully, waiting for the good news.

My heart sinks. What can I tell her? That I am seeing seventeen-year-old Bunko Kikazawa of Tokyopuppies? And half the webcam people in Adultfriendfinder? And all the buxom and accommodating young ladies in www.booblicious.com? Muttering something about writing I retreat to my room, and the dark, and the laptop, like Scrooge returning to his old bag of gold guineas.

It can't go on, and it doesn't. The absolute crisis point comes about six weeks after I first started, when I am down in Cornwall visiting my family. I am now missing so much sleep, staying up so late to surf, chat and pleasure myself, my health finally starts to suffer. One day on my Cornish trip I catch tonsillitis which, because I am so run-down, turns into a quinsy (a nasty suppurative form). Eventually I am rushed to the doctor's, who sends me straight on to A&E. It's a Road to Damascus moment. As I lie in the ward recuperating a few days later, the bitter truth sinks in: This is it Sean, I think, you've really done it this time. You've actually wanked yourself into hospital.

When I am able to talk again, my dear mum comes to visit me in Truro Hospital. She blanches when she sees me. I guess I must look pretty pathetic: I am on a saline drip, to replace all the fluids I lost during my severe tonsillitis, the tonsillitis I contracted because I was so tired and run-down, the tonsillitis I got because I had been surfing so much online porn.

'You look whacked . . .' says my mum. 'What made you so run-down?'

I look at my mum. What can I say? *'Well Mum, the diagnosis was: I'm wanking too much'*?

No, I simply can't admit the truth. I look at my mum again.

'I was working too hard on an article.'

Hey, come on, give me a break. It's a half-truth.

A week after my hospitalisation, I go home again, somewhat sobered. This sobered-up feeling is made worse one
chilly November morning.

I am about to access datingdirect.co.uk, to send a couple
of messages, when I notice that a bill has arrived. It's my
credit-card bill. The sight of it reminds me of all those
websites I have visited, and paid for. Slightly reluctantly,
I open the bill, and read the figure.

£550.

Wow. Normally it's about £100.

As I sit there, I assess my reactions to this sizeable figure.
My reactions are mixed. Put it another way: I'm morti-
fied. Much as I'd like to be perplexed by this, much as
I'd like to be outraged, much as I'd like to be mystified
as to where the money's gone, I can't. I know perfectly
well where the money's gone: to dubious companies in
Surinam, to the nice people in charge of Fetbot, to the
accounts department over at hootermania.net.

And now the questions are kicking in. I have to ask
myself: what's happened to me over the last few weeks?
What is it about Net porn that got me so hooked – in
contrast to ordinary porn? These are questions that have
been simmering on the rear hob of my mind for some
time. Now they're bubbling over.

A few moments' consideration and a very strong cup
of coffee gives me a quick answer. To my mind, there are

three huge, obvious and crucial differences between Net porn and old-fashioned porn, that may explain why Net porn appeals – to a dangerous degree – whereas old porn didn't.

First, much of the porn on the Net is gratis (you can pay if you insist, as I foolishly did, but you don't have to). Pretty important.

Second, there is no embarrassment in getting hold of the stuff; with the World Wide Web there is no quick furtive once-over of the top shelf at the newsagent. It's a shame-free environment. One of the reasons I never bought porn before was the sheer mortification involved – I never had the guts to go in and buy a sordid magazine in front of the girl on the checkout desk. This wasn't the only reason, but it was definitely a factor.

The third great advantage of Net porn is its infinite and remarkable variety, the fact it is so voluptuously and seductively diverse. If you want to find images of Russian girls in diving suits, there they are on the Net; if you want to explore images of Latino girls having threesomes in swimming pools, there is a whole site dedicated to the genre. Whatever you want, whatever you think it possible to sexually conceive – and way beyond – is on the Net. Waiting like a scorpion in your desert boot.

This last reason is the crucial one, to my mind, speaking as a man. The protean nature of the Net is dangerous, at least for men who are reasonably highly sexed (i.e. most men). That is to say: the Net can reveal to you, as it revealed to me, the various kinks in your teemingly sexual male brain – in an exhilarating but perilous way. For instance, I was never before remotely cognisant of the fact I liked lesbian dentistry – images of naked women giving each other fillings. It's not something that really occurs to you, is it? On an average day you don't wake up thinking, 'Oh I wonder if I like looking at women dentists with their breasts out, putting braces on Spanish girls with no underwear?'

But when I saw such images on the Net, I found the whole concept surprisingly erotic. It was something to do with the dominance of the naked lady dentist and the submission of the girl patient with toothache, and maybe also the juxtaposition of tender and feminine nudity with all the sterilised equipment and crumpled uniforms. Or maybe I just fancied a dental assistant when I was four-teen.

What does this infer? I think it demonstrates how the Net reveals to men that they may have peccadillos aplenty, hidden in the cellar of their libido. And this could be significant. Because the revelation of hidden kinks might be very dangerous – depending on which peccadillo is revealed, of course.

Look at it this way: Imagine there is a happy-go-lucky chap who has, in the corner of his mind, a weird but undiscovered penchant for looking at, say, sex with horses. In the normal run of things this would not be too disas-trous; after all, a man could easily go a whole lifetime without realising that he fancied thoroughbred yearlings.

But the Net has changed this situation. Such images –

of horse-sex, and worse – are there on the Net. So this happy-go-lucky ordinary guy could be surfing away, on an ordinary porn site, and suddenly an image of horse-sex flashes up and – bang – he's found that this kind of image pleases him and he's worried. But he also wants to find more. He's therefore hooked, and suddenly we have ourselves a potential criminal. Because horse-sex is illegal, at least in the West, if not rural Afghanistan.

There are two obvious answers to this. The first answer is that our happy-go-lucky chap shouldn't be surfing for porn anyway. The second answer is that, if he haplessly discovers that he likes horse-sex, then he should lock that thought away, and never return to it.

However, there is another way of looking at it.

The way I see it, male sexuality – maybe all sexuality – was never designed to cope with something like the Net. For sound genetic reasons, the male libido is constructed by evolution to be an unscratchable itch, a desperate, unsatisfiable urge. In this respect, it's essentially the same as hunger: it's meant to be unending, and overwhelming when brooked, and only temporarily satisfiable. Just as you aren't meant to wake up one day and say, 'Oh I've had six thousand meals, I think I'll stop eating now,' so men aren't meant to wake up one day and think, 'Oh, I've ogled five hundred girls, think I'll stop staring at them now.' Men are therefore the hummingbirds of sex, constantly up for it, perpetually famished, always seeking the nectar.

But because male sexuality is like this – so ardent, and

so powerfully insatiable – it has to be bridled by society, by social structures. And in the past, it was. Hitherto women were chaste, demure and/or hard to get; and pornography was naff, embarrassing and costly.

But now we've got the Net, which totally revolutionises things. To men, the Internet says: Hey guys, this is different, now you can have as much sexual stimulation as you want; now you can see as many naked teenies as you like. And men have not evolved with the ability to resist this kind of endless temptation. It's like giving beer to Eskimos; we don't have the enzymes to cope. Marry the infinite porn-resources of the Net to the endlessness of male sexual desire and men can end up practically frigging themselves to death. As I well know.

Make sense? Perhaps. But there is another big question going begging here. Maybe I am alone in these thoughts, in this experience, in my temporary but troubling Net porn problem?

If so, there's only one way to find out. The following weekend, instead of pursuing my Net-dating (put it another way, I haven't got any Net-dates), I have a big session with my closest pals, where I quiz them on their Net-porn experiences. Sure enough, on the third beer, the truth comes spilling out. It swiftly becomes obvious that many of my friends *are* also having Net-porn addiction problems similar, or identical, to mine.

One friend confesses he has cancelled his Web connection because he is so worried. Another says he has nearly lost his wife through his constant surfing. I think he is joking but he shakes his head soberly (well, semi-soberly). Still another chum tells me has gone on to mpegs – is mainlining the stuff – and is spending every hour of every weekend streaming porno videos online. He's also very surprised that it turns out he likes interracial hardcore. He's not at all sure why. A fourth friend goes further. He confesses to a kind of cyber-affair with a girl he met on one of the adult dating sites. They never physically hooked up, but the affair still paralleled the arc of a normal affair: they met, they flirted, they moved on to cybersex. Then his wife walked in and discovered him in flagrante delicto (or at least emailing a very saucy message). Happily, their marriage survived, but it was a close-run thing: the computer got soaked by a kettleful of water. My friend has now, at his wife's request, put a block on certain websites. He can look but he can't email, he can browse but he can't read messages. Like Odysseus tied to the mast.

Nevertheless, as we all finish our beers and move seamlessly on to a discussion of the England cricket team, I decide that this is all very fascinating and enlightening, but I still haven't proved anything. My friends themselves might just be an unrepresentative bunch, a self-selecting group of middle-class guys with too much time and bandwidth. What about the rest of mankind; does our experience hold for other men, too?

Further investigation reveals to me that my friends and I are quite the opposite of unusual; that Internet porn addiction is a burgeoning problem for men in the West, in the advanced world, maybe right across the globe.

Here's what I glean from a few minutes' research on the, er, Internet: There are reckoned to be two million pornographic websites on the World Wide Web; a thousand new ones are created every day. A *thousand*. The only words entered more often than 'sex' into Internet search engines are 'and' and 'the'. Thirty per cent of European companies have sacked employees for surfing porn or sending erotic emails at work.

I think this settles it. The problem isn't restricted to me and my friends. But in a way of course it *is* just me and my friends. Behind these statistics are men getting hooked. Me, you, your husband, that guy down the road, my friend Kenneth. Definitely my friend Kenneth. It's troubling. I'm not sure what we can do about it, but it's . . . troubling.

But does the above mean that I think the Internet is a bad thing for sex? Yes and no. I think the Internet is certainly a revolution in sexuality; and like all revolutions it has the ability to hurt, just as it has the capacity to liberate. Yet it's up to us what we do with it. Which is why, despite all of the above, and with several big caveats, I prefer to be positive. I may have nearly strummed myself to death on www.rasputeen.com, but I still like to think that the Internet has the potential to change human sexuality, human passion, passionate sexual love, in wonderful and life-affirming ways.

Because it frees us. It unslaves us. It opens us up to ourselves, and to everyone else. It makes it easier for lonely people to be less lonely. The Internet is a whole new way of looking at the world, a whole new way of looking at human relationships. Most of all, it's a whole new way of looking at middle-aged dinner ladies in the Wirral.

And now, finally, I really am done; I really am going to get back to good, wholesome Internet dating – to surf some profiles, to send some deft and wryly amusing messages. Or just some messages.

But when I sit down at the laptop, something happens. For a tiny moment my cursor strays to the Favourites button. I can feel my brain going down familiar and disturbing grooves: Go on, Sean – why not just a few minutes at The Hun? How about a quick visit to sublimegirls.net? Or a little one-on-one chat with Poonanny5? Where's the harm? Why not have a tiny peek?

But then I remember: lying in hospital, feeling a total dingbat, having to lie to Mum about the genesis of my illness.

Nope, I don't want that again. What I want is a real girl. Even if it's a girl I meet online, at least I might actually get to meet her in the flesh. There might still be a chance of love. After all, there are millions of women still waiting to meet me. And one of them is called Sandre.

This is Commitmentland

Is that a French revolutionary? If it is, why are his friends on rollerblades? Are they going to kidnap Freddie Mercury?

Yup, I'm at a musical. And I'm thinking it was a mistake. I'm thinking maybe I shouldn't have brought Sandre, my new flame from datingdirect, to the West End on our first assignation. Most especially, maybe I shouldn't have brought her to a crashingly amplified West End song-and-dance production where it's difficult to discern the plot amidst the mayhem, and it's so loud we can't even hear each other shout.

Thinking I should at least say *something*, I lean across to Sandre. Cupping my hand to her ear, I yell:

'It's loud, isn't it?'

'What?'

So why am I here? Because I got bored of the pub/restaurant thing, the normal first date rigmarole. I've had maybe fifteen Internet dating first dates now and I think I've been to a bar or an eaterie on every single one of them. Also, after my Net-porn debacle, I thought it might be time to try a new tack. And so I opted for a fresh first-date experience. With young Sandre here . . .

But now I'm not sure. Perhaps I should have remembered that, when you do this – when you want to try something new on a first date – you take a risk. A very big risk indeed: I can recall at least one similarly catastrophic first date that I had, years ago. The girl and I both wanted to 'try something different', so one Sunday afternoon we went to the Natural History Museum.

I thought this was a good choice, at the time. A few dinosaurs, dead butterflies, perhaps a stuffed polar bear. What could go wrong?

Quite a lot, as it turned out. We hadn't reckoned with the new-fangled museum curating, the graphic and interactive post-modern stuff. Within our first ten minutes we walked into a lurid exhibition called 'The Human Body'. This wide corridor had, at the end of it, a large, insistent, push-button model of human sexual intercourse. This model was massive: the size of a car. And there was no escaping it, as it was blocking the end of the corridor. Moreover, even if either of us had wanted to escape, I suspect we couldn't have, really – because if one of us had fled, that would have seemed gauche and unsophisticated. And so it was that this girl and I spent a fair chunk of our first date gazing with feigned interest at a three-foot-long penis inside a vagina the size of an RAF wind-sock.

The conversation afterwards, as I recall, was unusual. 'What did you think of that massive cock?' 'The whacking great cock? I thought it was excellent. And the clitoris the size of a scatter cushion was a deft touch.' 'Yeah, they're usually harder to find than that.'

We didn't actually have that conversation. In the end we both got the giggles and ran to a pub – where we should probably have started. But even if it turned out all right, it was a close-run thing.

So maybe I should be glad that I'm just bored, uncomfortable, and frustrated on this first date, rather than staring at an oversized celluloid todger. But still: this musical is *terrible*. And all the punters around me in the stalls aren't helping. I think there must be a busload of nitrous-oxide addicts in tonight, because they keep laughing at stuff that isn't funny. Perhaps they're only laughing because they paid £50 a head to watch this herniated drive – so they are determined to have a good time.

And now it's getting worse. A loud, silly woman in front of me has just sat down, and she is waggling her massive head in time with the 'music'. And of course I am trapped right in the middle of row J, right behind her. I can't see a damn thing. So what should I do? I can't just run away, because, even if I wanted to bolt, I'd have to barge past about fifteen tutting people, as well as explain to Sandre why I was baling twenty minutes into our very first date. My only choice is therefore to sit here; and suffer. And listen to this daffy woman asking inane questions of her friend, about every plot point of the musical. 'Why is she singing about starlings?' 'What's Freddie Mercury doing?'

The woman is a moron. She is a cretin. She is, I fear,

emblematic; in other words, she is crystallising a question that has been locked in the attic of my mind for some time. Just why *are* so many women so thick?

I know that sounds a little ungallant. But it needs to be said. Some women, lots of women, are just not up to speed – in my experience.

Take my old acquaintance 'Laura'. She was the long-term girlfriend of a friend of mine; and mentally speaking she was *not* the bushiest beard in the mosque. My friend used to tell lots of stories about his beloved Laura. Like this one:

One time, my chum and Low-Watt Laura were in the park, and they were watching a kite fly. The kite was making that rappling sound kites make when the wind is stiff. Laura looked at the kite in a puzzled way, and then she brightened and said: 'That one's got an engine.'

I ask you.

Another time, my friend and Laura went into a restaurant. After scanning the menu for about half an hour, she ordered 'garlic bread, *without the garlic*'. So that'd be hot bread then, with butter? *Hell*-o.

As for politics – bless! One time we teasingly asked her what she thought about Gordon Brown, and she said: 'I don't know, what is it?'

Here's another thing about women: about how not-necessarily bright they can be. It's a kind of mental experiment. Try asking a girl if a certain place is to the east or the north of where she is. It's fun to do this – because most girls *just don't know*. They bobble their pretty heads and say, 'Ooh, uhm, got me there! Is that up by the shoe shop?'

It's striking, when you think about it. How *do* women get around? You could almost feel sorry for them. In fact, I've often thought that there should be special maps for women. Instead of the cardinal points, or places of interest, or scientific information on rivers, earthworks and gradients, these special 'maps for women' would point out things that women need, understand and can reference. There would be pointers saying things like: 'Lovely dress shop here'; 'Janet's friend's flat is here'; 'Big house with those nice curtains'; 'This way to the ironing board, love'.

HEY GIRLS I'M JOKING. I'm just going barmy, trying to entertain myself while this interminable production grinds towards the interval. I am, as it happens, well aware that men can be just as dim-witted as women; that men have an equal facility for being ridiculous and numbskulled. It's just that maybe men are stupid in different ways to women.

To illustrate: I once asked a girlfriend to name the capital of Iran, and she admitted she didn't know. When I teased her about this, she pointed out, quite fairly, that this supposedly interesting and valuable fact would never have any relevance to her life, and would never come in useful. So why should she learn it? Her riposte rather stumped me, I confess. What's more, my girlfriend then asked *me* the date of our first meeting, our anniversary. I had forgotten, naturally. But when I asked her in return what possible relevance this fact could have, she said, 'Well Sean, it's very relevant, as I am not going to let you sleep in my bed now.'

So who was the stupid one there? Both of us; perhaps neither; maybe me. The point I am making is that men and women have different ways of understanding the world, both equally valid. Which perhaps explains why the genders sometimes stare at each other in blank-faced puzzlement, wondering: My God, are they really that idiotic?

But anyway, back to the musical. Here in London's famous West End, the interval has finally arrived, only seven hours after the musical began.

Together, Sandre and I shimmy off to the bar to get our G&Ts. In the crush at the bar we look at each other, stiffly, with a hint of nervousness.

Then she says:

'It isn't very good, is it?'

I feel a huge sense of relief.

'No. It's bollocks. Sorry.'

Sandre shakes her head.

'And it's so loud, too. Why is it so stupidly loud?'

'Dunno. Shall we bugger off?'

'Please!'

It's like bunking off school at lunchtime. With a joyous sense of illicit freedom, we swiftly down our drinks and step out into the night-time bustle of Shaftesbury Avenue. Outside it is raining, and polluted, and there are homeless people hassling everyone. Fantastic.

In the nearest pub, Sandre and I sit down for a drink

and a chat – at last. I am happy to discover that she certainly matches her profile, and her emails: she's a pretty, articulate, half-French girl, early thirties, who works in medical research and likes nice wine. However, she doesn't seem very happy. I know French people often look sour and disapproving, but Sandre seems really disenchanted. I'm starting to get bad signals here.

Perhaps the musical didn't help; I probably need to get her on to a chirpier subject. So I ask her about any other theatrical experiences she has had. Whoops. Big mistake. Not only has Sandre had quite a few theatre experiences; I soon realise, as she launches into an impassioned monologue, that she knows more about theatre than I do about Internet porn sites. She's been to Brechtian theatre in Clapham, theatre of the absurd in Paris; she knows stuff about Stanislavsky, Beckett, and Ibsen; she knows the entire programme at the Old and Young Vics; and she has a theory about the symbolic placing of a handbag in a recent fringe production of Strindberg's *Miss Julie*. Then Sandre asks me, inevitably, about my theatre-going.

'Well . . . erm . . . I thought that Abba thing was OK. And *Oliver!* is always a laugh . . .'

Her face is blank. I try again.

'*Oliver!*? The musical?'

Her face is still blank, perhaps with a new slant of sadness. That'll learn me for making jokes about stupid women. But why did I ask her about her theatre-going when I very rarely go to the theatre myself? Hello? *Sean?*

At a loss, I decide to cheer Sandre up, and lighten the

intellectual and rather oppressive atmosphere with a song from *Oliver*! (it really is the musical I like best). Doing a cheeky Cockney grin, and an Artful Dodger-ish waggle of the head, I launch into a lyric:

'*Consider yourself at home! Consider yourself one of the family! We've taken to you so strong. It's clear we're going to get along!*'

Silence. Some people in the bar are staring over. Sandre is gazing at me like I have just started masturbating in public. I'd better think about something else to say. Swiftly I tell her how I don't normally go to see musicals or plays on a first date.

'Normally,' I blithely add, 'I only take a girl to a play or the movies if I'm worried we won't have anything to say to each other. I had this one date and she was incredibly boring so I took her to see *Farewell My Concubine*, the Chinese film.' I look at Sandre for a nod. No nod. I carry on anyway. 'It's three and a half hours long. Perfect! 'Cause then I didn't have to talk to her . . .'

About halfway through that sentence I realise that my amusing insight is not going down too well. But it's too late to stop. So here I am, staring at Sandre. She's doing yet another unimpressed face.

'Hm.' She says.

Right. This is one of the most disastrous dates in my year of Internet dating. Which gives me an idea: why don't I talk to her about Internet dating? We have, at least, got that in common, if not an earnest appreciation of Pere Ubu. So I ask Sandre her opinion of Internet dating.

It turns out she's not sure she likes it. At all.

'When you go on an Internet dating site, it's like you see a sign saying "This is Commitmentland".' Sandre sighs, in a vaguely Parisian way. 'And when you actually go online it is so . . . so serious. "Hello everyone, I am here to meet a husband." You know what I mean? It is not playful . . .'

She looks very depressed. At a loss now, I ask her how long she has been online and searching.

She pauses. 'A year.' she says. Her expression remains downcast. 'It is too long, too long . . .'

A final silence settles between us. Eventually Sandre looks up and she abruptly says:

'I'm sorry. This isn't working for me any more . . . I am going to go.'

And with that remark, she leaves.

For a second I sit there. Resigned. Bemused. Deflated. Confused. I am staring at the door as it swings shut again. Then I think: Well, that was nice; I saw half a musical, and had half a drink, and made a total arse of myself. As ever, I decide to sweat off my disgruntlement with a walk, a walk home through the beery streets of Soho, the elegant streets of Fitzrovia, back to my little flat, and my single chair. Already I'm looking forward to my restful and stress-free isolation. Being single is so much easier. You can do what you like. When I'm home I might have a nice sit-down in that solitary chair. In my single room. And maybe after that I'll have a single meal. Then I'll stare out of the single window, at a single star . . .

If this was a film, and I were a woman, I'd burst into tearful song, right here. I'm frustrated and depressed. Why is it so hard to be Not Single? Is it something about me? Do I have some problem with shacking up, with getting together and then staying with one person?

I mean, there have been times when I have been Not Single, times when I have been all loved-up, and yet I let the relationships fade out, or they have imploded on me before I could make that commitment: the marriage thing. And maybe if I had made that commitment I wouldn't be single now? Is that my problem? Perhaps. I do have a fraught and nervy attitude to commitment. I think partly it's due to my parents' being divorced. I saw my mother and father unhappy in their marriage, so I don't want to repeat that mistake. I want to get it right.

Yet there's something else, too. I also don't want to get trapped. On analysis, I seem to have some kind of emotional claustrophobia, some fear of confinement. Tonight provides an analogy for this. When I was in that musical I got frustrated and agitated because I was in a seat halfway down a row, away from the aisle. That always freaks me out – at the cinema or the theatre, or on a plane for that matter. I like to be right by the aisle so that I can easily nip to the loo, so that I won't have to barge past people if I want to stand up or flee.

And I think I may be the same in relationships. In relationships I like to sit by the aisle. Just in case I need to escape. I want to keep my options open. Somewhere inside, I think that long-term commitment, i.e. marriage, would be like sitting in the middle of the row of seats at the theatre, forced to endure the whole show, like it or not. What if the show is *crap*?

Ah well. At least I'm nearly home now: the crowds are thinning out and I can see the trendy Thai restaurant at the end of my street. Inside, happy couples are spooning duck-and-tamarind sauce into each other's mouths. Good for them. I've never gritted my teeth so hard.

At my door, I key the latch, climb the stairs and go into my room, and I sit and spin on my chair (did I say it was a spinning chair? If you're only going to have one item of furniture, better make it a fun item, I say). Then on my third spin I stare across the desk and look at my pot plant.

The pot plant's dead. Irreversibly dead. *Dead*. Now, belatedly, I realise that I haven't watered the plant for about . . . ooh . . . two weeks. Or more. Why? Search me. It's not because I've been massively busy, not because I've been away. It's more that I'm just . . . scatterbrained, and easily distracted; it's also no doubt something to do with my tendency to be very self-absorbed and downright selfish. So selfish I can't be bothered to water a pot plant.

I've noticed this before in myself, this rhapsodic selfishness. Whenever I go down to Cornwall, I have to walk the family dog. This is fun sometimes – on the beach, say – because I'm quite fond of the dog; but most of the time it's a total chore. Most times I just tug the dog along the street and make phone calls while I'm doing it, all the time resenting the fact that this dog is using up about fifteen minutes of my day. And as I drag the dog seventy metres out of the house and then back again in double-quick time, I always think: What am I getting out of this? What's my end of the deal??

Let me repeat, I go down to Cornwall about once every two months, and there I have to walk the dog for about fifteen minutes. *And I resent the imposition.* I'm obviously incapable of looking after a dog full time. In fact I am probably incapable of looking after a mosquito full time. Moreover, my frigging pot plant's dead. Because I couldn't be arsed to water it, though the plant is three feet from my desk and I could probably, at a pinch, water it without actually leaving my seat.

In the light of all this damning evidence, what makes me think I *am* cut out for marriage? What makes me so keen to enter Commitmentland? What makes me think, for a moment, that I can cope with all the responsibilities, all the necessary compromises, all the required unselfishness of having a wife and family? If I can't look after a plant?

Hm. Perhaps another analogy from plane travel might help here. Recently I've started wondering if I am one of life's 'hand-luggage only's. Why? Because I reckon the dating game, assortative mating, is a little like waiting at the luggage carousel at an airport.

Imagine it: At the beginning you are all there, waiting for your particular luggage to trundle along. Then people start to pair off with the bags; you see people diving in and picking out their suitcases and rucksacks, and heading off for Customs. And still you're there, waiting for your bags. Now you're noticing that the people who checked in after you are picking up their bags; eventually you start thinking, Why am I always the last person to get his bag?! In the end they close the airport and start hoovering under your feet.

You see my point: maybe it is just better to face facts and admit that *your* bags are never going to arrive. You're never going to meet that right person, your designated life-long mate. So why not just accept this at an earlier point and go through life with hand-luggage only? Then you can fly in and out in a jiffy. Have smash-and-grab relationships. Quickies.

On the face of it, this doesn't look good. Add together the different mindsets of men and women, and my inability to commit, and my notable selfishness, and I could start to think that men and women just don't go together; that we are all doomed to mutual incomprehension; that I am destined for solitude. But I *can't* think that. Because I know how much men and women need each other, how badly we function without each other, how much we all crave a mixed-gender world. Because, you see, I've been to the one country in the world where there are *no women*.

It's called Mount Athos and it's a semi-independent ecclesiastic republic, set on a stunning peninsula in northern Greece. This place has quite a few men (maybe three thousand monks, hermits and pilgrims) – but it has absolutely no women. This is because, in the Holy Republic of Mount Athos, all women, and all images of women, are *verboten*.

The Athonite banning of persons and images female is not a new thing. It was first decided a thousand years ago, by the bigwigs in the Byzantine Orthodox Church. They reckoned women would distract the monks and rival the beauty of Mary, the mother of God, to whom beautiful, pristine, chauvinistic Athos is dedicated.

From the off, the monks of the Holy Mountain took this no-woman ordinance very literally. Not only did they banish all the washer-women and fishwives, they also drove off the female animals: the mares, sows and bitches. Even the hens were briskly shooed away. Eventually, only the female cats and songbirds were allowed, mainly because there was nothing that could be done about them.

And so it remains. These days, if you are an inquisitive female who wants to have a look at one of the famous monasteries of Mount Athos – like the Great Lavra – the best you can do is to hire a boatman at the border port, and ask him to sail you down the coastline of the penin-sula. He will approach within five hundred metres of the shore – and no further. And if you are a bitch or a hen – forget it, girls. Apparently there's also a monk still employed to sniff out the female creatures, and scatter them.

This emphatic lack of women has had, according to reports, a weird affect on the monks of Athos. A British traveller, Richard Curzon, went to Mount Athos in the nineteenth century, and he encountered a monk who had been left on Athos as a foundling. The monk had, there-fore, spent almost his whole life in the woman-free country, and consequently had *no idea what women looked like.* When this monk met Curzon, the monk asked Curzon if all women had haloes, like the Blessed Virgin. Obviously the monk had never encountered Vancouvergirl2.

A couple of years ago I myself went to Athos to write a piece on this weirdness; to find out what it was like in a world without women. The first place I arrived at was the minuscule capital, Karyes. The main street of this tiny town was lined with shops. These stores looked fairly ordinary on the outside, but inside they were a Dada-ist mess: huge great piles of old bananas were dumped on dusty ikons, selections of rosary bracelets were draped over packets of medieval-looking biscuits. The shops also looked like they hadn't been seen, kept, ordered – or cleaned – for centuries. The bachelor flats of retailing.

Then I went to visit the monasteries. Here I discovered that there is, occasionally, some contact with women on Athos. In one monastery I met a monk called Hector. After some cajoling, Hector told me about the difficulties of his womanless life: 'Once every few years, one or two monks may see a woman. Sometimes, you understand, women come to the beach here. It is illegal, but they come, and they make swimming. They often wear bikinis, and then . . . then it is very difficult for us.' As he spoke, I noticed Hector was doing a very pointed smile.

Short-wave radios can give access to the world of women for some monks. At another monastery, Dionysiou, I met a kind-eyed, thirty-something, Oxford-born monk called Jeffrey.

'You do have sexual desires, sexual thoughts,' said Jeffrey. 'The Evil One is always with you.' Then Jeffrey

added: 'You know we are allowed radios, very occasionally? The other day I heard a woman's voice on the radio;
it was the first woman's voice I have heard for many years.
It was so beautiful . . .'

He looked so sad, I thought he was going to burst into
tears.

My last stop on Athos was the little port of Daphne.
Although it was crowded with monks, pilgrims, roofers
and tourists, chatting and drinking in the pub, this place
had a spooky serenity, the calmest atmosphere imaginable.
Then I realised just why it was so calm and laid-back.

It was because there was no competing going on. There
was no need to jostle for female attention, because there
was no female attention. There was no need for the stags
to clash antlers in the forest, because there were no does
to fight over. The men were all equal in their womanlessness; this in turn was mellowing everybody out. So there
were few, if any, of the normal, boastful male conversations about football, politics, or cars. Even the bar was
notably serene – the oddest dockside pub in the West.

On the face of it, this sounds OK – even agreeable. But
my long hours in the docks, indeed my whole five days on
Athos, confirmed something else to my mind: for all its
meditative languour, Athos was a troubled and perturbing
place. The whole peninsula was sterile, somehow numbed,
enervated. The lack of women seemed to be inducing a
desperate torpor in everyone. Indeed such was the strange,
almost sinister affect of this womanlessness, the monks
seemed to be making up for it in their own way.

Some of the monks in the bars were acting like women (I know that's not hard when you are wearing a long black dress, but still): they were being coquettish, acting submissively or teasingly. Other monks were masculine, waving their arms in the air, flourishing their huge black beards, burping as they sank their retsina. And this taught me that, for all the differences between men and women, men desperately need women; because a world without women is a world without purpose and colour. Unthinkably drab. And we know this because when there are no women, men will actually try to invent them. And fail.

So there's my answer. Whatever my doubts towards commitment, whatever my anxieties about my own selfishness, whatever my fears about the differing mindsets of men and women, men and women need each other, on a strangely profound level. In particular, I need a girlfriend, because it 'just isn't a life without a woman', as Kingsley Amis once said.

So what do I do? I am not sure. But perhaps I should just stop fretting, and soldier on; and simply email some more girls. Because, who knows, I might eventually email a girl like me, and we can be totally irresponsible and crap together.

And in the meantime, I might get a cactus.

See you again, Marmaduke Skewes?

'*Wilma is looking for Freddie Flintstone. Only real cavemen need apply. Must have own brontosaurus.*'

Well – it's kind of interesting. I like the use of the word 'cavemen'. There's a hint of willing submissiveness in that word, a hint I find sexy, perhaps because there *is* a shred of Neanderthal DNA in the thick-cut marmalade of my chromosomes. And the hint of humour is good, too: maybe this one will be a little cheerier than Sandre.

Clicking on the message box, I send Kate a hopefully suitable email:

'*Not only do I have a brontosaurus, I've got a cudgel and . . . er . . . one of those cars made out of stone. Do you want to see my bearskin?*'

It's a naff message, so naff I am aware it risks not getting a reply; but I'm not sure I care that much. I am getting tired of prolonged email exchanges.

Two hours later (two hours!) I get my reply. The message is convoluted and obscure and it involves more terrible puns on dinosaurs and the like. For an hour I think about my own riposte, but before I can, I get a second message: '*God that was a stupid email!!!!! Can't think of anything funny to say about Barney Rubble!!!! Anyway you sound like a nice guy. I'm probably being really forward and a slapper but dya fancy a drink? LOL!*'

OK. This is a tad unexpected. My curiosity aroused, I go back to Kate's profile: she says she's thirty. Medium build. English. She's 'a waitress', yet says she's 'training to be a lawyer'. Then I scan down and see something I didn't notice before: under '*How sexually adventurous are you?*' she's put: '*Very*'.

'Very'? That's an unusual answer. Only a tiny proportion of women put this, and hitherto I've actually avoided these girls, as it seems so in-yer-face. But as I said, I'm feeling adventurous now; almost end-of-term-y.

Two more emails and we're done. We arrange to meet in a pub in west London, just off the Fulham Road. She says she will be wearing a yellow shirt, and when I get there I see she is spot on. Her shirt is acid-yellow, the brightest thing in the dingy pub. She's sitting by the bar with a pint, a just-cracked-open packet of cigarettes, and a boozy smile.

'Yay,' she says, as I look at the pint. 'I always get nervous when I do these dates. Drink too much!'

She does a modest burp.

I'm not yet sure what to make of Kate. She is pretty, in a buxom way. Dark haired, wide-lipped, nice jeans. There's something masculine about her; and something very sexy too. She's also got a checkered history, as she explains. 'Fuckyeah, I dropped out of uni to go travelling. Mistake of the year. I've done a ton of different jobs, never could settle on one thing so . . . I'm doing a law degree on the Q. Just what the world needs, another fucking lawyer . . .'

She swears a lot, does Kate. Again I am unsure of my reaction to this. I've always maintained, indeed I have previously written, that women should only swear in bed, just as men should only cry during wartime; but I think I said that just to wind people up or sound profound, or because I couldn't think of anything else to say. Kate's swearing is actually of a piece with her persona: laid-back, funny, honest, sexy.

She says she likes the fact that I'm a writer. 'What was that thing that Jilly Cooper said, "Lucky is the girl who lays the golden egghead"!'

With that she bursts into a laugh, and hiccups, and apologises, and tells me her dad is an artist. Then she says:

'So do you want to come back to my flat for large amounts of alcohol . . . ?'

I nod. Well, why not. She's a blitz of a woman. So we get up and we pace outside into the pizza-smelling air of the Fulham Road. As we walk, she takes my hand. Up front or what? Ten minutes later we turn into a mid-Victorian terrace, she keys the latch and we go into a flat that looks like it has been recently rifled by the secret police and then burgled to boot: there are shoes everywhere and clothes piled on a chair and a packet of cereal in the grate, and dozens of books haphazardly stacked on top of the CD player and some wine bottles in a row on the window-sill. There is also a big antique mirror on a wall with posh wedding invitations stuck clumsily in the frame.

Kate stops and looks at the tumult, the notable mess.

'Thank God I got the cleaners in yesterday . . .'

She bursts into a peal of ribald laughter. I like this laugh. It has that appealing mixture of butchness and girlish glee-fulness again, that is just so . . . well, so *Kate*. Scanning the flat one more time, I note that it may be messy but it's not that unclean. Kate's place is, like Kate herself, somehow likeable in its sincerity. It says: this is me; take it or leave it; I am Kate.

Seconds later, Kate returns from the fridge (which is in the hallway) with two pint glasses, which she near halfway fills with gin. Expensive gin. She then chucks in some ice and tonic ('not that sugarless crap, slimline my arse'). Finally she says, 'Do you mind if I skin up?'

Reaching behind a pile of artbooks she fetches out a pochette of tobacco and grass. I demur and say that dope sends me to sleep, or into a paranoid delusion. Unabashed, Kate grins and rolls a small reefer anyway, which she smokes herself, in between huge glugs of G&T. After about half an hour of giggling small talk, and of me getting pretty drunk on her gin, and lots of ambient techno on her stereo, and her getting aerated and high on her grass (which smells quite nice, I have to say), she does a lurid giggle and looks me right in the eye and she says:

'Hey. You know what? I have a strange desire to debut my underwear . . .'

'*I have a strange desire to debut my underwear*'?? Before I can construe this sentence Kate's hand is on my thigh and she says:

'Mnnnmnmnmnmnmnggggg.' She can't say much more because she is now kissing my neck in an imploring way.

Ah well. What the fuck, as Kate would say. Taking Kate's hand from my thigh I say:

'Bed or table?' Which is not a line I normally use on a first date.

Kate has her head tilted to one side, and her bleary eyes half closed.

'Oh bed I think . . .' she says. 'Got tons of legal textbooks on the table . . .'

Calypso.

It turns out, happily, that her bedroom is much less scruffy than her sitting room. It's got soft lights and another huge antique mirror and what looks like a fake tigerskin pinned to the wall. And prominent on the bedside table is a vibrator.

Ignoring this, sort of, I peel off my shirt. Kate and I are kissing now. Then the rest of our clothes come off, with a nice lack of awkwardness. But before we can go any further, naked Kate leans over to that bedside cabinet and abruptly pulls open a drawer, and I see piles of condoms, another vibrator, and velvet handcuffs . . .

Bashful, she is not. With a chuckle Kate reaches in the drawer, and grabs a handful of the condoms – like a greedy child reaching in the sweet-jar. Then she flings the multi-coloured condoms on her duvet, and sweeps a hand across the wide selection, and says:

'Take your pick.'

Ten minutes later, we are about our business. Everything is marvellous. There is a salsa-ish swing to our endeavours; we seem to know each other's dance moves.

That is, until Kate suddenly turns herself over, and says:

'Can you bugger me?'

Ouch. Ouch ouch ouch. Ouch!

Time Out!

Standing above supine Kate, I frown and look down. Her buttocks are white beneath me, like two snowy hills seen from an Alpine biplane. I am very attracted to her bottom, but I am unsure about this request, because, you see, I don't like anal sex. I may be into certain kinks, like spanking, or al fresco sex, or even a little light bondage, but I'm not into anal sex. Too squeamish, maybe.

So what do I do?

What I do is have a big think about kinkiness. About weirdness. Throughout this evening, as it has become obvious that Kate is very sexual, I have been thinking about sex and perversion and erotic adventurousness.

And so while I kneel here on this bed in the Fulham Road, on this mild winter evening, wondering whether to bugger young Kate, here are my opinions; here's my philosophy as regards sexual weirdness. Think of it as something for you to be getting on with – as I consider my next move with Kate.

The first thing to note is that 'perversion' (for want of a better word, and I don't want to offend my gay friends) is not restricted to people. Contrary to much received opinion, 'homosexuality' and 'deviance' are widespread amongst animals.

Time for a list. According to the boffins, deer, sheep, ducks, gazelles, giraffes, chimps, dolphins, woodpeckers, squirrels, worms, whales, herons, geese, buffalo, elephants, kangaroos, bats, seagulls, spiders, emus, hyenas, gorillas, wasps, shrikes, swallows, and the south-eastern blueberry bee (amongst many other species) all exhibit various forms of homosexual behaviour (to start with gayness).

What does that mean? I'm not totally sure, but it might suggest that homosexuality is genetic. I mean, can they all have dominant mothers? And gayness isn't all, either. The animal kingdom is rife with bizarre and unexpected sexual behaviour – way beyond simple queer action. Gibbons, for instance, like 'threesomes'. Chimps are said to use 'dildos'. Orang-utans like to fellate smaller monkeys. Weasels are known to masturbate. Spiders are sometimes paedophilic. Antelopes are prone to trans-vestism. Stags can come by rubbing their antlers. Ducks are fond of lesbian orgies. Many mice are bi-curious. American bison can be transgender. Certain lesbo seabirds like to douse each other with water – like porn starlets in a shower. And the bigger ocean-going whales are known to conduct extraordinary sessions of *soixante-neuf*, spiralling down into the depths for many hours, lovingly entwined.

Possibly my favourite animal in the department of deviant or imaginative sex (depending on your perspective) is the dolphin. Dolphin sexual behaviour is magnificently varied and intriguing, and they are also great show-offs. Dolphin-spotters have reported seeing three pairs of dolphins having balletic and simultaneous sex, with one dolphin under water in each pair – apparently for the amusement of the human spotters. Other dolphin experts report that male dolphins like to show their penises to humans, to exhibit skill in penis-fencing each other; the dolphins get more excited still if the diving dolphin-spotter is a menstruating woman.

Even when humans aren't involved, dolphins could give yer average sex expert a run for her creative money. Gay dolphins can have sex for entire afternoons, like Sting. Female dolphins will stimulate their clitori with coral, or rubber balls, or their partners' fins. Straight male dolphins like to put their beaks into their partners' vaginas and propel them along, with the linked couple joyously corkscrewing as they go. Male dolphins also employ the 'genital buzz', where a stream of rapid buzzing clicks is directed through the water at the genitals of the female, a kind of acoustic foreplay where the sound waves stimulate the sex organs. Spinner dolphins are even known to gather in groups of twelve or more, for prolonged orgies of caressing interaction, groups which are gloriously known as *wuzzles*.

So what does this prove? I believe that dolphin sex, at least, might be an insight into what human sex could be like – in space. But the whole shebang also, I reckon, throws an interesting light on our hang-ups and kinks, our penchants and propensities. For a start, almost anything you can imagine doing with your beloved (or a bus-load of cheerleaders, or truck-load of firemen) has been done by a swan or a stoat or the stumptail macaque. So – depending on your kink, of course – it may not be something you should feel so shameful about.

Yet that does not mean that we are *all* kinky; it certainly does not mean that we *should* all be kinky, in every way possible, just because animals are the same. On that basis, eating our mates after intercourse (the praying mantis) would be acceptable.

But does it mean that I should just relax and bugger Kate, if that's what she wants? I don't know; I wish I did. Because she's just lying there, with her bottom ready. And I do like her bottom. I love bottoms. I love bottoms almost as much as I love cunts (I'm very sorry, but I'm going to have to get graphic here). Cunts I adore. Cunts perplex me. Cunts (is there a better word? I sometimes wish there were, but no) . . . cunts are mystifying and wonderful and tyrannical.

In my time as a writer I've described cunts, or a cunt, as many things. As 'a stripe of pelt'. As a 'Gestapo officer's mistress'. As a feathered Aztec god. As a young czarina in her furs. As looking like the face of Robin Cook, the late Foreign Secretary. As the ground floor of a Venetian

189

palazzo, 'where she stores her furs and cinnamons' (I was particularly proud of that one, as the ground floors of palazzos are very prone to flooding).

What does all this show, apart from my propensity to make up overblown similes for the female parts? Most of my metaphors have the same theme: either wildness, furriness and animal vulnerability, or that there is something in a vagina that frightens men into adoration. I think this is true, when it comes to the vulva; we don't know why we adore it, but we do, we have to. It demands our feudal respect. The cunt, indeed the entire naked female body, is, for a man, like an imperious ruler; we men kneel before it like peasants. I'm getting overblown again. But I can't help it. Kate's nudity is very exciting. Yet . . . I'm still less than keen on buggering her.

Here are some more thoughts on kinks, while I wrestle with my anal indecision. In my late-twenties, after my TV-star relationship, after my most important promiscuous period, after I lost my job on a proper newspaper, I started working for the first 'lad mags' – the British magazines, like *Maxim*, *FHM* and *Stuff* – which are all full of jokes, breasts, sex and football. These magazines, aimed squarely at young men, have now been successfully copied around the world, so they obviously appeal to all kinds of men.

A few years writing for *Maxim* taught me a lot about kinks, and just how many people like them; and how much they like them. One of my first assignments for the mag was to go to a 'punishment festival', in east London.

It was an extraordinary evening. I took along a couple of friends and we rolled up to a disused art gallery. We thought it would be a demure event with perhaps a little over-the-skirt paddling.

No. The place was chock-a-block with interested parties from all over England, Britain, Europe. And these people were up for it. By nine p.m., there were girls being spanked by middle-aged men, there were young women in nighties being thwacked by mature lesbians, there were men spanking men in one corner and women caning transves-tites in another corner, and in the middle there was a stern woman dressed as a headmaster spanking a large young man dressed as a baby. The atmosphere was effervescent and intoxicating: at the end of the evening one young woman got so carried away she had her entire naked pelvic area publicly cast in plaster.

One notable thing for me, as a neophyte journalist, was how 'ordinary' everybody was at this 'function'. There were lawyers, lorry drivers, surgeons, educated housewives from Yorkshire, a Spanish man. These people weren't freaks (though they were behaving fairly freakishly). Yet they were so into their chosen kink, they were prepared to drive across the country, or fly across Europe, just to join in the show with like-minded folk.

Another notable thing about the evening was this: one of the friends who accompanied me to the gig had brought his new girlfriend along. It was their first date. This may seem odd, but we had expected the evening to be fairly mild and only slightly outrageous. Once we were in, and realised it was a lot more hot-blooded and naked than we had expected, it was way too late to turn back.

So how did this girl react? She was a nice, mild, bourgeois estate agent; you might have expected her to be fazed or appalled or even to flee. She didn't. She loved it, she laughed, she used a lash on some guy. She might even have gone back the next week of her own accord. That gave me another inkling that this sexual deviance business is big business, that most people, perhaps – not just men – have some strange things lurking somewhere within.

Since then I've seen plenty more bizarrerie. For instance, I once went to a 'live sex' art class where a couple had sex and other people had to paint or draw them. The couple having sex certainly enjoyed it (the woman orgasmed); the painters and drawers definitely enjoyed it. I found the whole thing surreal and intense, and in truth I couldn't wait to get out. But still, it was another pointer of how wild the world is, how the avocets and baboons of the human sex zoo like to get it on in so many different ways.

Friends of mine in the lad-magazine trade have also encountered odd goings-on. I have one friend, Rob Arkell, who worked on these mags from the off. A few years ago he started a column called the 'Laboratory of Love'. The idea was that each month he would try some new sexual act or kink and report back in his column just how much he enjoyed or abhorred it. This column was read by about two million British men, every month.

So it is that I learned from Rob the pleasures and

displeasures of tribadism, urolagnia, sprinkling, glory holes, scarfing, switches, hosing, frottage, coprophilia, enemas, undinism, yohimbine, urtication, cupping, rhabdophilia, kokigami, love beads, bottom-mittens and the Mongolian cluster-fuck. His column was always entertaining, sometimes shocking – and again it showed the infinite variety of human sexual endeavour, the lengths some people will go to gain that pleasure, and just how weird the Japanese are (kokigama is the Nipponese art of dressing the penis in a paper costume).

Sometimes Rob's column did rebound on him. There's a true story about Rob's mother, a gracious, rather posh Englishwoman. At the time of the story, Rob's mother was living in Spain. Despite never having had the chance to actually read Rob's journalism, she was very proud of his work – 'my son the columnist, one of the most popular writers in Britain'. As I understand it, Rob fully intended to enlighten the old girl, but never found the right moment.

One day, the inevitable happened. Rob's mum announced that she was flying to England, and very much looking forward to reading her son's work – at last. Rob did everything possible to put her off, but it was too late. She landed, and practically the first thing she did, in the airport bookstall, was to buy this magazine where Rob's column regularly appeared. The month she bought it, Rob's column described how, in his laboratory of love, i.e. his bedroom in Camberwell, he had been sodomised by a woman wearing a strap-on dildo. In the column he described how he had found the activity 'oddly comforting'. The column was never mentioned by Rob's mother. In fact she never mentioned his journalism ever again.

Anyway. Back to the factory floor. I'm still here in Fulham. Seconds are passing. Kate is starting to wriggle her little bottom impatiently. She wants me to do it. Why?

Could it be because she thinks *I* will like it? Could she be doing this to please *me*? A fetish for anal sex is one of the commonest kinks – in men at least. So common is it that some women do, I believe, almost expect their men to be into it. Perhaps that's true of Kate here. I recall one past girlfriend who offered to let me have anal sex when it was my birthday – as a *present*. I demurred, because, as you already know, I don't particularly like to visit Buckingham Palace by the Grosvenor Place gate.

But my feeble squeamishness, or physical laziness, is arguably unusual. I've got plenty of friends who think anal sex the very acme of sexual pleasure. I had one friend at university, now a well-known banker in the City of London – a man now in charge of billions of euros – who as a student was so keen on anal sex he used to snip out pictures of female anuses from pornographic magazines and keep them in his wallet. When he was feeling mischievous he would walk around supermarkets and drop these little photos into the handbags of unsuspecting young women.

He found it deeply amusing and also, I suspect, sexually arousing, imagining these women opening their handbags and finding these tiny pictures. Men! I hope he has stopped this now, not only because it is probably illegal and certainly distasteful, but because it could cause a fracas at the Bank of England.

What is it about bottom-y sex (and related kinks like enemas and watersports) that is so appealing to some? Two possibilities, interrelated. First, it's partly the sheer naughtiness of it. When we are kids we are taught that things to do with going to the toilet are filthy and dirty and best kept to the lavatory. The reintroduction of these things into sexual play adds to the naughtiness of sex, and the naughtiness of sex is deeply important.

As Freud said, civilised man puts barriers (physical, social and moral) between the self and sexual gratification not just because rules are important for social harmony, but because, perversely, breaking the rules is a naughty pleasure. The more clothes you have on, the more deliciously teasing and laboured is the process of taking them off. Delayed gratification, dontcha know.

The second reason we like bottom- and toilet-type sex is surely because they are demeaning. Degrading. This is arguably an unhappy aspect of human sexuality, but it exists. Some like to demean others sexually, some people like to demean themselves sexually; it's surely something to do with domination and conquest, and also symbolic of true love.

'Facials' are another symptom of this – ejaculating on to the face. Plenty of men find this idea a turn-on, coming on to the face of their partner. And plenty of women, as I have discovered by asking my friends, find the idea of being ejaculated on to a turn-on as well. Some women ask for it. Want it. Why? Perhaps because it says: 'I love you so much, I let you do this to me.' And because, yes, it is naughtily dirty, as well.

While I'm going through the list of kinks: what about the sexuality of pain and bondage? Giving it, receiving it? This is the second broad area of kinkiness, after anal and toilet stuff. Why do so many men and maybe just as many women like to be tied up, restrained, chastised, ravished, even pretend-raped? Perhaps it comes from evolution. Women in our evolutionary past would yield only to the strongest man, as he was the fittest. Perhaps the appeal of ravishment still lingers in the female mind, and maybe in all human minds (through our shared genes), way beyond its evolutionary usefulness. That's why women love bastards. And *Gone with the Wind*. And Daniel Cleaver in *Bridget Jones*. *Girls!*

As for the restraint/bondage thing – a factor at work here is that helplessness is erotic. Putting yourself in the hand of another, utterly trusting someone else, allowing your partner to use those velvet handcuffs: it's sexy and loving. It also reminds us pleasurably of when we were naked and helpless as babies – yet utterly adored. And of course there's the rush of endorphins, of the body's opium, from pain and fear. It's why people start laughing after they've been in car crashes. Well, I did once.

Voyeurism, scopophilia, swinging, wife-swapping, 'husband wants to watch' – that's the third and last broad area of kinks; and to my mind it's the most obscure and

intractable. Why do we get turned on by watching partners we love have sex with someone else? I reckon that
this is related to masochism. Watching someone you love
have sex with a third person is surely an exquisite pain –
and therefore a sexual pleasure. Put it another way: jealousy is emotionally painful, and emotional pain is
pleasurable, because of the endorphins it produces (this
is also why we like weepy films and horror movies). Put
it still another way: we like to be in jealous torment
because this turns us on. No one told us our sexualities
were going to be uncomplicated. As for orgies and
swinging and 'cluster-fucks' – in my limited experience,
these things tend to be better in the mind than in reality.
The reality is so often disappointing, or at least confusing.
A friend of mine once came home on his birthday to find
his fiancée and her best female friend naked and willing.
That was his birthday present: a threesome. Unfortunately
my friend got so flustered with excitement he was unable
to achieve an erection; he actually had to sit in the toilet
for an hour to calm himself, by the end of which the girls
had lost interest and put their clothes on. My friend totally
blew it, and he still gets mournful about it now.

But in this he merely repeats the experience of other
friends and acquaintances. I've heard so many tales of
orgies being not-quite-what-was-hoped, of jolly threesomes turning into horrible arguments, of swinging
turning into bleak and destructive adultery, that I've come
to believe that the human mind isn't equipped to cope
with all the emotional permutions of multiple sex. The

human body certainly isn't equipped to deal with the physical permutations. You've only got one penis. I hope.

'Hey! You asleep up there?'

Oops. It's Kate. She's still waiting. And very ready. I'm going to have to make my mind up very soon.

But in the meantime I'm going to think about . . . lesbianism. I often do this when confused or at a loss. Because lesbianism is a fascinating subject, and one that starkly divides men from women (I mean that in an unobvious way). A majority of men are, I think, highly enthused by the idea of lesbianism. Yet women are notably less thrilled by the thought of gay men getting their rocks off. I'm not sure there are any websites aimed at women devoted to gay-male dentistry for instance. Yet as I have myself discovered, the obverse is gloriously true. The Net further proves the gender differential, through the number of adverts of happily attached heterosexual women looking for 'female playmates'.

During my Marmaduke Skewes days, for instance, I came across www.wewantfun.co.uk, a UK swingers website. One of its members was an exceptionally lovely, twenty-three-year-old blonde English girl called Sabrina who had posted a series of pictures of herself fellating her boyfriend; yet in her profile, she said she was looking for girls to have fun with. She was just one of hundreds. But were they, are they, really all lesbians? I'm not sure. I suspect, after some thought, that a number of these girls are not necessarily lesbian but are being asked to have lesbian sex by their boyfriends – so their men can watch.

This is just a grossly ill-informed hunch (I have a lot of those), but I still think I'm right.

And why do men like looking at lesbians? Several reasons have been advanced over the years. Some say it is simply that lesbianism is a twofer: you get to look at two naked women rather than one. Perhaps. Another reason sometimes suggested is that lesbian porn is a way for men to look at women being extremely sexual, in pornography, without having to worry about other men butting in. There is also a sociological theory that says that men like lesbianism because they have been conditioned into it by society and the sex industry. A feminist perspective into men's attitudes to lesbianism tells us that men like lesbian porn because it is yet another way of objectifying and therefore demeaning women – these theorists cite the fact that the lesbians in lesbian porn for men are always 'femme' (feminine), unlike in real lesbian sex. Therefore this porn is designed to titillate men at the expense of women. True? Maybe not. I do think the feminists have a good point about the unreality of lesbian porn, but I don't quite believe men view lesbian porn as a way of 'validating and affirming their superiority over women'. You may as well say that women like reading magazines about interior decoration because it validates *their* superiority over Georgian fireplaces. And anyway, all porn is unreal. That's its beauty and its tragedy. And its comedy. Those Estonian haircuts!

So how do I explain the fascination of lesbian porn? Here's my final opinion, before I get back to Kate's plump and expectant bottom. I reckon that, throughout their lives, men harbour a secret suspicion that women don't actually like sex. Or at least, they don't like it anywhere near as much as men. This is because women are more demure and opaque about their desires, and because women are so obviously less enslaved by their ravenous libidos than men. A corollary of this suspicion is that men subconsciously think women have sex mainly to get boyfriends and have babies.

But lesbian sex introduces the idea that women like sex the same way as men, as *sex*. There's no chance of a baby in a Sapphic encounter, therefore these women must be doing it simply because they like getting their rocks off. And that is a deeply exciting idea for many men.

I don't pretend this is absolutely the right answer. Or even the right answer. It's just the best I've come up with in the last five seconds. Who knows, maybe the sociologists are right! There's gotta be a first time.

All this brings me on to the very relevant topic of the DIFFERENCE BETWEEN MEN AND WOMEN AS SEXUAL CREATURES. For most of my life I have made the lazy presumption that men are just more wildly and variously sexual than women. But now I'm not so sure. After surfing the Internet for several millennia, and talking to all my friends, and a few bemused strangers, and not least meeting young Kate here, I am coming to the conclusion that women are a lot hornier than I presupposed.

I still think men are more deviant than women. There are very few, if any, female fetishists, for instance – and that's a good thing for girls; do the ladies really want to get turned on by chickens, gloves, spectacles or pavements? But my in-depth research is showing me that women evince extraordinary sexual variety themselves, and are certainly as sexually imaginative. Perhaps after centuries of sexual repression, when the female libido was contrarily viewed as either dangerous or non-existent, women are finally showing that their secret garden has quite a few herbaceous borders too. You've only got to look at the Internet to see that. There may be more men doing weird stuff on the Net, but there's no shortage of women either.

Like, for instance, Kate.

Ah yes. What's happened to us? Well, while you were reading all that – I've been and done it. Yup, I've closed my eyes – and done the deed. I've proved myself a toffee-wombler, I've recently landed at Terminal Two, I've set the controls for the old folding star, I've sodomised her.

Now she is leaning back on her noon-blue duvet. Happily. Because she has orgasmed. A moment ago I looked down at her black-haired vagina, and it was panting like a frightened mink, caught in a mantrap in the snowbound forest.

'God I love fucking doing that,' she says. 'It's my favourite thing!'

Her favourite thing? *Her favourite thing?*

Ah well. It could have been so good.

Lovemelovemycat

For all the ups and downs of the last few weeks, the ones you've just read about, I think I am beginning to get the hang of this Net-dating lark. In fact, I think I'm becoming something of an expert. Over the last six months (six months!) I've learned various crucial tips, and some disparate Dos and Don'ts, vis-à-vis Internet dating. For instance:

It's best not to lie. I confess, when I first went on the sites I thought I could juice things up a little. So I fibbed: 'for a laugh' I told everyone my salary was £80,000. But then I looked at this monstrously incorrect sum and I got the heebie-jeebies and decided to be honest and dropped the figure way down. Then I didn't get any responses for a day or two, and I doubled it again the next weekend. Everybody must have thought I was on quite a career roller-coaster.

Soon after that, I resorted to the truth once more. It had dawned on me that honesty in cyberspace is as essential as honesty in real life. Even if you do start a relationship online (where lying comes easy), if things proceed as you wish, you're gonna meet these people in the flesh – and if you've claimed you're a six-foot-three billionaire with a yacht in Marbella, it will soon become apparent that you've over-egged the pudding when you can't afford to buy the girl a pizza. Or indeed reach up to kiss her.

The same requirement for honesty applies to women's Internet dating profiles, albeit differently. The place where women seem to lie most, I am finding, is in their online photos. Some women seem blithely happy to post a shot of themselves taken five or even ten years ago. This is surely counter-productive. Do these women think their dates somehow won't notice the discrepancy when they finally meet?

I certainly did. On one of my dates, I met the girl and quickly realised that she wasn't quite the same girl as shown in her photo (by about a decade and a half). The girl noted my surprise and puzzlement, and by way of explanation, she airily waved a hand and said, 'Oh, I've changed my hairstyle since then.' To which I felt like replying: And your dress size? And your beard-shaving regime?

Another good tip, for guys, is this: when emailing a girl, try and hasten things along a little. Pin her down to a date within a week. One of the first mistakes I made was to let my email relationships drag on for weeks, politely waiting for the girl to make a move. Not good – the same arcane rules as to 'who goes first' sometimes apply in cyberland as they do in real life. Just because some women write the first message, asking for a date will probably be up to the chaps – so do it! If you don't look lively, you'll only get to meet three women before you die – thereby obviating one of the crucial advantages of cyber-dating over normal dating, which is, in case you haven't guessed, that there are millions of people just waiting to meet you.

And here's another tip: always have a get-out clause. A first Net-date is essentially a blind date, for all the email fandangle that precedes it. So make sure you are in possession of that essential accoutrement of any blind date: a get-out option. The best way to ensure this, is to arrange for a friend to ring your mobile phone half an hour into the date, to tell you that your uncle has had a ballooning accident. If you don't like your date, turn to her and say you have to dash to hospital. If you do like her (or him, or them), tell her you were never that fond of your uncle anyway.

Finally, here are a few tips just for the guys (we need them), tips that I have gleaned from all the women out there:

1. Never use a supposedly 'sexy' nickname. Really. 'Bigdong66' isn't really going to attract the nicest girls, unless this is a pretty downmarket website we're talking about.

2. No matter how tempting it may be, strive not to blurt 'I like your hooters' in your very first email, even if the girl is showing some cleavage in her photo. Instead, compliment her on her dress, maybe (if she's wearing a dress in the photo); this shows that you have checked her photo and you appreciate her looks without your directly mentioning her nipples.

3. Do not, under any circs, post a picture of your car on your profile. Even worse, do not call yourself after your

car (Porscheboy5, etc.). I myself managed to avoid this sole-cism, not least by not actually owning a car (I suppose I could have called myself Carless4, or posted a picture of a Tube train); nonetheless, more than one girl mentioned to me how off-putting this car-related sales pitch can be.

4. Spell right.

Is that any help? I hope so. Even if it isn't, I'm not done yet. Here's some more advice (again, this is for men. Women can skip this bit. But they may also find it useful).

In my experience, women use certain phrases, clauses and descriptions in their profiles, which can be decoded by men and lesbians with a little thought. Here's a handy table:

The Sean Thomas 'Millions of Women are Waiting to Meet You' Official Profile Decoder™

If she describes herself as . . .	She's really . . .
Curvy	Tubby
Cuddly	Huge
A cat lover	Desperate for kids
A traditional home-maker	Looking for a meal ticket
Scatty	Bonkers
Fun-loving	Drunken, possibly a crackhead
Adventurous	Fond of a threesome
Demanding	Impossible
Sensual	A good kisser

The 'more about you' section, the arena where women are given space to be more expansive in their answers, will also contain tell-tale giveaways. Here's another table to help you through that particular maze:

If she uses the phrase . . .	She really means . . .
I'll send you a photo privately . . .	I'm married and I don't want my husband to know I'm doing this
I'm from St Petersburg	Marry me
I like rugby-playing types	Dominate me
My favourite things are theatre, clubs, dancing, restaurants, sport, reading, football and walking	Can't think of anything else to say
I'm right wing	You'd better earn more than me
I hate cruelty to animals	I'm predictable
I have three tattoos	S&M?
I'm tired of the singles scene	My looks are going
I've got a pierced navel	Honky Tonk Woman!

It's merely a rule-of-thumb guide, but I hope it's of some assistance.

Now, I imagine there are people out there pooh-poohing this, or thinking me a terrible misogynist, or even a misanthrope. In which case I'll tell you about my most recent date, which I believe proves my point; at least as regards this 'cat' thing – what a liking for cats can mean, in terms of emotional code.

Her name, of course, was Lovemelovemycat. I met her on Loopylove. She looked rather pretty in her photo, sitting in tight blue shorts on a rock somewhere in Peru. Machu Picchu, I think.

The photo was, however, slightly misleading – as there wasn't a cat in it. Throughout the rest of her profile there were plenty of cats. For a start there was her name: Lovemelovemycat. Also, her interests were, she said, walking, reading and 'my cats'. She even made a lame little joke about cats in her 'More About Me' section: *'Some people think I'm catlike, I certainly like cats'*. Even her apparently cat-less photo might also have been feline-related: she was staring with rapturous interest into the distance, over the photographer's head; perhaps she'd spotted a cat.

But she seemed pretty. And amusing. So last week we agreed to meet in a rustic pub in a secretive corner of London: the Albion, in Barnsbury, Islington. If you don't know it, it's a rickety, cosy, rambling Georgian coaching inn with roaring fireplaces, and a disconcerting number of burglars and playwrights in its clientele (I know this, because it used to be my local). Perfect on a cold winter's night, ideal for romantic trysting.

The date went well. We talked about lots of stuff; I can't remember what. But I remember laughing. She told me she worked in a legal practice, a serious job. She was thirty-five, curvy, affable and perky. Her real name was Sally.

After the drink, we went back to her expensive City flat for a coffee and hopefully a cuddle. It turned out she had four cats, sharing her costly space. She introduced them to me by name. Told me what food they liked. How old they were. These cats had personalities, apparently. 'Oh, that's Canasta, you have to watch her, she's a wild one!' Canasta was fat, old and snoring contentedly, on the CD-player.

But Canasta's torpidity was in stark contrast to Graham. Graham the tom-cat. As soon as I walked into Sally's bedroom (cat pictures on the wall, a couple of Peruvian souvenirs on a chest) he hissed at me. For no reason. All I had done was rest my jacket on a chair and Graham was spazzing out. Edgily I moved closer, and sat down. Sally and I started chatting, but I couldn't take my eyes off 'Graham'. As I watched, Graham seemed to calm down – and subside into sleep.

But then he attacked my jacket. One moment Sally and I were enjoyably gossiping over the espresso, the next thing Graham had leapt across the room and was clawing at my silk lining. It was the cat-versus-jacket equivalent of the Second Battle of Ypres. I stared. Graham stopped clawing and looked at me triumphantly; he had an expression which said, 'Fuck you, Jacket Man.' Sally shooed him away and explained that he was 'just a kitten' and 'he was just playing'. Tell that to my jacket, I thought.

And that was that, really. Graham the Cat's heathen and unprovoked assault had put the kibosh on any romance. Ten minutes later I was out of the door, shredded leather on my back, walking for a cab by the Barbican, wondering why so many women get so dippy about pets.

Didn't take long to work out. Sally was thirty-five. Sweet and kind, and soft and big-hipped. In other words, her body was urging her to have babies. But a good career and a yen for adventure (those pictures of Machu Picchu?) were perhaps getting in the way of that maternal instinct; which meant she was desperate to have kids and she was desperate not to have kids. So she'd decided to go for the middle way – and have cats instead.

In this, I couldn't and can't blame her. I wasn't exactly turned on by Sally's cat-thing, I knew she and I weren't hailing the taxi of marriage anytime soon, but as I slipped home in the chilly dark night, as I stared out at the lonely night-buses with the lonely-looking people on board, I felt a pang in my own heart. Why? Because I've had my brushes with near fatherhood; I know what it's like, that yearning. I feel it too, sometimes. Sometimes very badly.

My first brush with fatherhood happened in my twenties. It was during one of my briefer forays into philandering – another roll on the log of promiscuity. One evening around this time I joined some friends in a restaurant. There was a lot of banter and wine and we ended up hugger-mugger with another rollicking table of girls and boys – and more wine was shared. Finally a friend suggested that, as the restaurant was closing, we should all pile down to south London where a chap he knew was looking after a disused swimming pool. It sounded unlikely

– but also potentially fun. So we taxied south and sure enough, this strange guy was temporarily living in an apartment overlooking an abandoned (but warm and clean) indoor swimming pool. Given that we had all drunk six bottles of Rioja, the inevitable happened: everyone stripped their clothes off and we had a skinny-dipping session. Cue lots of whooping and laughing, and lots of surreptitious glances at each other in the buff.

There was one woman in particular, amongst all the naked young people, who seemed to be taking a shine to me. This despite it being rather cold underwater. She was about twenty-eight. A doctor. She had amazing breasts (remember we were all naked). Towards the end of our whooping skinny-dipping hootenanny she fetchingly breast-stroked over and asked me to help push her up and out of the pool even though the ladder was only about five yards away. Why not? Obediently I heaved her naked ass out of the pool. An intimate moment.

The next day, we had sex. Followed by a relationship. I was quite keen on this girl. She was a very amusing, very smart woman. A doctor at a central London hospital.

Actually, I think I'll stop there and get regretful for a second. Looking back at this woman – I'll call her Teresa – it has occurred to me more than once, since that time, that she might have been 'the one'. She was certainly the whole package. She was clever. She made me laugh more than most people. We could talk all night, we did talk all night – and all morning, too. She had a fine figure and was really pretty. It turned out her breasts were fake, but they looked great anyway.

So why did I dump her? I have no idea. Perhaps because I am a nitwit. Perhaps because I was on another philandering jag and I wanted to sleep with more women. That was maybe it. Whatever the case, I remember when I dumped her I felt an awkward sense of making a mistake – and I have felt that pain ever since. *Maybe she was the one. Maybe she was the right turning off the motorway, maybe I missed my connection.* Etc.

The pain was about to get worse. Two months after I chucked her, Teresa rang and informed me that she was pregnant. At first I felt a surge of cock-a-hoop smugness (I'm fertile! Not only am I fertile, I can impregnate women through a broken condom – I'm super-fertile!); then I felt a sinking feeling. I didn't want kids. I was twenty-nine, just making my way in journalism, writing a book, sleeping with different girls.

Babies? Marriage??

So I met Teresa in a coffee shop and I briskly signed a cheque to pay for the abortion. She looked at me weirdly as I wrote it. Can't blame her. Then the day arrived and I got a soft, plaintive call from her: 'I've done it,' she said. Just that. So I replied with a remark that I hoped was kind and fitting, and then I put the phone down and nodded to myself, thinking: Yep, good, that was the right thing to do. But a still, small voice somewhere near the nape of my neck was saying: What have you done what have you done what have you done . . .

Consequently or no, my life span out of control a few months after that. The willing women dried up, the jobs went astray, I ended up broke, drinking and feeling quite miserable. This went on for a couple of years; it got so bad I decided to move out of London.

I retired to Cornwall to lick my wounds at the family house. And there, a year on, as I pieced my life back together, I fell in love for the third time in my life.

What's more, I fell in love with a schoolgirl.

Yes. I know. I was thirty, she was seventeen. In some countries it would be illegal. But love laughs at lawyers.

I met her in a pub in Devon. Her name was Tamara. She was a sixth-former. She was underage so she couldn't buy a drink, so I bought a drink for her and that's how it began. Tamara was dark, short, and punchy. She liked doing car repair. She was a scholarship girl. She was eccentric and funny. She was so shy she wouldn't eat in front of me, not at first. She made me wait to have sex with her, for months. But those months were strangely blissful. We would just lie there, on the hills around Cornwall, in the garden, on the soaring clifftops, in the sun, listening to the skylarks, listening to each other breathe, listening to the seals have sex on the beach.

When I first put my hand up her jumper, my knees shook. I remember that. That hadn't happened to me for a decade. Then again, I hadn't been out with a schoolgirl for a decade and a half.

Eventually the time did arrive – the time when Tamara was going to let me have sex with her. To do the deed we went to a little village called Lamorna, which is right on the cliffs at the far western end of Cornwall. There, with the moon staring through our hotel window like a disapproving old pensioner, we made love. It was everything you could expect, if very brief, and I wanted to do it again several seconds later. But I couldn't. So I waited an hour. But no go. Then a week went by – and I still couldn't do it.

It was my old impotence thing. A wildcat strike in my underpants, a French farmers' roadblock in libidoland. I was flummoxed, angry and highly aroused, which made it worse. I couldn't get it up because I so wanted to get it up. Unlike some of the other women I had been seeing in the previous year or two, I *really* wanted to impress Tamara, to love her properly, to be a good lover and all that; so I was deeply anxious, and this anxiety bred the old anxiety, like dull roots and spring rain, and consequently I was cruelly unmanned by the young woman I most wanted to be manful with.

For weeks, even months, I raged. Tamara thought I was nuts. She must have thought all men were like me.

But then I discovered Viagra. *Bliss*. It was like someone taking the madman in my head around a corner, and shooting him. Or at least tying him to a chair and gagging him. That lifelong anxiety was short-circuited. I was a man again. For the next three or four years, Tamara and I had a thunderstorm of a relationship. We had lots of sex; she dumped me regularly; I dumped her regularly; she was smart and she knew how to twist me, to tease me; sometimes I quite liked being teased. Once I fell ill and she decided to jilt me, then and there – she marched into my sickroom and said, 'It's over,' chucking my things on the bed. I kind of admired the callousness of her teenage confidence, as I lay there panting with agony. She was very pretty when she was angry. But then she was even pretty when she was doing car repair. That big spanner in her little hand. A week later, we were back together again.

You may think this was an unhealthy relationship. But fuck you. We were happy in our own way. We had a lot of fun, we had a lot of sex in cars by beaches. That's when she wasn't surfing. She liked to surf, did Tamara. I can still see it now: big waves splashing over her wetsuit; her dark smile flashing; her strange plodding run as she carried the surfboard, which was twice her size. She looked like Aphrodite in a fetish film.

And when she stripped off to change, that was even better: I loved to gaze at her sallow mixed-race skintones; she was a quarter Jewish, a quarter Scottish, a quarter Chinese – and a quarter geek. I found the geek bit very sexy: I used to get her to do her Maths homework topless. But then again, I also got her to drive topless. Best of all was when, just before her A Levels, I made her study in the nude. Impossibly sexy.

And then, and then. One morning, a year later, when Tamara had made it to university (nude revision *works*) I was driving back to London, because I was slowly getting my head together, preparing to return to the temptations and turmoil of The Smoke – I was in a good mood. But then I got a mobile phone call. It was Tamara.

'I'm pregnant,' she said.

'What do you mean?'

'What do you mean by that? I'm pregnant.'

'But . . .'

'Yes it's yours.'

It was the same dilemma, but worse. I really did love Tamara; even if we didn't have much in common, we had love in common. Sometimes the cliché is true: love is all you need. Plus money and a nice car. But still, was I ready for this, for parenthood? I was already acting *in loco parentis* to Tamara, given how much younger than me she was; I'd only just stopped buying her drinks because she was under eighteen. Were we truly and ideally suited to have kids together? No. That was my thinking. It sounded a sensible line of reasoning. But there was an undertow, too, an undertow tugging me swiftly out into the Sea of Selfishness: unacknowledged, I was also thinking, Jesus, I've just got my life back in gear, I'm working again, I'm heading for London once more. What would I be doing with a kid? With Tamara? Now??

So Tamara and I got together, and I gave her my opinion: that I believed 'we' should have an abortion. When I told her this, she looked at me with a kind of pained under-standing, a perplexed and knowing frown. I ignored it. A few weeks down the line, when Tamara's bulge in her little tan belly was getting cruelly noticeable, we went ahead and she had the abortion.

I shall always remember the day. I remember picking

her up from the clinic. I remember the sadness, the white-ness of her face, the faces of the other girls in the clinic; I remember the sense of error, the silence in the car on the way back, the staring out of the window. How can something so sensible be so wrong? Maybe the Pope is right. It certainly felt agonising and weird. Then we started having sex again and everything seemed OK. But it wasn't OK. It soon occurred to both of us, independently, that the decision to abort a baby had been tantamount to a decision to abort our relationship; if we weren't going to have kids now, when we very much in love, we probably weren't going to have kids ever. So what was the point in our going out?

From that point on, Tamara started fooling around, seeing other guys at her university in Bristol. I couldn't blame her, because I'd started fooling around before that. It was, in other words, an unholy mess, getting messier.

Somehow, though, we managed to keep this apology for a relationship on the road for a couple more years, right up until the time Tamara was about to graduate. Why did we continue to see each other after all that had happened? Looking back, I think it was because it suited us both in a way: together, but apart, we could mess around with people (in London, for me, at Bristol Uni, for her) yet we both had the security duvet of knowing that ultimately there was someone out there who loved us, whom we could return to when things went wrong. *Yadda yadda yadda.*

Eventually the last wheel came off, and the hub-cap

went spinning down the road. One day I just thought: Do it. So I did it. I finally dumped Tamara. I told her we couldn't go on like this; she was too young, I was living too far away, we were too unsuited long-term. Then she gave me that look again, and she got out of the car in tears and went running up the stoop to her block of flats in studenty Bristol, while I sat there in the car looking at her tears and her litheness and her dark jeans, and the door closing behind her, thinking: So this is how it ends, after five years, five long and tempestuous years; this is the last time, the very last time I shall see her, on a windy day in April, in a humdrum road, with the traffic roaring blithely past, watching her close the door. This is the last time.

I saw her again about two months later. I wanted to sleep with Tamara again. I still fancied her like mad; moreover I wasn't getting laid anywhere else. So I drove to her city, her street, her flat, and this time it was nearly summer and the sun was shining cruelly down and her flatmates were away on vac. And in her lonely room we gave our relationship a fiery Viking funeral.

It was urgent sex: sex with the brakes off, lost sex, a boat heading out into the sea with the sails on fire. And then I buttoned my flies and I walked to my car and she waved at me with a sad little smile from the curtainless upstairs window and this time I thought: This really is it. This really is the last time, no more going back.

Two months after that she rang me and said: 'I'm pregnant.'

For a moment I felt like checking the calendar, or my own memory. Then I remembered that last ardent coupling, in the dusty student house bereft of students.

'Fuck,' I said.

Before I could add to that, Tamara said:

'And I'm keeping it this time. I can't go through that again . . .'

This was sudden. This was frightening. This was . . . well, this was wonderful. Quite unexpectedly, I felt a joyous release at this news; I felt a strange weight lift from my shoulders. It was done, the corner had been turned. I hadn't had to make the fateful decision to commit, she had. I hadn't had to face up to my inability to make a decision, she had faced up to it for me. She had forced me into it, she was obliging me to be a dad, she was making the executive move; not me. At all of twenty years old, so many years younger than me, she had slashed through the mangrove swamps of my immaturity and said: This is it, dude, from now on, you're going to be a dad. Love it or loathe it.

I loved it. I didn't expect to love it, but I loved the idea. Perhaps a sense of regret had been burning inside me, for years, like one of those underground coal fires in Pennsylvania; perhaps I had long nurtured but ignored a sense of terrible error vis-à-vis the two abortions.

The next day, I drove to meet Tamara and we had a summery beer and we toasted the decision in the West-Country sunshine. We would let fate decide our long-term fate, we were going to have this kid. And I was glad for it. At last something was going to happen, at last I had found the right slip-road, at last I was moving on in life. The baby, as I saw it, was going to sort out my problems, my sense of directionlessness, my feeling of anomie, the dull weight of pointlessness that was plaguing me more and more.

I was, in other words, keen on having this baby for some very dubious reasons. I wanted to be a dad because I thought that being a dad would sort out my life; give me a compass point, tell me to get a move on, get me restarted, redirect me.

Then something happened.

One evening, about three months into the pregnancy, Tamara rang me and said, 'I feel weird, I have a weird pain in my stomach, I think there may be something wrong with the baby.'

Nonsense, I replied, this happens to pregnant women all the time. My sister (I wisely explained to Tamara) had had three kids and with the first one she had lots of weird pains and scares. *You'll be fine, just call me if it gets worse.*

Then I put the phone down and went to a church to pray. I hadn't done that in years. I felt pretty stupid doing it, with old Italian women staring at me in the smoky Soho church. But in my soul of souls, something was telling me: You deserve this to go wrong; you wanted the baby because you are a selfish idiot. The brief glimpse of a sunlit future, of the way out of the mess in my head, was clouding over. I was heading back for the mangrove swamps, with an awful sense of inevitability.

Tamara miscarried.

The following morning she rang me in tears and said, 'It happened, I've lost it.' I asked her if she wanted me to drive down and she verbally shook her head and said, 'No, don't worry, there are people here looking after me.' She said the word 'people' with a certain weight, an emphasis. I wasn't one of the *people* looking after her; there were *people* she knew who cared enough to be there, where she was. I imagined that one of them might be a guy she liked.

I was right. Tamara had met someone else, someone who cared. She and I were finally kaput, and the only souvenirs of my third and far final love were a nagging sense of inadequacy and a feeling that I was royally fucking up my life.

And what do I think now? I really did love Tamara, as much as I loved Eleanor or Briony. Perhaps more, even though Tamara and I were much less suited – ostensibly. This is confusing, but it's true. Tamara and I just had a laugh; for all our difference in years, outlook and character, there was some profound and subconscious fit between us. This may have been because her father left her when she was young, so she wanted an older man in her life; likewise, I have this urge to protect, as well as a physical taste for chasing elfin and elusive girls. Therefore Tamara gratified and aroused me, just as I maybe stabilised her, and made her feel not quite so fatherless.

I was certainly broken-hearted when we split. Surprisingly broken-hearted; almost as moonstruck, doomy and obsessive as I had been after Briony. I was surprised by this because I had expected that as I got older, any heartbreak would be less intense, less destructive and disabling – because I had been through it before. Turns out that's not true, of course. Heartbreak hurts practically as much the third or fourth time as it does the first. The only advantage of age and experience is that you know what to expect and how long it will last. So that helps you prepare. The pain is precisely the same. Of course, the pain I suffered from breaking with Tamara was exacerbated enormously by the baby thing. That really upset me, the nearness to fatherhood, the happy expectation that was snatched away. Now, years later, I accept, when I am in a logical mood, that it was arguably for the best that we didn't become parents. Tamara would have had to give up college to have the baby, we didn't have anywhere to live, I would have had to work a lot harder – and get over that selfishness thing.

But then, when I am being less logical, I think: Maybe we would have been great parents. It's possible. Who the hell can say? You can self-analyse too much; sometimes you just have to do it. But fate took away that option.

All this has left me with one final insight. Virginia Woolf once wrote that many childless women have significantly large and hollow eyes (she was referring to Thomas Hardy's wife and perhaps, indirectly, to herself). I think that can apply to men, too. Men may not have quite the same biological clock as women, or at least a clock that doesn't tick quite so insistently – once a month, tick TOCK

– but they do have a kind of genetic time bomb. A terrorist device planted at the end of the road. A bomb that explodes without warning, that makes everything else seem unimportant, that leaves you wandering in a daze, that makes you realise that you are mortal and that if you want to be a parent you'd better get your rollerblades on.

As I see it, the device is designed to go off when you are about thirty-seven.

Income: any

For the last fortnight, this Mexican girl has been emailing me. She says she is a banker in the City. She loves London but finds it 'alarmingly cold' sometimes. Juanita's emails are not the wittiest I have encountered but I am nonetheless excited. I think this is partly to do with Juanita's foreignness. I have always liked foreign girls: many of my girlfriends have been mixed race and/or foreign in some way. Tamara, Amelie, Eleanor . . . Why not a saucy Mexican lass?

Another week goes by, with a few more messages exchanged; Juanita and I dance around the handbag of dating. Then I decide to take a stance, and I suggest we meet Thursday. She briskly replies: Nope, she can't do Thursday. Or Friday. Or the week after that. However, she could do lunch two weeks away . . . that is, if she's not too busy.

Perhaps I should be insulted by these caveats? Maybe; but she does look fetching and sultry in the photo. So I suppress my misgivings and we arrange to meet at the champagne bar in Tower 42 in the City, at her suggestion. I've never been there, but she says it's nice.

It turns out that the Tower 42 champagne bar is not just 'nice'; it's superlatively cool. Situated at the very top of the tower it has spectacular views. Two dozen soft blue seats are positioned around the plush circular bar-space, facing outwards, so that you can see the planes in a holding pattern right across London, as you sip at your fizz. St Paul's Cathedral looks majestic in the winter sunshine; the traffic on London Bridge less so.

Holding her flute of Taittinger, Juanita sits down and tells me about herself. It turns out she was born in Mexico City, she grew up with just her mother, her truck-driver dad having done a bunk. Her mother, it seems, was a bit eccentric – she worked extremely hard to bring up her four kids – but this meant Juanita's mum was out of the house doing one of her many jobs by five or six in the morning.

'She felt guilty I think,' says Juanita. 'So she used to make us get up when she did and she gave us this special kind of soup she made, with liquidised vegetables. That made her feel better . . . she knew we had at least one decent meal inside us.'

Juanita smiles. 'Every day for about ten years I had to get up at five in the morning and eat this horrible soup. Can you imagine that?'

I nod, though I can't.

'And now . . . now I don't eat so much soup.'

We chuckle. The cold champagne is ticklish and dry; Juanita looks at her expensive watch. I ask her what she does, to make her so busy. She goes into an obscure spiel about Spanish Treasury Bonds and the variable prospects for peso futures, then she smiles again and says:

'I know it sounds boring but I love it. I like handling money, and . . . it pays very well.'

Now she asks me the standard questions: What am I doing Internet dating? How long have I been doing it? etc. Experience having told me that honesty is the only policy, I tell her the truth: that originally I was commissioned by a magazine, and that I wasn't keen on the idea at first. I add that I now think that Internet dating is fun, intriguing, entertaining and possibly the future of romance; at least, for people over thirty (I don't tell Juanita some of my growing doubts about Internet dating).

Juanita nods:

'One day last year I woke up and looked at myself and I thought: I have this great flat and this great job, I travel all over the world, yet I am single. At thirty-two. And all my friends are married back in Mexico.' She suddenly laughs, 'Well, most of them married when they were about fourteen years old. But I was different and I moved to America and then I came here and . . .' she sips some more bubbles and goes on, 'and now I find the only men I meet are my colleagues at work . . . and taxi drivers who take me home. So I thought I'd try Internet dating. Because I don't want to marry another banker.'

'And taxi drivers?'

Another warm smile. This is going fairly well. She is obviously very smart. And I am getting *very* excited, not least because of the one thing about Juanita I have yet to mention. She is beautiful.

No kidding. She is ravishingly pretty. When I look at her profile I feel that eerie sensation you get when you witness someone truly beautiful: that strange and sad feeling; that doomy vertigo. That feeling that's hard to describe.

But it's my job to describe it. So I'm going to try – with a weird analogy:

When I was on a trip to Iceland about ten years ago, I remember standing on the harbourfront in Reykjavik, and looking over the blue fjord north of the city. Across the choppy blue waves was a glacier, maybe twelve or twenty miles away – a big, dirty white tongue of ice crashing down from the bald black mountains with infinite slowness. Intrigued, I asked some hungover local about the glacier, its name and whereabouts. He told me the name of the glacier. Then he told me the name of the sea-channel: Faxafloi. But then he added that the glacier wasn't twenty miles away, *it was two hundred miles away*. The air in Iceland, he explained, is so clear and unpolluted, things look nearer than they are.

I turned and looked again at the glacier, framed by the imperial blue waters of the fjord. I felt a bloodrush in my heart. The scenery was so breathtaking, and so majestic – I was moved and gratified – and yet I was obscurely troubled at the same time. The sense of unexpected

226

distance was dizzying and confusing as well as exhilarating.

This may seem far-fetched as an analogy, but it's the
best I can do. The feeling I had by that fjord is, somehow,
the same weak and head-spinning feeling I get when I look
at a truly beautiful woman. Like Juanita here.

Do women suffer this knee-buckling sensation in the
face of male beauty? I'm not sure; I somehow doubt it.
Camille Paglia – the possibly lesbian American writer –
once described how she had a testosterone injection in a
clinic, for a medical complaint, and when she walked out
into the streets of Manhattan she looked at a pretty young
girl and she felt this sudden crippling urge, this desperate
sad lungingness, this feebleness. Then, and only then, did
she understand the power of male desire, which is of course
a function of the power of female beauty. Hitherto, she
had had no idea. She could of course have simply read
Kingsley Amis, who summed up the incomprehensible
affect female loveliness has on men. 'I know why I like
breasts, I just don't know why I like them so *much*.'

This incomprehensible effect can be crippling, not to
mention tongue-tying; it can also be oddly piercing. As I
know from my relationship with Jen, the beautiful girlfriend of a friend of mine.

When I first met Jen she was going out with my best
friend, Trevor. Indeed she and my friend were in love, for
months. This affair of theirs came after my torrid break-
up with Tamara, after I had returned to London.

About eighteen months into Trevor and Jen's relationship,

things started to go awry. At this time in my life, our group of friends had a habit of heading out for enormously long, gastropubby Sunday lunches, where we would sit around chatting, smoking, swearing, and guzzling endless Merlot. During one of these sessions I started to notice a chilliness between Jen and Trev; the touching and hand-holding had gone, replaced by tiny, stifled sighs of boredom at each other's anecdotes. Not a promising signal.

Another sign of the impending death of their relationship was that, during these lunches, Jen started to peel off and come and talk to me, hang out with me, asking me what I thought about her and Trevor – whether I thought they had a chance of going on. I just reckoned she was being needy, that she needed a neutral male voice to talk to, so I gave her my honest opinion. I didn't think any more of it.

The next wildly inebriated Sunday lunch (we used to drink a lot) was different. Trevor and Jen were really bickering this time; eventually my friend threw his arms in the air and said he would rather sleep off his incipient hangover in our shared laddish flat than argue with Jen any more. This left me and Jen and a couple of others to carry on playing ironic darts in some rackety Bayswater pub. Just as I was picking up the darts, Jen came up to me and said:

'I'm in love with you.'

I dropped the darts. Then I picked them up again and threw them. I missed the board.

I thought she was joking; she wasn't. Urgently, softly, pressed very close to me, she confessed that she had fallen in love with me over the past few months.

I was nonplussed. So I threw another dart. It nearly hit the barman on the shoulder. And then I turned and looked at Jen. She was twenty-seven or so; she had lucid grey eyes and fabulous bone structure, and a bottom you could bounce ping-pong balls off. She was smart, demure and feminine; she was, in a word, stunning – and she was telling me that she was totally in love with me, despite her having a (faltering) relationship with my best friend.

We kissed. Then we kissed some more. Then we started walking around Bayswater, kissing and drinking. My mind was afire with guilt, but I was also incredibly turned on. She was so lovely. What do you do?

OK, I know what you do. At least, I know now. You say 'no'. But she was so beautiful . . . petite, intelligent, and trying to kiss me lots with her lissom pink tongue in a dingy rock 'n' roll pub on the Moscow Road. So we carried on snogging as I tried to work out what to do, how to handle this. Could I betray my friend for this girl? Could I *not* betray my friend with this lovely girl?

I needn't have bothered trying to work it all out. Jen had it taped already. At the end of the evening, on our own now, our scandalised mates having drifted off, we walked down to the busy Bayswater Road, hand in hand. The cars were whooshing by in the sweet evening blue, the trees of Hyde Park were soughing in the summer breeze, and as we stood on the pavement Jen got down on her knees, unzipped my flies, and started sucking my cock.

On the street. In broad lamplight. With cars going by.

I think I nearly fainted. This was the greatest and most flattering sexual thing that had ever happened to me. A beautiful girl was so in love with me, she was prepared to fellate me on one of London's busiest streets. Without my asking. But she was my best mate's girl! I went to stop her. I did. But then I stopped trying to stop her. It felt so good, for so many reasons. I think at this point I might have actually stared at the dizzy stars, seeking an answer (and sighing with confusing pleasure); then I realised that people on the bus heading for Marble Arch were staring at us avidly, so I tried to stop her again. But . . . but . . . but . . .

I finally stopped her. I thought about Trevor and I put my hand under her chin and then I zipped up my flies and I said, 'I'll call you,' and I walked to the Tube station. Then I kicked myself for being such a wuss all the way home.

For a week or two I boxed with my conscience. I really wanted to sleep with Jen; she was still going out with my friend. But I wanted to sleep with her: the image of her sweet young face kept rippling through my brain. I dreamed about her. I woke up knowing that I must stop this now. Two hours later I was masturbating about her again.

We arranged to meet in a friend's flat. We obviously had to be clandestine. So we met in a bar and we kissed and then we went to the friend's flat, but then we decided it was too sordid so we went back to her place where her friends were living and it was sad and exciting at the same time. Could I betray my friend? Of all people? At the end of the night we went to bed . . . and I couldn't do it. She was so lovely, and naked, and I was stricken with guilt. So we fooled around, and then in the morning she looked at me with grave disappointment, when I was hoping for moral approval. I'd failed. I had all the guilt of betrayal without the actual fun of penetration.

That might have been that, but she was still, apparently, in love with me, and I was falling for her. Six weeks later she rang me up and said she really wanted to see me. We went to a party, but again we were foiled; this time she felt guilty as well as me. At least I kissed her breasts. They were like pale white lilies in a Japanese garden.

Our constant fuck-ups were destroying what chance we had. We did try one more time but again we were paralysed and she might have cried a little and told me she loved me again; then there was silence, for months. The denouement came about a year later. I'd almost forgotten about her (well, almost) when I got a phone call out of nowhere. She and Trevor had long since broken up and I was doing my own thing, cutting back on the drinking, reining in the partying, sorting out a life for myself; and then my mobile rang and it was Jen.

'I've met someone else', she said.

'That's good,' I said, thinking immediately of that kiss in the pub. With a stab of grief.

'But . . .' Her voice sounded distant and yet intimate, tremulous. 'But . . . you know I'm still in love with you.'

In my heart the cars were still whooshing down the Bayswater Road. O, the ceaseless London traffic of Love . . .

'Well . . .' I said. 'Well I . . .'

I didn't know what to say. I still wanted her. She was so lovely. Yet it had never worked out. So instead of saying what I wanted to say – *Meet me, now* – I said:

'Good luck, Jen. Really.'

There was a silence on the end of the line. I couldn't tell if she was crying or not. I felt like crying. But instead I closed the phone call. I put the phone down; I've never spoken to her since.

Why the fuck did I do that? I don't know. Did I still feel guilty?

Hardly. Trevor had got his own back, without realising.

About six months after the Jen-and-me debacle, after Trevor and Jen had properly broken up, I met a Swedish student girl in a pub. She was very cute and about ten of us hit on her, including Trevor; but I was the one who got to escort her to various clubs and pubs that evening; I was the one who got to take her back to the flat.

When we got back to the flat, Trev was asleep in his room. The Swedish girl asked me who slept in the other room in the flat. I told her it was my friend, the one she met in the pub a few hours previous, the funny one with the dark hair. *Ah*, the girl said, with a rather starry expression. I didn't clock this expression at the time.

An hour later, we were in my bedroom. She was naked, so was I. But she resolutely refused to let me do anything. I was allowed to fumble around, kiss her nipples a little, but that was it. Frankly it was a bit boring after the third hour and anyway, we both seemed tired. I flopped back on the bed. Then she got up and said, 'I need the toilet.'

She got up and disappeared out of the room, into the toilet. I heard the toilet door close and I think I slowly drifted asleep at that point. After all, she was taking a long time. Then, suddenly, I woke up again. She was climbing into the bed. I checked my watch: about an hour had passed, maybe more.

'Long toilet visit,' I said, only half computing what might have happened.

She said nothing. But she seemed in a different mood. She was still naked and so I decided to have one last bash -- but she still wouldn't let me penetrate her. However, she did let me go down on her and try oral sex; she seemed to enjoy this. She was certainly very wet. Very wet indeed. Early in the morning, I yawned and looked over and I noticed that my girl was already awake, staring at me with a strange and shocked expression; then she quickly climbed into her Swedish student-girl clothes and scooched out the front door.

Later, Trevor woke up and wandered blearily into the kitchen. He saw me making toast and he nodded a coughy hello and then he said:

'The weirdest thing happened last night.'

I stared at him. He went on:

'I was asleep. But then this girl, that Swedish bird from the pub, she came into my room and got into bed with me. Weird or what?'

I ignored his question. Instead I said, very slowly:

'So what did you do?'

'Duh!' He chortled. 'What do you think? I shagged her. How did she end up back here anyway?'

I took a deep breath. I thought about the way the girl let me go down on her; her sudden, unexpected arousal . . .

I nodded at my friend and said, 'Oh, she slept on the sofa or something. I think she was very drunk,' and then I stepped into the bathroom and brushed my teeth. A lot.

So, Trevor, if you are reading this, here's how it stands. Your girlfriend gave me head on the Bayswater Road, but I went down on a girl just after you'd slept with her. I reckon we're quits, old pal.

Yet even if we are quits, my heart still feels troubled. The image of Jen's lovely face is imprinted on my mind – more than is the case with many women I have been with, maybe women I have loved. Even though I never actually slept with Jen. So why does she have this frightening power when other girlfriends don't – or at least, not as much?

Perhaps Thomas Hardy can help. Again.

When Thomas Hardy saw a beautiful girl on the streets of London, he would sometimes spend the whole day just following her, watching her on and off trams, observing her nip in and out of shops, as he stood there yearning in the sooty London shadows. Today this would be called stalking, and the novelist would be arrested. But every modern man can understand the plaintive note in his words about these women. One day he saw an especially lovely girl on a London omnibus and he wrote that 'she had one of those faces of marvellous beauty which are seen casually in the streets but never among one's friends . . . Where do these women come from? Who marries them? Who knows them?' Recognise the sentiment? I do. But Hardy's words are not just echoic and true, they are also suggestive. Hardy was a great one for elusive women. He liked nothing more – as those words infer – than tormenting himself with untouchable or unreachable ladies. When his first wife was around he was obsessed with other young women; when his first wife died and he married one of these other young women, he spent the rest of his life mooning after his first wife, now utterly unreachable in her Dorset grave.

This leads to an interesting possibility: that it is unreachable female beauty that truly crucifies men. I think this is true. Something in the unattained is especially lovely: the more elusive a beauty is, the more piercing its quality. Certainly, the fact that I never actually had sex with Jen, the fact that she was ultimately ungrasped, makes her feel more beautiful to me than almost anyone else.

So what am I trying to say? I think we, men, are haunted by such unattainable beauty because it tells us something troubling and profound about life. When a man glimpses a truly beautiful woman across a street, a bar, a banging disco, he is stunned and perplexed because he glimpses something that he can never attain, yet something that demands adoration. And it's the same with the world: we love it, yet we die. We adore it, yet it leaves us. It is beautiful, yet it must fade. And so we stand on the shoreline, and look across the icy fjord, and stare at the blue and regal mountains. Wishing we could reach what is so very far away.

And now back to the beautiful Juanita, who is not so very far away at all. About three yards, in fact.

While I have been finishing my drink, she has stood up and said:

'One forty-five. Meeting.'

This is quite abrupt – but I know she is a busy woman. Standing up I offer a hand; I sense that she is going to leave without any further remarks. But then she grins and says:

'That was very nice. Shall we do it again?'

Yes! Comparing diaries (hers noticeably more crowded than mine) we agree to meet in a week. Then we head off in our very different directions. For a week I am giddy and happy. After all, a beautiful Mexican girl wants to meet me . . . again!

But then, when the evening comes, Juanita phones at the last minute and cancels. She has to go to Norway 'for business'. Not to worry though: we re-arrange for another week. But then when that day arrives she phones again and says, 'Hey look I'm really sorry but . . .'

'Norway?'

'Zurich.'

At this point I could get disheartened. But she is smart and, as I say, utterly lovely, and . . . I like her. I think. Or maybe she is so beautiful I am making up other reasons to like her, so I can fall in love with her beauty. Who cares? She's beautiful. Three weeks after Juanita's and my first date, we finally have our second date. We agree to meet near her flat in Knightsbridge.

Unfortunately, in the interim, Juanita has been skiing and she has come back with a broken wrist; when I meet her outside the Tube station she is standing rather awkwardly with a big white plaster cast. For a moment I am taken aback, then I dutifully admire the impressive cast on her arm and say at least it looks like she's been doing some heroic off-piste-ing. To this she replies 'yes', but she actually broke the wrist falling down the icy front steps of a bar at two a.m. after a lot of glühwein and schnapps. Funny girl.

So far everything is upbeat and OK. We happily chat some more, and then move on. But while we are walking down the road, something happens. We are looking for a bar that I remember, tucked away down a side road. However, as I don't know this area so well, it's taking me a little while. After five minutes of searching, Juanita lets out a taut sigh, and then she says:

'Oh for God's sake. Can't you find it?'

I'm taken aback. This seems unduly sharp; rude even. Swallowing my concerns, and an angry riposte, I put this down to her mild incapacity, her irritance at her plaster

237

cast. So I smile and reassure her, and then we scout around some more, and eventually we find the bar (after some more tutting from Juanita).

Six or seven cocktails later, we head back to her flat – her lovely, expensive flat, with its automatic blinds and plasma TV screens and real Aztec *objets d'art*.

But here we start squabbling again. We just seem to . . . butt heads. Something is not quite right between us; there is some conflict, a search for dominance maybe. I am finding Jen's company irksome, even as I gaze adoringly at her profile.

I think, partly, it's the money thing. One thing that is putting me off Juanita is her obvious success, her very expensive flat; I confess I am daunted by her status, wealth and ambition. As well as her beauty. And my discomfort is making me satirical, even aggressive.

I know this is pitiful and myopic, but the boy can't help it: there is something deep in my caveman brain that seems to respond in a resentful, atavistic and negative way when presented with a woman who comprehensively out-earns me. I don't mind heiresses – evidently, as Eleanor and I proved. But I do have a problem with women who earn their own money and do a lot better than me. And frankly I wish I didn't have this hang-up. Given that I am a free-lance journalist and a moderately struggling novelist and therefore on the same wage as, say, a provincial teacher, many of the women I meet in London are going to out-earn me.

In the past, this has been dealable-with. If the discrepancy is not too big – if the woman has no more than double my income – I have found I can cope. I satisfy myself with my high social status as a writer, which evens things out. OK, I delude myself with the idea of my high social status as a writer – but nonetheless the mindgame works.

But if the woman out-earns me by, say, four or five times – and in London that is well within the realms of possibility – then I get a bit nervy. And more macho: I then feel I have something to prove.

What's weirder about this is that I have often found that the most successful, affluent and dominant women (in terms of career) often turn out to be the most feminine and yielding when they get the chance.

For instance, I had this one girlfriend, after Tamara, who was a very successful thirty-something TV executive. But when she wasn't being a dynamic TV executive and influential media bigwig, she liked nothing better than ironing shirts. Domestically speaking she was, likewise, a very keen cooker and caterer and even washer-up; she also loved a good tumble dryer, and liked to get her pelmets just right. And when we hit the sack, well then she hated to go on top, and instead liked best to be taken pretty brusquely from behind.

Having said that . . . she did make a memorable interjection during one of these from-behind sessions. We were having this from-behind sex and I penetrated her so vigorously that I slipped out (as you do). Before I could readjust, she reached around and slotted me blindly back into place while saying, in a rather withering tone, 'I have to do all the work around here.' Huh? But then she started doing her kittenish whimpering again, which was a relief. And then when we'd done she made an onion tart and stacked the dishwasher.

In other words, it appeared to me that this high-earning, high-status, highly successful girlfriend had these nurturing and submissive female instincts, which just came bursting forth when she wasn't trying to be ambitious and aggressive with other TV producers. It was like these instincts had been suppressed by her day-job. Or maybe she just liked cooking.

Whatever the case, no such Jekyll-and-Hydeness is discernible in Juanita. As I am discovering, she is the same forthright woman in person as she is in her emails: she is as decisive, firm and impatient in her flat, as I imagine she is in her office.

This isn't good. This doesn't look good in terms of me and Juanita as a potential item.

Why? Because, after a year of Internet dating, and twenty years of ordinary dating, and thirty-eight years of being alive, I am belatedly coming to realise that I have psychological types, as well as physical types. And what I have discovered is this: as much as I like small elfin girls, I also like rather submissive girls; girls with a feminine yielding-ness; girls with a coy and fluttering demureness. Eleanor, Briony, Tamara . . .

Moreover, my requirements are even more complicated than *that*. Within that submissiveness, I also like to find, even need to find, a subtle but serious streak of rebellion, a girlish ability to tease me (as Tamara did); I like girls to be yielding but *not* wholly conquerable, to be ultimately elusive, though superficially subservient (like Eleanor). Coquetry is maybe the word. I can't think of another one. 'You are a helpless idiot, Sean' is maybe another one.

I sometimes wonder if I am unusual. Or, indeed, just an over-demanding fool. I know my tastes are far from universal. I have plenty of friends who much prefer obviously bossy women, seriously dominant women. These men like to be nagged and told what to do, to be ordered about by the wife, although they might rebel like naughty boys. These men, I have noticed, often seem to have bossy mothers.

So is that where my tastes come from? The dominance/submission dynamic of my parents' relationship? I'm not at all sure. Actually, it doesn't feel like it, to me; I could be kidding myself, but my desire for this coquettish type feels like it comes from somewhere much deeper than my upbringing, somewhere way down there. Somewhere primeval and unalterable. It feels like it's in the architect's plans. I'm at a loss to explain precisely this psychosexual desire, but I'm also unable to ignore it.

Which, as I say, doesn't augur well for Juanita and me. Unutterably gorgeous as she is, she is also bossy, and slightly hectoring. Not at all the coquette. As a case in point, she's just told me in firm and not-to-be-argued-with tones precisely how to make her coffee. And I'm bridling, now. Almost seething.

But maybe I should give it one more go (she is beautiful). Maybe I should kiss Juanita and I'll know for sure. This is normally the acid test.

At the end of the evening I get my chance. She is showing me to her door, she's looking relaxed and happy, even as she sets her mobile phone alarm for five-fifteen a.m. (another business trip). Standing in the doorway I lean to kiss her; for a tiny second she seems uncertain but then she bends to kiss me too. But it is not a good kiss. We seem to be struggling for dominance even as we kiss; there's a nose problem; who is kissing who is an issue; abruptly we both pull back; then she smiles inscrutably and closes the door, leaving me to trudge to the Tube station wondering who did the blueprints for my psychosexuality.

Two days later I get a not-entirely-unexpected email from Juanita. But if the sense of the email – 'goodbye' – is not unexpected, the way she phrases it comes as a mild surprise.

'Hope you aren't offended . . . but I don't think there can be more than one star in a relationship! Adios, J.'

Once I have gotten over my grievous disappointment – she *was* gorgeous, as I may have mentioned – I sit down and analyse that 'star' reference. It's intriguing. Is she on to something? Do I need to be the one that shines in a relationship? Do I need to be the funny guy in the comedy duo? It's possible. I like a fair amount of attention in a conversational group; it is arguable I would have felt outshone by Juanita's beauty and success. Maybe that's the flipside of my desire for submissively coquettish girls: a stupid need in me to be the 'star'.

As I sit here, disgruntled, I recollect the relationships I have known where there have been two loud extrovert people, or two arty people, striving for attention in the one marriage or partnership. These relationships were often not good. Often they have been argumentative and doomed, in my experience. But is my stupid wish to be ostensibly (if not actually) the dominant member of the relationship any better? Any more promising in terms of happiness?

All this is very enlightening and rather sobering. Through all these dates I have finally come to see what I want, what I like in women, what women might like in me. And what I like, it seems, is quite precise.

Psychosexually speaking, my romantic ideal is this: short, petite girls, with pretty curves, who have a good sense of humour, who earn between half my salary and twice as much (unless it's inherited), who are submissive but teasing, who are feminine but slightly devious, who are preferably mixed race or even foreign, who are bright and well-read without being heavily intellectual, and who eschew anal sex – but who might be into spanking. I don't mind if they are blonde or brunette. Well, not much.

Put like that, it's not such a list, is it? I mean, why don't I just log on to www.pretty-curvy-foreign-smart-unstuffy-feminine-elusive-affluent-professional-submissive-coquettish-spankable-teases.com? Forward slash notintoanalsex?

243

Funnily enough there isn't one of these websites (I have just tried. Well, you never know. The Internet is an amazing place).

Or is it? Is the Internet such an amazing place? I'm starting to wonder. I'm starting to wonder if all this Internet dating is so very good for me. Maybe it's actually making my job, of finding a lifelong partner, more taxing. Because all this choice is making me way too choosy . . .

What the F. I think I'll give it one last go.

Please pay £21.99

At least, I'd like to give it one last go. But I can't. I don't know if it's a kind of Internet weariness, a jaded outbox, a lack of zest on my part; but it's not happening for me. My last three Internet dates, since Juanita, have all been crap, and not even amusingly crap. They just petered out into nothing.

The last one in particular was lamentably poor, because after one date the girl simply disappeared into cyberspace. We exchanged about three emails, had one brisk lager-shandy, and then she vanished without even a goodbye: like a fading vapour trail in the blue summer sky, like a genie after your three wishes are up.

I am beginning to see this as another downside to Internet dating. For some reason, people find it easier just to disappear brusquely online. There was another girl, Lenina (Lenina?), who I was also emailing recently. She was blonde and cute (from her photo); she looked a bit like a chipmunk in blusher. I really liked her profile because it was funny and oblique and she said she had a penchant for *Flash Gordon* the film, and she said she wanted to meet a guy who could match her 'Brian Blessed obsession' and she really wanted someone who could say, 'Gordon's alive!' at crucial sexual moments.

I don't know what it was about this whirl of weirdness in her profile that so appealed to me, but it did, and Lenina and I exchanged the usual spry, wry, mildly flirtatious emails – and then she just vamoosed, disappeared, went AWOL, faster than a Swedish girl-student who's just bonked your flatmate. Because when it comes to calling things off, Internet dating is brutal like that. Much crueller than real dating. In a real-life situation, when you are chatting to a girl or a boy, someone you have just met, and it turns out things aren't going well, then the person who is going to bail, to bow out, is obliged to offer an explanation, a valedictory line, e.g. 'I'm sorry I'm already attached', or 'God I've got to go and feed the hedgehog who comes round my garden at midnight.' In other words there's a sign, a signal, a courteous brush-off; at best people will also give you a risible excuse as they scoot away – to sugar the medicine of rejection.

In cyberspace, by contrast, people just think 'Fuck it' and leave, without a word. They don't reply to your last email and that's that. It's the equivalent of that-someone-you've-met-at-a-party dematerialising in front of you, being transported to the mother ship. Unnerving. I know I've done this myself to my own cyberspace admirers –

just stopped replying to emails – but that doesn't make it OK. It's not OK.

And another thing. I'm starting to worry about this criteria fetish again. As you have surmised, I like short girls. As you also know, I am consequently whittling down my Internet dating options quite fiercely, burning off the unwanted ones, only going for girls with heights under five foot six, hopefully five foot four.

But maybe, in doing this, I am missing out on the unexpected but wonderful affair with a giantess, or at last a woman taller than The Artist Formerly Known as Prince. Why should I be such a slave to my template? Yes, I know that my first Net-date – that first date, all those merry and confusing months ago, with Bongowoman – came a cropper when I realised she could outreach me in a boxing bout, but that could have been just a disaster anyway. Maybe it wasn't size that did it. Perhaps our pheromones didn't alchemise, maybe our neurochemicals didn't click. But I presumed it was my template; and then went on applying the template, rigidly.

But what are templates for if not for breaking? Maybe it's time to shatter the mould, to look at women of all sizes and shapes. But then what criteria would I apply to all the millions of women who are waiting to meet me? Only women who use semicolons correctly? Do I only go for women who don't mention cats? Brunettes with tattoos? Indian women? Lawyers? Dentists? Nude dentists?

Time to rethink the situation. As I now realise, with

Internet dating, I am sieving out some people who might possibly be the one, the girl, the lifelong love affair, just because they seem unlikely on paper, or onscreen: too tall or normal or redheaded. Whereas in real life, you and I are open to all. You may not expect to like the six-foot-seven gingernut with alopecia but when this person turns and smiles at you across the Paddington Station booking hall she may well turn out to be the wildest lover you could imagine. Or what about that forty-three-year-old French matron with a bachelor pad in Ealing who made you laugh so hard you forgot to breathe? You didn't expect to have so much fun with her, did you Sean?

Yes: it's the unexpected. I'm missing it. By contrast, the Internet feels mechanical, statistical, bleak – and I've got repetitive strain injury from surfing so many sites.

And then, as I am thinking all this, as I am having major doubts, one day a bill arrives, by email. Sitting at my laptop, I open it up. *Your Udate account is up for renewal*, it says. *Please pay £21.99.*

At this point, something snaps. I know that I'm not paying for these subs, but still. *Someone* is paying. Someone is forking out money, and the fact of that payment is beginning to feel wrong. Why should you pay to find love? Doesn't that tarnish the whole experience? Doesn't the exchange of money, make it all pretty grim and commercial – and therefore doomed?

If it seems like I am over-reacting, I should explain: because of a recent, bitter experience I am somewhat conflicted about paying 'for love'. And this is because I have several times paid for *sex*, and the last time I did that, it went terribly and utterly wrong.

But let's start with some background. My first experience with a working girl, or at least the world of commercial sex, was probably similar to most guys'. It came on a school trip to London, aged fifteen, when a bunch of us bunked off from the 'Vikings in England' exhibition at the British Museum, and went to a Soho peep show.

I was there for an hour or more. I must have got through a dozen fifty-pence pieces, gazing through that slit in a rusty metal panel – gazing with adolescent seriousness at some bored young nude woman writhing 'suggestively' on a bed not five yards away. Was this erotic? It possibly could have been – if it weren't for the fact I could also see, through my slit, a dozen other slits with lots of furtive eyes staring desperately at the openly yawning girl. This ruined it for me. For the first time, and not the last, I felt used by commercial sex – exploited, even humiliated – and the smell of cheap detergent in the peep-show cubicle wasn't ideal.

A few years later and I was ready for something harder. At least, I thought I was. Not long after Eleanor and I broke up, I flew out, broken-hearted, to visit my friend Trevor (yes, Trevor), who was then living in Thailand. His advice to me, after he'd listened to my self-pitying, over-romantic, super-poetic spiel about me and my lost true love, was this: do lots of drugs, drink lots of beer and go see lots of lap dancers. It seemed good advice at the time. Especially as Trevor was cheerfully doing it anyway, even without a broken heart.

I lived in Thailand, with Trevor, for about three months. Three wild months. Every night we would put on our cool cotton shirts and we would tuk-tuk through the hot, humid, noisy, trafficky Bangkok night and then we'd go and hang out in Patpong bars and sex clubs. There we'd drink Singha beers and watch the naked Thai girls on stage do the fucky-fucky sex shows: shooting ping-pong balls from their vaginas, blowing smoke rings from their vaginas, shooting a dart from a vagina to pop a balloon held twenty yards away by another girl.

Actually I wasn't that excited by the sex shows. I liked the *idea* of being at a sex show; I liked the idea, even more, of being *blasé* about being at a sex show, of occasionally glancing up from my Singha beer to look, with worldly acknowledgment, at the naked teenage Cambodian gyrating her bare brown arse ten feet away – and not particularly caring because I was too cool. But did any of it turn me on?

Not really. My erotic moment usually came later. When Trevor and I had had our fill of Klosters beer and ping-pong balls, we would go back to our druggy hotel and drink more beer; and when Trevor was snoring away happily and the rest of the city was fitfully asleep – then I would lie there through the watchful night, masturbating about Eleanor, furiously, imagining her golden breasts, conjuring the way her pelvis moved as she ground away on top of me, the way she curved away beneath me like a leopard stretching on a tree bough. For hour after hour I would bring to mind select images of Eleanor naked with which to torment myself into orgasm – this after I had been in the presence of at least twenty naked girls that night, girls I could have shagged for five quid.

Eventually Trevor and I got bored of the sex shows – we realised we had been going to them a little too much. The realisation came like this: every night the go-go girls had a rigmarole where, along with the banana-slicing and the ping-pong-ball-shooting and the actual live shagging with a blank-eyed Thai bloke, they would put a marker pen in their vaginas and, by moving their pelvises, write some pithy or 'amusing' message on a placard. Then the message, written on the placard, would be held up for desultory applause from the men in the bar. Usually it would say *Hello Boys*, or *Guten Abend* or whatever. But one typically hot, mosquitoey night a naked girl put the marker pen in her vagina, wrote the message on the placard, and held it up. It said: *Hello Again to Trevor and Sean from London.*

We were flattered, obviously. But we realised we had possibly been over-attending. So the next week Trevor suggested we actually move on and get a couple of hookers, a couple of hookers to shag, not just to watch. My mind still full of the glory, the unlikely perfection, of Eleanor's breasts (getting ever more perfect in my nostalgic imagination), I nodded unhappily and agreed unwillingly. I wasn't keen, yet I was desperately, desperately horny and therefore very keen.

So we went to a bar and chose two girls, and took them back home, and Trevor spent the night rampantly coupling with his girl in the room next door, and I spent the night just looking at my lovely, naked seventeen-year-old Thai girl. Just looking at her body. I did have a sadly persistent erection, but I was unable to penetrate because I was so confused, morally conflicted, in love, short-circuited. At first the girl tried to coax me out of my inhibition, to relax me, but in the end she got so bored she put on my Walkman and started singing tunelessly along to 'Transmission' by Joy Division. The next morning I lied to Trevor and told him I'd had a great time. Than I told him the truth and he shook his head and laughed long and hard and called me a 'sad bastard'. Then we drank some more beers.

And that was how it remained for quite a few years. As my twenties and early thirties motored by I deliberately eschewed the whole commercial sex thing. Partly because of some residual moral distaste (maybe); partly because of a kind of arrogance ('I never pay' etc.); partly because I never got the opportunity again. If I was going to do it I knew it was going to be somewhere safely far-away like Thailand, where it seemed more acceptable, more fun, certainly cheaper, and where of course the girls were sweet and elfin. Seeing prostitutes at home was a simply impossible idea. For a start, the scene in London seemed to divide between £5-a-night street girls in King's Cross, and £500-a-night call girls from the King's Road. Neither pole was appealing.

All through this time, however, my friends were behaving very differently. They kept coming back from their holidays, or their nights out, with debauched and amusing stories of their forays into the *demi-monde*. When I was about thirty I became good friends with an American journalist based in Dublin, who – though he was happily married – had an utterly outrageous whore habit. He had at least one strumpet a week. He would have a whore any time, any place, at almost any cost. He would call a call-girl just after breakfast with his wife; he would visit a lady of the night just after celebrating his son's fifth birthday. I used to quiz him on the 'morality' of this. I knew he truly loved his wife; and she really loved him. If she ever found out about his other life she would probably leave him, and break up the family he loved so much. How could he do it? How did he square the moral circle?

At this he smiled, sadly, and said, I know, I know. But his answer was that he and his wife had married young, and he was highly sexed, and he needed to sleep with different women, and if it wasn't different whores, well then it would be different girlfriends. Which would have been worse, and much more threatening to his marriage. In other words, he believed he was using prostitutes to keep his family together. I really wasn't sure how to react to this. Maybe he had a point? Yet the idea of his pretty wife's face crumpling into tears if she ever found out . . . I couldn't have coped with that, I don't think.

But I was sometimes jealous of his surreal stories. One day he came back from an assignment in Amsterdam where, naturally, he had indulged. Indeed he had indulged so much he had run out of money early, had spent all but

253

his last few euros. So what did he do when he was down to his last few shekels? He went whoring again.

'But,' as he chucklingly told me later, 'you see because I only had so much money, she wouldn't take her bra off, she would only let me shag her with her knickers off. She kept the bra on. And you know how much I'm into tits.'

I affirmed this.

'So,' he went on, 'about halfway through shagging her I said, look, please, how much is it to take your bra off, I really want to see your tits? So she said, it's thirty euros more, and I said I've only got fifteen euros. She shook her head at this – but then I had an idea and I said, well can I just look at one of your breasts? For fifteen euros? And she said yes, and so I got to take half her bra off, and fool around with just the one breast. Well worth it.'

It was this guy, this American, who finally push-started my stalled commercial-sex car. We were on assignment in Russia, in some God-forsaken ex-Soviet town, and he, of course, was having a whale of a time with the plentiful women willing to do it for *valyuta*, hard currency. At the end of the week the discrepancy in our fun levels was starting to get to me. I was becoming frustrated about going to my hotel bedroom to stare at the mini-bar while he screwed half of Novosibirsk down the corridor.

So I thought, Fuck it, I'll join in. But I had to get my courage up first. So we went to a banging Siberian night-club and drank ten vodka-tonics (me eight, him two) and when I was finally ready, finally up for it, well then we repaired to our concrete slab of an old communist hotel

– only to find that it was so late, most of the lobby-whores had gone home. There was just one left. But she agreed to have sex with both of us for a hundred bucks.

We got the lift to my friend's room. In the room she immediately took her clothes off, and then took my friend's clothes off. Then she and my American friend immediately started having blatant sex, while I pretended to look in the mini-bar. I was embarrassed. This was ridiculous. I couldn't even think about getting an erection. Perhaps I should have some Pringles?

No, this was ridiculous. I had to join in. But when I turned around she was on top of him and he was sitting on the sofa and it was very peculiar seeing my friend's testicles jiggling as this woman bounced away on top of him. So instead I watched a bit of late-night Russian telly. Then again I thought this is just stupid, so I took my clothes off, but still I was so nervous I couldn't get an erection (this was the mid-nineties, still, just, pre-Viagra) so I had a bright idea. I nipped into the bathroom, where I managed to tease up an erection by thinking about Tamara or Eleanor or some other girlfriend, and then I hesitantly stepped out into the bedroom with my erection, where my friend glanced over (he was still having sex with the girl) and saw me hovering in the doorway and he called over:

'Fuck's sake Sean, are you in or out?'

And with that I ejaculated, prematurely, on to the dusty Russian carpet.

As I put my clothes back on and stepped quietly out

of the room, leaving them to it, I decided this was not the most successful of threesomes. Nonetheless it had been fun. I resolved to do it again. Perhaps. Perhaps, yes.

Over the next couple of years, therefore, I went successfully whoring – twice. First there was a girl in Thailand (of course); I was on my way back from a trip to Japan. I hadn't had sex in a month or two and my airline ticket had a scheduled stopover in Bangkok. Staring at my ticket in Tokyo airport, remembering my Bangkok debacle of years previously, remembering the way I enjoyed myself standing in the doorway in Novosibirsk, ejaculating on to the carpet, I went to the airline desk and turned my three-hour stopover into a two-day stopover.

In Bangkok I got to work fast. Soon as I had jettisoned my bags I went to a go-go bar in a steamy Bangkok street called Soi Cowboy; there I found a girl in one bar dancing naked on the dais (with about a dozen other girls). Like all the girls, she had a number on a disc attached to her wrist; I wrote her number on a slip of paper, thereby summonsing the girl.

An hour later she had changed into jeans and climbed in my taxi and she and I went whizzing through frazzled Bangkok, and we went to my hotel room where she immediately had a shower. For the few minutes she was in the shower I had my usual moral and emotional brainstorm: What am I doing? Am I exploiting this girl? Maybe she is a sex slave? This is terrible! Will I be able to perform with a condom? I am a monster! Have I taken enough Viagra to make sure I can get it up?

But then she came out of the shower all beautiful, brown, wet, naked and nineteen, with her dark wet hair coiling down her supple back, and I grabbed her and kissed her bottom and flung her on the bed and then I actually went down on her; and after that I moved up her body and I penetrated her and as I did it felt so good I actually said, 'I love you'. And for that moment I really did. I really did love her. She cost £20.

A year later I had another assignment, this time in Vietnam. The same thing happened, only in Ho Chi Minh City it was cheaper, and just as fun. She smelt of almonds. She told me I was the biggest etc., which I was now discovering they always do: to reassure you. Except, that is, for the whore my American friend had in Kenya, who told him that 'he was nice because his penis was so small; her previous customer had been so big he had hurt'. My friend was not reassured by this.

What had happened to my moral doubts, my ethics, my cavils? I was starting to dispense with them. I had dispensed with them. I was starting to think: What's so wrong with whoring? There is a certain honesty to it. No one lies to anyone else (apart from 'oh you so big' and all that). You get laid; she gets paid. Is that any worse than taking a girl for dinner and lying to her by telling her you really like her and probably want a relationship just so you can have sex with her? Is that better or worse than whoring, or similar somehow? I was starting to find these clichéd questions harder to answer. I was starting not to care what the answer was. I was getting into prostitutes.

My next chance to have some sad, bittersweet, deliciously easy paid-for sex came a few years later, a few
years ago. 2002. By this time I had sorted my life out;
sort of. I was certainly more sober, and not distractedly
in love; I was older and wiser too, and still horny. Plus I
had lots of Viagra.

It was time to go to Thailand again, to do it seriously:
with no hang-ups, because all my hang-ups had gone. It
was time to fill my boots; have lots and lots and lots of
girls; have all the sex I could eat.

So I did. I flew out to Bangkok for the third time since
I first visited the place as a callow, feral, boozy young
Englishman. This time it was very different. My partner
in crime was a Scottish lawyer friend, David, a man not
unknown to debauchery. Together we went for it. On our
first night in Bangkok we cabbed to a bar in Patpong and
I didn't even wait for the ping-pong show. I chose a girl
and took her back to my room. And of course it was fine
and dandy. The second night I did exactly the same, as
did my friend. Over the next week I must have had five
or six more girls, culminating in one night when my friend
and I got two girls into the shower with us and had a
foursome.

And I was happy. I have to admit: I loved this bonanza,
the freedom, the carnal satisfaction. Those two weeks in
Thailand were, you see, one of the only times, possibly
the only time, when I have felt utterly free of sexual
yearning. Instead, I was sated. I was full up. The chat-
tering monkey was off my back. I felt relaxed at last. It

felt like a car alarm had just stopped blaring; an alarm that had been blaring so long, I was starting to forget it was there in the background. What I experienced was close to serenity, a unique period of blissful liberation from the insistent and tedious demands of my libido. Maybe this is what Zen monks feel? The final absence of desire. The silence. Nirvana. At last.

Perhaps this doesn't make sense; perhaps it's over-wrought. But this is what it felt like for me. I may have said this before, but for me the urgency, persistence and overwhelmingness of male sexual desire is not fun. It is exciting and energising and all that – but it is not 'fun'. It doesn't make me happy, and it sometimes makes me very sad. I actually don't want to spend the rest of my life, half my waking life, looking at girls, desiring girls, wanting to view the naked bodies of girls, yet I have to, as it's just the way I'm made. I have to do it, even if it bores me. It sometimes bores me. Even if I'd rather be reading Tolstoy or chucking paper darts, if a cleavagey young thing walks down the street I am going to have to look at her. My hormones tell me to. I am a soldier obeying orders. I've had a message from HQ.

Incidentally, I am rewriting this bit of the book from Trieste, in Italy. I'm writing a travel piece about the city, you see. And my experience here this weekend may provide an illustration of what I'm saying. Yesterday afternoon I went for a walk down the sunlit Barcolo, the big concrete embankment that stretches west of Trieste.

The Triestines use this embankment as a bathing place

259

– which means, at this summer time of the year, that it is wall-to-wall with tanning young Italian chicks, topless, bethonged, semi-naked. So, like I say, yesterday afternoon I went for a walk down this avenue of naked Italian beauty, and it was gruelling. It felt like being under fire, being in the trenches.

Everywhere I looked there was a bare breast or a firm young buttock or the beautiful laughing face of a bikini'd principessa putting cream on her nipples and saying, '*Ciao bello!*' It was so distracting and depressing and yearningly harrowing, I actually started walking fast. I almost broke into a run to get through it: to escape the incoming bullets, like Mel Gibson in the film *Gallipoli*, where he has to make that fatal sprint through the withering Turkish fire.

But I have digressed. Back to my story. Me and Dave in Bangkok.

As I was mentioning, me and Dave were having a wonderful time in Bangkok, with lots of girls and sex and booze. The last hurrah of our over-long youths.

And then we made a mistake. Then *I* made a mistake. We'd flown down to finish our vacation on Koh Samui island, in the south of the country. We were staying on Chaweng Beach, a raunchy strip of pubs, hotels, and hippie shacks. At seven p.m. I walked into one of the many thumping go-go bars. As usual, there were a dozen young Thai girls gyrating on the bartop; some of them had that sad, fixed smile of the long-term whore; some of the girls were having a genuine laugh, I think.

Then, one of these girls caught my eye. Petite, black-eyed, extrovert; she was wearing a stars-and-stripes bandanna. She was very sexy; about twenty-eight years old. When I first saw her she was being chatted up, unsuccessfully, by a German guy; even though she was available for money, it was clear she wasn't available to just anyone for money. Or so I told myself.

I sat down and ordered a beer. Within half an hour Min and I were playing Connect 4 on the bar, as you do; within two hours we were both on her motorbike heading back to my hotel. I waved at Dave as I disappeared; he grinned and nodded: Another girl, good on you, see you tomorrow for a debriefing session, Sergeant Thomas.

But this wasn't just another girl. By the end of the first night, Min and I had dispensed with condoms. Looking back this seems incalculably reckless and foolish, disturbingly dumb, and I can't believe I did it. But . . . but there was just something about the night and the beers. The night and the beers – and Min. And so it went on from that evening.

Two long, Min-filled weeks later, I was almost in love. I knew this was ridiculous, but still. Reluctantly I started packing for London. As I packed Min looked at me and cried a little. I suspected this might be a performance; I was well aware that Thai girls can cry at the drop of a hat for western men, as the men depart – then the next day the girl finds another 'farang' boyfriend and she cheers up all of a sudden. But still. Something in Min's tears seemed sincere. But I had to go, I wanted to go. I'd had a great holiday. I kissed little Min on the top of her little brown ear, and Dave and I went to get the plane. I was sure I would never hear from Min again.

I was wrong. A few weeks after my return to London I got a shy, plaintive mobile phone call from Min (we had exchanged numbers and email addresses). 'I miss you!' she said. Then her phone cut out. I ascribed the weird call to a slack week in the go-go bars, and got on with life.

Three months later I got my first email, saying she had moved to Bangkok and inviting me to visit. I was startled; I was also slightly seduced by the sincere inarticulacy of the email. It had real charm, like Min herself. So I wrote back: a light-hearted email explaining how much fun I had had in Samui.

She wrote back, telling me she had given up working in bars, and was working in a 'shower-curtain factory' in Bangkok. She said she was OK but a bit lonely. And so it continued; we exchanged more emails. By the fourth or fifth email she was dropping the first hints of a hidden secret: '*I have something to tell you . . . I hope you will not laugh.*'

I ignored this at the time, not least because I had recently begun a relationship with a very loveable new girlfriend in England and Min was drifting from my thoughts. Happily, the emails dwindled into silence. This was good. Then, six months after I had first met her, sitting down at my laptop, I opened my email inbox and saw there was another message from Min.

In faltering English, it began, '*Hello Sean. How are*

you? I hope you are fine.' Then, after a few friendly details about the rainy weather in Bangkok, came the bombshell: '*I am six months pregnant.*'

At this point, I stopped reading. I sat back, stunned. Then I read the paragraph again and again, followed by the whole email, filled with its references to 'hospitals', 'baby', and my surname.

Despite the pidgin English, the meaning was obvious: Min was pregnant and she was sure that the baby was mine. Either that, or she was trying to blackmail me.

What do you do at this point, if you think you may have impregnated a hooker? Do you disown the child, Victorian-style? Do you offer to marry her, absurdly?

Or do you do what I did: think about the missed opportunities for fatherhood, the abortions, the miscarriages, the time in the clinic with Tamara. And then do you think: I do really want to be a father, and if this is how it happens, so be it . . .

After the initial shock had sunk in, I poured out online questions to Min: How did she know it was mine? When was her last period? How many other 'boyfriends' had she had at the time? I was rocked, perturbed, and wary . . . yet, as I say, a fairish-sized part of me was secretly a little hopeful that Min was pregnant, and that the baby was mine.

It was truly perplexing. I was somehow optimistic, yet also wildly suspicious.

My friends were simply suspicious. 'Sean', they said, 'she's scamming'; 'She's a whore, this is for money'; 'How do you even know she's pregnant?'

They had a point. But naïve though it may sound, some-thing struck me as being different in my situation. There was an air to Min, to the way she wrote those gushingly inarticulate emails. Taken together they suggested she might be telling the truth; that she might be pregnant, that it might well be mine. Or was this just my own wishful, unreproduced heart telling me what I wanted to hear?

Over the following months I attempted to examine the matter coolly. I spoke to a Kiwi expat in Bangkok who did 'private investigations' of Thai girls who had 'ensnared' western men. His perspective was illuminating. He told me of many such scams by Thai girls. He told me about a ruse where a Thai girl would simultaneously pretend to be pregnant with about eight or ten different 'farangs'; at least three of the guys would fall for the bogus pregnancy, and start mailing cash to Bangkok.

This panicked me. Was I just one of a number of pale-faced dupes sitting at home in the cold, getting anxious about a non-existent baby? Was Min trying to siphon money from dozens of guys like me?

Three weeks later Min asked me for money. It was not much, but it was enough to tip the delicate balance of my mind. I snapped, and angrily rang her: I accused her of setting me up, of fabricating the pregnancy, of shoving a metaphorical cushion up her top.

The response was fierce and immediate. Min sent me a dozen long emails in the next twenty-four hours. They were angry, passionate, fractured, compelling . . . and even a tiny bit mad. Yet the message was clear: Min was pregnant; she really did think the baby was mine. And if I didn't want to help or get involved, well, fine – she would do it by herself.

I took the message, and backed down. Over the subsequent weeks I managed to adopt a more philosophical angle on the whole thing. Also, I decided to send Min a little money, on the basis that even if the baby wasn't mine, Min was still a lonely Thai girl in a lot of trouble, and helping out was therefore the right thing to do. I sent Min about £300; not a lot for me, but enough to make a difference in Thailand.

Sometime later I received proof that Min was indeed pregnant. She sent me some digital photos of herself, looking big and radiant in her Bangkok bedsit. Two weeks further on, as I sat in my then-girlfriend's flat, I got a text message from Thailand, breaking the news: Min was sitting in a hospital in Bangkok nursing a seven-and-a-half pound son, delivered at thirty-six weeks. Immediately, I booked the air tickets, and started preparing myself to look into the eyes of this newborn child.

Min and I had arranged to meet in my Bangkok hotel. I was sitting in my room, anxiously eating some sushi. Then Min knocked on the door. Taking a deep breath, I walked over.

She was carrying the tiny newborn. For a second she blinked at me, and then she started crying. I hugged her, wordlessly – because I didn't know what else to say. I didn't feel *great* passion for Min any more; but I felt huge affection and a lot of sympathy. I really wanted to help; I wanted to do the right thing; but what *was* the right thing?

And then I cradled the baby. It was a shattering moment. I hadn't expected the surge of emotions, the overwhelming and conflicting sensations that flooded me. I was thirty-eight: childless and unmarried. And now here was this perfect, vulnerable thing in my hands. My *son*, maybe. How could I be so cruel as to test it? How could I be so ruthless and cold?

Somehow I got a grip. Before I'd flown to Bangkok I had established the best method of DNA-testing a small baby. This, it turned out, was the 'buccal swab' method, where you sweep a Q-tip across the inner cheek of the child, gathering cells. These cells can then be tested for DNA. Unfortunately, the buccal swab method was not available in Bangkok – that is to say, I was going to have to courier my swabs back to England, for testing.

Putting the baby on my lap, I got out the Q-tips. As I did, Min looked at me, sorrowfully, and perhaps contemptuously. It wasn't hard to sense what she was thinking: How can you do this? How can you not trust me? How can you do this to your own child?

I did it. I scraped the Q-tips, sealed them in an envelope, and sent them off to the UK. And then I waited. And waited. I spent days sitting by my Bangkok hotel swimming pool, fighting my feelings. Half of me, maybe more, wanted this child to be mine. Yet I had to find out the truth, and stay calm. In the end I couldn't help myself.

Before I got the test results, I went to see Min and the baby one more time. I had firmly resolved not to do this, because I was scared of that surge of unmanageable emotion, that upwelling of paternal love.

It was a long drive across Bangkok, to a distant, humid suburb. There I sat with Min and the child, in her tiny flat. We chatted and sipped tea, and I helped her feed the baby. As I did, I started marvelling at the little boy, at the way he looked like me. Weren't those my eyes? Surely that was my nose, my mouth, even my Celtic complexion? Why did I need to do a test when I could see with my own eyes that *this was my son*?

I very nearly cracked. Back at the hotel I decided to cancel the DNA tests, and accept the child as mine. But when I picked up the phone, a small voice inside me was saying: No, this is wrong. You will always have doubts, if you don't find out now.

I put the phone down.

A day later the results came through. '*We are 100 per cent sure the alleged father, Sean Thomas, is not the true father of this child.*' The boy wasn't mine.

My first reaction was anger. At Min, at life, at myself. I refused to see Min or the baby before I left; when she rang in tears, I rang off. I packed my bags, and went home.

On my return to London the anger slowly – very slowly – abated. It dawned on me that Min had probably convinced herself that I was the father because she so desperately wanted me to be the father. And she was a single and frightened young mother, without any options.

But even when the anger had gone, the melancholy remained. I felt like someone had given me a son, and then snatched him away. I was aware that my feelings were irrational, but that was no help. I was bereft.

Over time, however, these feelings began to mellow, and to change. One day I woke up and realised it was something of a blessing. Because I realised that if I had not done the test, I would have spent my life helping to bring up a child that is not mine; and thus I might have foregone the chance to have real children of my own. Moreover, if I hadn't done the test I would have prevented the true father, whoever he is, wherever he is, from knowing his son.

I also believe that I have learned a lesson. A harsh but salutary lesson. What exactly was I doing in Thailand? How stupid can you be? If my adventures ended up giving me some terrible anguish, maybe that is what I deserved. Maybe all the stress and angst of those weeks and months were my own misdeeds and irresponsibility of the last few years, coming home to roost. As ye sow, so shall ye reap – right?

Incidentally, three weeks before writing this chapter I had a friendly email from Min. She told me she had finally re-registered her child in her own surname; she said they were going on holiday together. She attached a picture of her son. He looked bonny, and happy.

I hope one day he will find his real dad.

Still single?

'Not bad,' says Simon. 'I like it. Even if it did take you a year.'

We are sitting in his gleaming, bronze-hunk-photo'd *Men's Health* office, nearly ten months – not a year! – after Simon first gave me my commission. Simon has just finished reading my piece, my article, my Internet dating essay. This is a good and important moment. I have done it.

'I do have a couple of tiny points though.'

Ah. He gazes at me, frankly. Then his eyes slide away and fall once more on to the sheaf of papers in his hands – my article. He picks up the papers:

'I mean . . .'

'Er, yes. . . ?'

'Well . . . It would've been nice if you could have had a happy ending.'

I shrug. What can you do? I didn't have a happy ending; there wasn't a torrid kiss in the London rain, a blissful

269

ascent in the hot-air balloon of happiness. As I have said, my Internet dating just . . . petered out. Dwindled. And then came my Road to Damascus moment, when I got that spasm about paying, and had those memories of Min.

And so one day last week I thought, That's it, I'm done, I've enough material. *Finito.* Consequently I wrote the piece and emailed it off to Simon, and waited for a week while he put the last issue to bed, until he had time to read the article – and now here we are.

'I suppose I could have lied?' I say.

'Oh please! Who do you think we are?'

We look at each other. We start laughing. Then we move on and start talking about various small changes I can make, ideas for possible extra bits, and how we're going to handle the images ('We'll get some girls from the office to pose').

Finally he sits back, with his eyes half closed, like a vet in his surgery, listening to the last farmer of the day. Evidently his mind is moving on: another issue of the magazine, another batch of ideas in his inbox. But then he looks at me and says:

'So I guess that means . . . you're still single?'

'Terminally.'

'Hn.' His eyes are slyly bright. 'What are we going to do with you?'

'Dunno.' I shrug. 'Maybe I'm all set for lifelong bachelorhood. . . ?'

'Very nice,' he replies. 'Individual apple pies. Wanking. Great life.'

I regard him:

'And being married is so fantastic?'

'Yes . . .' He shakes his head. 'Well. There are worse things.' He thinks. 'Like the Holocaust – that was worse.'

I see that his gaze has left mine. Again. Instead he is openly surveying the prospective cover versions for September. So that's that: we're done; it's over. Quietly getting up, I go to the shiny new Rodale Incorporated door, but as I do I hear him say, without lifting his head:

'By the way, the expenses are fine.'

Yay. I close the door behind me. Quickening my steps past the open-mouthed office workers, feeling like a hunter-gatherer amongst the farmers, like a spearman who has brought a gazelle back to the tribal cave, I press open the final door and step into the fresh air.

Outside, London is being London: busy, impersonal, drizzly, vivacious. For a moment I stare about me, slightly disoriented. What is this feeling? I have a weird void in my stomach. It feels like I am finally being let out of jail, or released from the army, or . . . rejected from a long-term space mission, or . . . But hold on: rejected? Why do I feel rejected? What's this sense of mild depression? Am I just disappointed that my paid-for dating spree has ended with such a dying fall? Or have I lost a little purpose in life? Something that gave my bachelor days a sense of direction?

Whatever the answer, the fact is I didn't meet the right woman. So what do I do now? I go home, that's what.

I'm back on the chain gang: from now on I shall slowly accede to reality. To a non-Net-dating life. To meeting prospective partners in the normal way.

The normal way . . .

Two weeks into my new life, my old life, the bitter truth sinks in. One morning I find myself at a bus stop contemplating a difficult question.

Just what is the normal way – of meeting women? Is there such a thing? I'm not sure. All I know is that I've been meeting women online for so long, I've quite forgotten the niceties and rigmaroles of regular courting.

Really. What do you do? How do you meet women casually, i.e. not through the Internet? Do you just start talking to them at bus stops, like this girl here? What if they run away? As she just did?

Perhaps instead you have to rely on luck: the accidental meeting on the street, when fate forces you into a collision? That's certainly how it works in Hollywood. One day you are walking down the busy summer street and on your left a shop door swings open as a woman comes out carrying lots of pink hat boxes, and she bumps into you and drops everything and you look at all the spilled shopping and you say, Here, I have a taxi, and you go back to your flat and she takes off her clothes and . . .

Unsurprisingly, this doesn't happen to me much. Certainly not over the month that follows my closure of the article. Over the following few weeks, I actually fail to meet anyone at all.

But then there's a party. A friend's thirty-fifth birthday.

(Thirty-five! What happened?!) It's a fun party; it's also a tad poignant as it reminds me just how paired-off most of my friends are; how advanced in life-changes. As I look around the boozy, noisy, happyish room full of people doing fairly bad dancing, I realise that many of my friends have had kids, got divorced, swapped partners, gone bald, gone bankrupt, had more kids, in what seems like the last six months. And what have I been doing in all that time? Crochet?

Amongst the jitterbugging marrieds, there are, at least, some apparently single people. Like Sarah here. She's pretty and sweet. And very smart. An osteopath. I'm not sure what that is; a cross between brain surgery and aromatherapy, I think. But she's cute and I'd like to chat her up. A lot. Yet the hangover from my Internet dating abides: I've rather forgotten *how* to chat someone up. I'm so used to Net-dating, I've quite mislaid what I like to regard as my normal subtlety. My urge is to go up to Sarah and say: 'Hi I'm Sean, I'm thirty-eight and consider myself quite attractive. Are you looking for a serious relationship, or just fun and maybe sex?'

Can't do that, natch. But what do you do? Well, you do your best. And my best is this: I go over to Sarah and talk to her for about an hour, then I get excited because we are laughing together a lot, then I move away from her because I think I'm being too obvious, then I go back and talk to her for another hour before finally asking her for her number, after which I go home all drunk and happy and optimistic in the cab, then I text her the next day –

and she texts me back saying sorry, she's married.

Brilliant, not. That wouldn't have happened online. Online you know everyone is single. Well, ish. But my debacle with Sarah is, I suppose, a start. At least I've talked, in the flesh, to a woman I have never met before – and she didn't punch me to the ground in anger or scream and squirt mace at me, or indeed run away from the bus stop.

And so, in the normal way of things, this faltering start leads in time to a period where I am not starting any more; slowly, I get used to normal dating again. Yes it is a painful re-education, but gradually things move into gear: now I am meeting women, I am talking, laughing, drinking, and dating. And, one fine day, having sex.

Yup, I even get to have sex. Her name is Petra and we meet at a party and she is quite tall and fun and we break up soon afterwards and I don't really mind.

But . . . maybe I *do* mind. Not so much the break-up, but what it represents. Another miss, another failed chunk of my love life. Put it another way: what is troubling me now is how all this normal living and normal courtship is taking time.

Lots of time. Too much time. Time I haven't got.

The morning after the painless 'break-up' with Petra, I stare out of the window of my flat over at the law college and I see another group of eighteen-year-old law students having their induction day. It's a painful sight: they all look so . . . young. So fresh. So like me, so long ago. That's the problem with living in a studenty area: every term is an audible tick on the clock; every influx of cheery young teens with implausible complexions and magnificent breasts on the street outside my flat makes me realise how long it is, and getting longer, since I was eighteen.

With a palpable shock, I realise that it is late May. Nearly summer. The seasons are slipping quickly by. And that is starting to panic me again. Because I'm thirty-eight, going on thirty-nine. To put it bluntly: I need to meet the right woman soon, if not now, because, well because when I am sixty or dead it may just be too late. Since I stopped Internet dating I've returned to my normal course, just dawdling along, affably waiting for life and love to happen to me. But maybe that attitude is a luxury, a luxury only the truly young can easily afford.

The young, the very young, they are time-billionaires, they are the plutocrats of time. Only the truly young have endless months to spunk, have great big yachts of years; only the very young can slouch around the world, knowing that if they drop a few months here, lose a gap year there, it doesn't matter. But people in their thirties and forties, they are not so time-rich: they have used up a lot of their time-capital, they are glancing anxiously at their time bank accounts, they know that time is finite, and that one day they will go to the time-ATM and have their time-cards eaten (I think I'm done with that metaphor). And so they – we – have to get cracking with the marriage-and-kids malarkey.

And that's how I am starting to feel again. So what do I do? How do I hurry things along, increase my chances, get the stats and the maths on my side? Well . . . *can* I go back to Internet dating? If I do, I'd have to pay for my own dates. A sobering thought.

The next evening, coincidentally enough, I go to meet my friend Joe. The transsexual.

This isn't just any meeting. Joe's coming to the bar as a real woman. That is to say, this'll be the first time I've seen him in his full kit, in the outside world, since he (rather shockingly) announced his transvestism to me in an Ealing pub, about five years ago. In those inter-vening years I have seen him in unisex gear – or with flouncier than usual haircuts – but never as an actual *woman*.

Feeling the tension, I pace the floor of the pub. Then the door opens and Joe comes in. He's wearing a blue dress and a blonde wig. It's a sight I am conditioned to find comical, and so I do. But after a while I stop giggling, and I look at Joe more studiedly, and I begin to find the sight of Joe as a woman rather inspiring. Certainly it's gutsy and brave, to confront the world like this. Standing here, I realise that Joe's got balls – at least for the moment.

Taking up my wineglass I go up to Joe. He stands there, with an unsure expression.

'You know,' I say, 'you look OK . . . Not bad at all.'

In his blue dress, Joe smiles with relief.

Later that evening, we get to talking about other stuff. Joe tells me that he has been following my example. I look askance at him, then I realise that he is talking about Internet dating.

'It's great . . .' he says. 'Before it would have been impossible; I mean – before the Internet, it would have been very difficult to meet women, women who might want to be with a transsexual.'

I nod. 'Certainly a niche market.'

He goes on:

'Course there are clubs and stuff, but it's a tiny community. But with the Internet I'm able to meet the few women in the world, in Europe, or wherever, who are happy with the way I am, who might be willing to get it together.'

My mind is bubbling with questions. Not for the first time, I want to know what Joe intends to do with these women.

'Oh, dressing up and stuff. Putting on make-up. Just being intimate.'

'K . . .'

'It's not all about sex!' He shakes his head at me. 'It's about love and emotions, finding the right person, someone who fits. The Internet is great for that. It just makes it so much easier.' He continues. 'It's a revolution. It gives someone like me a chance for happiness, a chance that maybe wouldn't have existed before.'

At this point, I feel an urge to confess to my good friend. With a tepid shrug, I tell Joe that I've stopped Internet dating, because it seemed repetitive, rather bleak. And, I add, perhaps I also stopped because a part of me still bridles, deep inside, at the stigma of meeting someone 'that way'.

He stares at me, almost pityingly.

'And real life isn't ever bleak and repetitive? How bleak are singles bars?' He is shaking his bewigged head. 'If you meet someone that you like, that you can love, how does it matter the way you meet them?'

He puts a hand on one hip and pouts, quite effectively.

'Sean. Did you meet women you liked when you were Internet dating?'

'Sure, but . . .'

'Well then.'

A pause. The pub is noisy and boisterous. Joe and I are staring at each other.

'Hey. Nice wig,' I say.

'Ta,' he says.

Then we both chuckle and talk about football. Some things don't change so much.

But on the way home I think some more about Joe. Being with Joe, knowing Joe, has taught me a lot. About myself, about how much I've changed. For a start, if you'd told me when I was, say, twenty, that I would one day be close friends with a man who likes to wear miniskirts, I would have been pretty sceptical. That's not to say I haven't had my own brushes with gayness. I have. I remember once when I was a fifteen-year-old lad in rustic, bumpkiny Herefordshire, a bunch of us mates went night-fishing and we all ended up wanking together (but separately, if you know what I mean) around the camp-fire. Looking back, I do wonder what that was about. Also I have, over the years, done the normal metrosexual stuff – talked about food and Georgian architecture in a foppish way for instance. And finally – big confession coming up! – there was this other time.

Me and a close friend of mine, we got very drunk one day, perhaps the drunkest I have ever been in my life. Which is to say, a lot. The entire day we went from pub to pub to flat to flat and by the end we were having such a good time, for some reason we started openly wondering how it would be if we were gay – how much better it might be, because it would solve so many problems: we could talk like chaps, then have a brisk shag, then nip down town for a curry. There wouldn't be any need for any of that emotional, touchy-feely sometimes-annoying girlie stuff.

Normally, a conversation like that might have ended there. But because of the beer and the wine (and the night! and the stars!) my friend and I suddenly started . . . snogging – and then he slid his hand down my jeans and started fumbling. However, given that neither of us are actually gay, all this was rather awkward, not to say clumsy. His fumbling was uncertain and amateurish. So in the end I got impatient and bored and snapped at him, saying, 'Look, are you going to suck my cock, or what?'

At this point, there was a shocked silence, while my words sank in. Then I started giggling, and he started laughing, and finally I went upstairs and got into bed with one of my female flatmates. I woke up with a hangover of Korean War dimensions.

Not my greatest moment. But that doesn't matter; what I'm saying is this: I've had my own mild and brief experiments with gayness, though in the end I've decided that I just fancy girls, not guys. I think it's the facial hair. So I'm not intrinsically closed or inimical to the concept of gayness. Let a million lilies bloom, is what I have long believed, vis-à-vis homosexuals.

Nonetheless, transsexuality is a big step beyond simple homosexuality – and one I might have expected myself to find difficult, even in a close friend – yet Joe has taught me that I can be tolerant, that friendship maybe means mutual tolerance. He has even shown me that such a bizarre life choice can be a courageous and admirable thing.

So. Perhaps this *is* what Joe has ultimately taught me: *tolerance*. And maybe, just maybe, it's time I applied that tolerance to *myself*. Maybe it's time I cut myself a bit of slack, stopped demanding so much of life. After all, I don't have to meet the woman of my life in a perfect situation; I don't have to meet the perfect woman, for that matter. I just need to meet a woman I can love, and who loves me, for all my imperfections.

Put it another way: I just want to be happy, to drink some nice wine and have a laugh, to find someone to cuddle. What does it matter what other people say? Why should I give a toss what the world thinks of me if I seek this happiness through Internet dating? Joe doesn't care what the world thinks of him when he wears a *frock*.

I'm going to have a long think about this.

Welcome back to Loopylove

This serious cogitation actually continues for about an hour. Maybe more. Then I open up my laptop, click on to the sites – and to my surprise I find that my profile and photo are still there, ready and waiting. All I have to do is get out my credit card and pay the fees myself (an admittedly difficult moment) and I am able to 'Send and Receive'.

And so here I am again: up and running. I'm on.

For a week or two nothing dramatic happens, but this doesn't phase me; I'm an old hand now – then I chance upon a Korean girl called Denni. Thirty-two-year-old Denni hasn't got a photo online but she has an intriguing profile. As I'm in a giddily hopeful mood – presumably because of Joe's pep talk – I decide to email her anyway. Swiftly she emails back; the usual sly badinage is exchanged; eventually we arrange to meet. I am now quite excited; I'm not even put off by her final email, in which she 'warns' me that she looks like 'Lou Ferrigno, the Incredible Hulk'. I am presuming this is a joke.

Oops – not a joke. I am standing on Charlotte Street in the warm spring evening when I see, ambling down the road, a female figure that bears an uncanny resemblance to Lou Ferrigno, the Incredible Hulk. Could be a coincidence, except that this woman is also Korean.

For a moment I panic, and actually think about not turning up. Just bolting. She hasn't seen me yet. I could do it – just run away. But then I think about how wanky such behaviour would be. I've heard stories about other online daters doing this – standing in a shadowy London streetcorner, like a latterday Thomas Hardy, waiting to see what their prospective date looks like, before skedaddling if they are not impressed. And I think such behaviour sucks. It's rude and ungallant. Shame on you, Kazzagirl44.

So Denni and I do meet up, and actually she's very pretty when she smiles and we have a few beers and a Thai meal and yes, we have fun. She's a stage designer, and droll. She tells me how she lost her virginity to her dentist, after he did her fillings. Denni is, in truth, pretty damn sexy – which just goes to show something. However, the carnal biochemistry isn't quite right between us, so at the end of the evening we part on affable good terms, and she gives me a kiss and wishes me *bon chance* – only in Korean.

It's been a pleasant and agreeable encounter; and it's got me thinking. Of that blonde girl who stopped emailing me several months ago. Lenina. Lenina's was perhaps the funniest profile I have read these past months, certainly the most surreal. I loved her *Flash Gordon* thing. If I had so much fun with Denni, what fun could I have with Lenina?

Back in my flat, paging the sites, I find her profile again. Going to my messages section, I read through my exchanges with Lenina, and see how our emails dwindled. Perhaps this was due to a lack of chutzpah and assertiveness on my part; perhaps because she thought I was a dork. How do I find the answer? I'd truly like to know, I'd sincerely like to try and rekindle this; yet I don't know how.

Actually, maybe I do know how. I reckon I'm going to use a method I have long considered, but always dismissed. I'm going to Tell the Truth. I'm going to email Lenina and tell her the Real Facts about myself. The long and the short; the wild and the weird.

That's not to say I normally lie. I don't. I don't lie outright. What I do, normally, in an online email exchange – and when I'm chatting up a woman in a bar or a party, for that matter – is present a version of myself, a censored and selected take on my character which is hopefully attractive and . . .

OK – I fib. At least by omission. But this time it's going to be different.

And so I start. One evening at my laptop I compose a long email to Lenina, a long email which points out that I have a wildly varying income, that I can be moody and impulsive, that I have the odd run-in with trouble, that I am a nitwit sometimes but romantic other times, that I like sex a lot but that it's led me into disaster on occasion. That is to say: much of the stuff you've just read, in a necessarily shortened form. Although in the end I do leave out the gay encounter.

Is this email of mine stupid? Probably. But what have I got to lose? We haven't emailed each other in many weeks, and Lenina herself has not visited the website for a fortnight or more. By now she's probably met some respectable doctor with a steady income and no immoral history and they're happily living in a maisonette in Clapham. And if she hasn't, well maybe, just maybe, this missive will work. It may even be the best way of doing it, of finding the right woman.

After all, I want to meet a woman who is going to like me – for me, for what I really am. And what I really am is written here; what I am is what is in this email; what I am is this: a mildly screwed-up, generally optimistic, sometimes happy-go-lucky, sometimes horribly depressed, sometimes disastrously inept thirty-eight-year-old single man who owns just one thing: a chair. So I'm going to say all this; I'm bored of pretending.

Moreover, if I'm ever going to fall in love successfully, this is a good way of working out who not to fall in love with, who will never love me – because anyone who could possibly want to meet me after reading this ridiculously long, over-honest email, is the kind of woman who thinks like me, i.e. who understands why I would do something as stupidly candid as this. And therefore that woman is the sort of woman I could love, just as I may be the sort of man she could love.

Make sense? Yup, I think so. Confidently I click and

send the email. And, of course, immediately – practically before the click is complete – I deeply regret what I've just done. I particularly regret the sentence where I admit to a 'fondness for nude dentistry'. What the hell did I send it for? Who on this green, good earth would ever reply to an email as stupid as this? Shaking my head at my own imbecility and impetuousness, I close the laptop and retire to bed, feeling dire and hopeless.

The next morning, I have a message.

'*Lenina has read your email.*' Uh-huh. At least she's still online and 'active'. But I can picture her now in 'north London', scanning my idiotic confessions and grimacing. And resolving not to use a computer for a while. Tschhh . . .

A week goes by, and there's no reply. It's just as I thought. Nothing doing. What a jerk!

And then . . . then one mild Saturday morning I access my inbox. The good people at the website have passed on some information.

'*You have a new message from Lenina.*'

Right. OK. Here goes.

Heart actually pounding, I open up the message.

'*Well,*' it says, '*never had an email like that before. Not sure I want another one. But . . . let's say I'm intrigued. Do you want to meet? L x.*'

Lenina and I meet in the lairy London pub near my flat. It's the pub where I've met several people before. It's the pub once used by Hitler, Stalin, and Lenin, at various

285

times, and by Aleister Crowley the Satanist. It's the pub where I first met Bongowoman nearly a year ago; the beginning of this strange and enlivening adventure.

Lenina walks into the pub and she sits down. She says her real name is Claire. She does indeed look like a chipmunk in blusher. More to the point, she also looks very lovely: twenty-nine-years-old, blonde, smiling, nervous, curious, talkative, keen to get a little tipsy. I tell her about Hitler and Stalin and Lenin. She says maybe Stalin bodged Hitler's pint when they were here in the pub, hence the Second World War.

I ask her about her job. Advertising, she says. She makes a face and laughs. She asks me about my flat and I tell her. I ask about hers and when I do I brush her knee by mistake but she does not flinch; she looks at me straight. We drink a few more glasses and she asks why I sent such a nutty email and I try to explain but she says:

'No, I liked it. I get loads of messages from . . . you know . . .'

'At least I could spell?'

'At least you could spell.' She eats a handful of crisps and regards me, and says, 'My friends all thought you were . . . well, they thought that I should be careful – or not even meet you.' She glances at her mobile phone, placed on the bar. 'They'll probably call in a minute, to find out if you are actually a kidnapper.'

'And?'

She looks at me. Her eyes are a distant, sad, amused, Hebridean blue. Her blonde hair is as yellow as the sun on Raasay sands. She has just told me she is Scottish. She shrugs and smiles. I lean nearer. She doesn't lean back; she has slightly closed her eyes. We've only been together for three hours and I feel an odd sparkle in the air and . . .

Four seconds later we kiss.

Several times. Then we stop. Then we both laugh. Then I nearly fall off my chair and we drink and joke and time does an impression of a seventies car-chase, and finally, at the end of the evening, on the way to her taxi, she squeezes my hand and says: 'Call me?'

Watching her climb in the cab, watching her taxi disappear, I get a first, strange sense of something-different-about-this-ness. Like spotting a limousine without a numberplate. Like seeing a celebrity you can't quite name. An obscure and juvenile excitement.

How can you explain this? The first possible feeling of possible right-ness? I'm not sure; it's difficult to pin down. In a way it's like when you fly to a warm country from a cold northern winter. That moment you come out of the plane and you turn your smiling face to the sun, and you feel your shoulders relax; only then do you realise how stressed you have been by the cold back home, how braced your muscles, how tensed and stiff. I'm probably being way too optimistic, but these first hours in Claire's company have felt like that: like a milder climate. Like the glorious sun in winter. Like I could relax, at last . . .

A few days later we have a date in a pub in Islington. I am running late and I text Claire this news. She texts back this message: '*Don't worry, same here – progress being mildly hampered by stupid shoes.*'

I stop on the street and read this message. I halt on the road where I was pacing to the pub and I look at the text again and I actually smile and nearly laugh and when I get to the pub she is indeed wearing impractically feminine shoes but she is also wearing the loveliest dress I have seen this year. We spend the night laughing. It seems we have lots in common.

Again I feel the giddy optimism rising fast inside me. Because it seems there's something else too, something else between me and Claire – a sort of fittingness, a match. My masculinity/her femininity; her desire/my desire; they seem to knit together. They feel good. I feel good. The world feels good. In fact I have just got the impression that God is somewhere saying, 'I'm bored of screwing this guy over even if he is a knob, let's just give him a break.'

Which itself is unnerving. This really is too easy; Claire and I are getting on so well, we are having such a nice time. Will it now go wrong? Surely it will go wrong? Surely a really nice relationship with a really nice girl can't actually be . . . happening?

Worse still, as I sit here drinking and chuckling with Claire, I start to wonder: How do I know I am not deluding myself? Maybe I am so keen to meet someone I really am kidding myself. Maybe I could delude myself through the entire relationship and never actually realise that it was, in fact, not right all along! And what about the way I met her? Can I really meet someone through cyberspace? OK she's lovely and funny and all that (and I love the dress!), but what about the fact she was online anyway? Why was she online? And how can a relationship found this way be compared to real love, the love I had for Tamara, or Eleanor, or Briony, or . . .

I hear a voice in my ear. Joe's voice. Trevor's voice. My voice.

SHUT UP.

At the end of the evening Claire and I arrange to meet again. This next date we meet by the river, where she eats a big pizza and makes a good joke about refried beans. However, I can't remember the joke because I've just noticed that she is wearing her first low-cut top and I can see that she has a wonderful cleavage. This is terribly shallow of me – but then I notice that she has a marvellous bottom too. This is even more shallow of me but I am now verging on happiness. The happiness is confirmed when we embrace on Blackfriars Bridge, with the stars of London twinkling smoggily overhead and the streets and palaces and towers all gleaming down the river.

That night is the night. We make love, and it is notably unawkward, sensual, relaxed, delicate, and cherishable. In the morning I wake up smiling. Smiling before the coffee.

But as I make the coffee another spasm of anxiety kicks in. What's happening to me? Could that incredible thing really be mine? Could I be falling . . . in love? How do you know? Is this truly what proper falling in love is like? Because, you see, I've forgotten. Every time you fall in love it's different, even though it's just the same. As for me, I feel *totally* different. Taking the coffee back to Claire, I feel like a young huntsman out with his king. I feel like drinking less alcohol in future. I feel like giving money to orphanages. I feel nervous – but also absurdly hopeful and good-humoured.

Later that day I also have an odd and heady need to tell someone what I am experiencing. So I text my friends about Claire; then I regret it. What a twonk! How will I feel if this isn't 'it'? What kind of fool am I? Why am I getting so carried away? Entrusting my heart to someone I met online? Here is the key to me, stranger, you can use it. Jesus!

For a while, I embark on another rearguard action. The forces of defeatism, the army of negativism, the Napoleonic regiments of pessimism, cynicism, flippancy and nihilistic self-destructiveness aren't going to beat the retreat from the wintry Moscow of loneliness without the bitterest of struggles. I haven't spent a whole lifetime regularly screwing things up without at least trying to screw this up too; I didn't get where I am today – single, thirty-eight, in possession of a solitary chair – without having a serious capacity for turning impending triumph into tedious disaster.

Once again I go into mega-critical mode. How can this girl, this lovely girl, Claire, be the right one? Isn't she just a bit too easy? Do I actually like blue eyes? She isn't foreign either (apart from the Scottish thing), so what happened to *that* criterion? And what about her job? She said she worked in advertising. But wasn't I looking for an heiress? Maybe I should have gone for a banker? Moreover, I'm starting to think her hair could be a tiny bit curlier. Even though I don't actually like curly hair that much. And her eyebrows are a bit brown. I prefer black eyebrows, don't I? And, come to think of it, do I mind the way she eats? Well, no. But I could probably find something to complain about if I tried. Because that's precisely what I'm doing. I'm looking for things to complain about. Digging up pointless flaws, and some that don't actually exist. I'm actually trying to demolish the prospect of happiness, to attach bombs to the struts, just in case it – happiness – comes off.

Fortunately, throughout this fugue of doubt, this pointless dirge of anxiety, my hormones, instincts and genes are doing everything for me. However hard I try to crash the plane, I seem to be on the most marvellous autopilot. I'm simply falling in love with Claire – whatever I think or do or say. We just get on. No matter how much I try to mentally sabotage this relationship, I *can't* sabotage it.

And the reason for this, as I realise by the seventh date, is that it's a good relationship, a good and fine relationship. We laugh at the same things: each other, ourselves. We dance just as stupidly as each other. She's worse at tennis than me, and I'm terrible. We complement each other, in an odd but profound way: if she is Lake Windermere, I am the over-revved motorboat; if I am the baffled professor, she is the sudden equation. Claire and I, we are like two amateur astronomers, working through the night, who have just discovered our own supernova.

I am in love.

And then one day, six months into our relationship, I even tell her this. That I love her. Glory be – she tells me she loves me, too.

So what now? Now . . . now . . . now . . . oh God – now comes the marriage question, the commitment bit. We've been going out for eight months; it's seven and a half months since we both logged out of the dating sites (harder than it sounds – you can get addicted to those out-of-the-blue messages); it's two months since I told her I loved her and she told me she loved me too. We've been on holiday twice together. We've had sex on a train; she's made me her weird pasta sauce. She's even – incredibly – seen my lack of furniture, and not worried about it overly. I cannot conceive that I will ever again be this lucky, this well-matched, this happy, this content, this relaxed, this sighingly relieved, this sexually and emotionally stable, this surprisingly not-bored, and so the terrible question is looming. Can I? Could I ask her to marry me?

It's here that I hit a wall. I have two remaining questions, two hang-ups, that are still blocking me, are making me think all-too-hard about proposing.

The first is: Have I slept with enough women?

I know this is a tremendously trivial question. It is also a question many men – and women – ask themselves before they get married. Because it's an important point.

Have I done enough sex? Have I seen enough naked girls? Am I happy to retire here, at this point? Can I call it a day?

Well, can I? If I sit down and think, I reckon I have probably slept with about . . . sixty women. Maybe seventy, if you include prostitutes. Is that good or bad? Is it a lot or a little? Where does it put me in the league table of lubriciousness?

On reflection, I reckon this figure compares favourably (if that's the right word) with several friends of mine. I have one friend who has only slept with one woman: his wife. And I have quite a few friends who have slept with only a few women. But then again, I also have several friends who have slept with hundreds of women. Literally hundreds, or more.

So I'm about halfway up. Or a little higher (I said this was shallow). But what makes this picture more complicated is this paradox: the friend of mine who has only slept with one woman is one of the happiest people I know, and is devoted to his wife (though he does adopt a poignant expression when we are all swapping saucy anecdotes). Equally, a few of those super-promiscuous friends of mine are some of the unhappiest people I know – driven, compulsive, obsessive.

Like I said: a paradox. My wide-ish experience of male sexuality tells me that a compulsive pursuit of promiscuous sex does not necessarily lead to happiness; it may even be inimical to long-term happiness. It also tells me that monogamy might be the better route to contentment.

Yet I still want to sleep with lots of women, and envy men who do.

OK, I'm getting nowhere. So perhaps I should rephrase this question. I am, actually, pretty content with having slept with sixty women. Not least because I have started to forget just how many women I have slept with; this shows to me that above a certain number or notches (thirty, forty?) the number becomes meaningless, and the memories start to blur. And that is surely Nature's way of telling a man that he has had enough. At least for the foreseeable future. Therefore, what is really worrying me is perhaps a slightly different question. Whether I will – given my libidinous nature, my jealousy of sexually successful men – be able to stay faithful to Claire.

And here I reach my second hang-up. The big one. My background. My childhood. My parents. I'm talking about my father's nature – and what his nature means for my own nature.

How can I explain this conundrum? Here's a stab.

For most people, I suppose, their earliest impressions of their father are of a presence – a deeper voice in the room, an unshaven smile over the cot, that sense of a taller, darker figure hovering somewhere behind the mother. For me it was different. When I was growing up my father was an absence. This absence could take many forms. Some of my very first memories of my father are of him writing and working in the bedroom he then used as a study. Occasionally I would decide I wanted to talk to him about something – the ants in our garden, the relative size of sabre-tooth tigers – and I would tentatively open the door. However, although I knew that he was in there, I couldn't really see him.

Partly this was due to all the cigarettes he smoked – the room was so fuggy you couldn't properly see the walls – but he was also not there because he was so definitively unapproachable. My mother was constantly telling the family that my father's work – his writing – was so important he should never be disturbed when he was working; as he was always working, we could never disturb or approach him. He just wasn't available.

Other times my father's absence was more serious and dramatic, and related to my parents' marriage, or lack of. From an early age I became aware that my parents were fundamentally mismatched. Where my mother was resourceful, feisty, loving, pragmatic, my father was airy, aloof, intellectual, libidinous; he also had a fear of hugging and suchlike whereas my mother was warm and tactile. Indeed, just about the only things my mum and dad had in common were that they had both married too early, and that they both came from Cornwall (although we had all moved to Herefordshire).

Predictably, perhaps, my father began to stray. Almost as soon as he was married to my mum (as I later found out) he began to have flirtations, then flings, then full-blown affairs, often with female students at the college where he lectured. In turn this meant that his appearances in the house, in my and my sister's life, grew more sporadic and fleeting. My sister and I never knew what evenings

Dad would be in; or what mood would then obtain between him and Mum; or how much attention Dad would eventually give us.

Paradoxically, and unfairly, this made my sister and me all the more hungry for Dad's attention. Even though it was my mum who was breaking her back to keep the home together, to keep us all sane and healthy, it was often my dad that my sister and I really wanted to see, simply because we so seldom saw him. It also helped that my father, despite it all, maintained a kind of distant, opaque charisma, the charm of a largely silent man whose presumably important thoughts we could never quite fathom.

But his lack of knowledge about his kids was painful. I remember one time, when I was about fifteen, I was avidly watching the rugby on TV. My dad came in and stood there, silent, wreathed in smoke from his Peter Stuyvesant cigarettes. As per. Then he looked at me quizzically. 'I didn't know you were interested in rugby,' he said. I turned and gazed at him. 'Dad, I play rugby for my school. I've been playing for my school for the last four years.' I'd like to think he looked bashful and contrite at this point, but as I remember it he merely nodded in surprise, as if he'd been told an interesting fact about Roman mythology. And then he walked away. Back to his study.

The 'open' marriage that my parents were concocting led to other bizarre conversations. The fact that my dad obviously had girlfriends (and latterly, that my mother had boyfriends) led me to believe that this was the case with all marriages. So when I started – at the age of, I don't know, ten or so – visiting my friends and staying over, I used to innocently ask them: 'Where's your dad's mistress?' As if that was most normal thing in the world. But of course it was not the most normal thing in the world, at least not in provincial bourgeois England at the time. The way my friends reacted told me that my family was moderately odd.

Yet somehow, perhaps because of my mum's sterling efforts, perhaps because we were all intelligent and healthy despite our bizarre arrangements, the family stayed relatively cheerful. But in time the underlying contradictions started to drown us; in time the superficially cheerful tone of our family life departed.

One of the catalysts for change was my father's moving his mistress into the family house; this proved too much for my mother and she finally flipped. The mistress swiftly moved out, but the damage was done. During my mid-teens I began to hear my mother crying in her room, alone and privately – something she had never done before.

This had an inevitable result. It made me start to resent and distrust my dad. Where before I'd seen in my adolescent mind at least a few logical excuses for my dad's misdeeds – he'd married too young, etc. – now I began to see simple weakness and selfishness. No longer did I buy the old excuses (hitherto trotted out by my mother) that my dad had 'artistic temperament'. The iron was entering my seventeen-year-old soul and I just wanted out.

Thankfully, London, and London University, beckoned. So I did get out. But while I was partying in London – escaping from the weirdness of my home-life – my family was moving on. One morning, to my surprise and delight, my mother told my sister and I that she had met someone else, someone she finally wanted to marry (my parents were already divorced, although they had carried on living together – an even more bizarre arrangement). A few months later Mum was ready to pack her bags and move in with her new man.

The effect on my father was revolutionary. He proposed to my mother again. He guiltily renounced his old ways. He told Mum he couldn't bear to be without her. Bless.

But my mum, splendidly, kept her resolve. Then one day I came home from university to the newly Mumless house in Hereford, and I found my father silently watching a kid's programme on TV. At ten in the morning. Mum's departure had pitched him into a nervous breakdown.

Of course I was concerned for Dad. But inside me I also felt a bit righteous, even callous about his downfall: You asked for this, Dad. What did you expect? And as my dad slowly recovered, as he moved in with the long-term mistress – still confessing his guilt the while – this feeling of mild contempt remained. Furthermore, when I wasn't feeling self-righteous I was now sensing something else: that I could use my father's new-found guilt to my advantage. My father, when he hadn't been having break-downs or fathering half-siblings (it was around this time he told us we had a half-brother of twelve living in the same town), had all along been writing books. Now, his best book had found fame and fortune in the USA. As a result he was, for the first time, flush with cash; and I was flush with ideas of how to spend that cash. I also knew that my father now felt so guilty about the way he'd been to us, he was in no position to refuse my increasingly frequent requests. So I made the phone calls, and he wired the funds. Again and again. I knew he was buying off his guilt, amortising his regret. I didn't care.

This was a very unhealthy relationship: I resented and had no respect for my father (even as I loved him as a dad and respected his work). In turn he felt guilty, used and unloved, and he was still too detached to get emotionally close. It was, therefore, a distant and dissatisfying relationship. And we could have kept it like that unto death.

But as it happened – no. Fate intervened. In my early twenties I started heading into some deep shit. Doing drugs, breaking the law, trying to get myself killed in foreign adventures, the works. My nihilistic attitude to life – fuck it, I don't care, let's have a laugh even if we screw up – may have been a result of my upbringing. Alternatively it may have been because I am an idiot. Either way, when I was in the very deepest trouble – my late twenties, my early thirties – my dad reached out. He helped. And he didn't just help financially; he helped emotionally. He took me in when I was messed up. He tried to talk to me when I was out on the edge. He tried his damnedest to fix things. And even if – in the end – I had to fix myself, I was seriously grateful for his efforts. I looked at him, and us, and me, and my family, afresh.

And, so, somehow the breach between us – the contempt from me, the guilt from him – was healed over time. And now, me and my dad have a pretty reasonable relationship. Amiable, even affectionate, in a mild and English way, though sometimes it does come with Too Much Information. The other day my dad told me that he was worried that he wasn't having enough 'explosive sex' with his latest (and fourth) wife. My dad is seventy-one.

Actually that remark is very relevant to what I am trying, struggling, to say. The thing is, I may love my dad now, but I also know, because I have seen, because I have suffered from it, the dark side to his personality. The selfishness and the philandering. And I also know that I carry his very red blood in my veins. I am my father's son, after all – and I well know that I am also capable of extreme selfishness, that I am also hugely driven by my libido. I may not be quite as carnally obsessed as him (I hope) but I'm still at his end of the spectrum. So: if I get married, will I be able to stay faithful? Will I treat Claire the way my father treated my mother? God, I hope not. I don't want to hear Claire crying privately, I don't want to be the cause of her tears.

And there's another thing: fatherhood. Over recent years I have come to see, through the prism of my father's travails, how daunting and difficult fatherhood must be. Dad, I now realise, wasn't a totally bad father; more a fairly decent man who was a pretty bad father at certain times. So can I be sure that I will do any better, as I begin to contemplate the role of fatherhood myself? Maybe I'll be worse? I'll have the same conflicts, after all.

It's a momentous dilemma. And I'm not handling it very well. With these thoughts tumble-drying in my head, I approach the idea of asking Claire to marry me, and I begin to think about baling out. I'm now thinking I shan't ask her. I can't. I just . . . *can't*.

And then one day I speak on the phone with an ex-girlfriend. Ex-girlfriends are very good people to speak to on troubling and confusing personal matters – they know you, they understand you, they've already dumped you. They can cut through the crap.

This particular ex-girlfriend listens to my self-doubts, my neuroticising, and then she sighs impatiently and says, 'Sean, you are not your father. Genes aren't everything. You may be different. Who knows. You can learn. You have learned already.'

This hits home. She is right, of course. Just because I had a philandering dad, that does not mean I have to be the same. Nor does it give me some kind of moral cop-out. I am a sentient being; I am capable of making choices for myself; blaming the parents is just too easy. How bad must Hitler's mum have been?

Yet I am still unsure. Residual anxiety, maybe. Can I ask Claire to take me on, with all this rubbish in the background? But then, crucially, my ex adds, 'By the way, I am in love too, and love is a good thing. Give it a chance. Relax!' And . . . somehow this snaps me. This does it. This spurs me on. Maybe I would have spurred myself on anyway, but this final advice comes at just the right time. I am newly resolved. I'm going to do it. It's time to lay the bet. To take a chance on love. To be as bold in my love life as I have been elsewhere – in jumping out of planes, or heading into war zones, or doing all the other stupid impulsive stuff. I'm going to ask Claire, I'm going to fight off my doubts . . .

Oh God.

And so here I am again. This is where you came in.

I'm sitting on the roof terrace of my flat, on this warm summer evening, and eventually I get the words right: I turn to Claire and I say:

'Will you marry me?'

Your dating dilemmas: solved!

I want to tell the entire history of the Internet. It began with the Victorian mathematician Charles Babbage, who was born in Devonshire in . . .

No. Only joking.

She said:

Yes.
Yes!
yes
YES

which is nice.

So that's that then?

Well, yep – or very nearly. As I write, Claire and I are still together. In fact she is here in the room right now. Last night we went to a knees-up in town, not far from my flat; we both drank a little and danced like loons. Now, I'm sitting at my desk typing quietly into my laptop, nursing a hangover, and she is over there in bed. Snoring. Snoring quite loudly. In a few moments I may actually go over to the bed and biff her with a rolled-up magazine to make her shut up.

But despite the snoring, and the hangover, I have to confess: I am happy. Happy as a llama with a new spittoon. I'm happy because it's still there; the feeling, still there after quite a long time. It's weird. It's rather nice. It's good and slightly frightening. I've never felt quite like this before.

Anchored, harboured, tranquil, happy. I'm glad I made the fateful step; it wasn't half so bad as I expected. It was great.

And so we come to the ultimate question. What do I think about love and the Internet after all this? I think you know what I think. I think it's a wonderful thing. The Internet is a revolution, a whole new way for people to interact, an astonishing advance in socialisation. It's more important than the phone, maybe as important as print or writing. Like those other inventions, it can and will be used for evil, for bad things; but the potential it has to add to human happiness is virtually limitless, too. And I'm not necessarily talking about www.no-panties.com

But what about online-dating in particular? Well – how could I not be in favour? Online-dating helped me fall in love; I'm sure it can do the same for you, for your brother, for anyone. And that is, surely, a good thing. We all want to fall in love, we all need to fall in love, we are all expressly designed to fall in love: the medium is almost irrelevant, as long as it works. Put it another way: when you are looking for love, you are shooting for the moon. Who cares if you get there in a gondola, or in a minicab?

Just get there.

And finally, a few weeks later, comes The Wedding.

No, not ours, not yet (we're now thinking of Skye, where the waves pound the cliffs by a lonely Celtic church. And where the catering is cheap). This wedding is my ex-girlfriend's – the girl who gave me that final advice to chill, to stop fretting, to propose. The man she told me she was in love with has, in the interim, popped the Q (is there something in the air?), and consequently they've organised a small, impromptu wedding down in deepest Sussex.

Claire's away for the day on business, so I go on my own. It's a wistfully pretty summer morning. The train from London rattles through the suburbs, then makes a break for the real countryside. Half asleep, I stare out of the window, at the rolling scenery. There's a man setting up a swing in his garden, there's a young girl on a pony paused at a farm-yard gate; there are fields, and cows, and sunlit downs.

Almost too soon, we are there. One of those tiny Sussex stations, improbably caged in by beech trees. It's so anciently scenic, I half expect to see a waistcoated porter come out and blow a silver whistle, before guiding me to a pony-and-trap. Instead I exit the station and climb into a hot taxi, and make it to the church just in time, in a minus-cule village five miles down the road.

The church, if anything, is even prettier than the station. Flint, chalk, sun-shadowed graves. My ex-girlfriend's mum is standing in the gravelled drive, wearing an anxious blue hat. She looks at me curiously, then smiles, remembering who I am, and no doubt relieved to think things could have been worse – I could have been her new son-in-law. With that she grabs my suited arm and says:

'Congratulations! I hear you're next!'

I do a modest smile. She nods towards the porch, and dramatically crosses her fingers. 'Here's hoping!' Then we step into the cooler church. It's a sea of suits and more hats. And crying babies. And relatives fanning themselves with order-of-service pamphlets. At the altar, the groom is tapping his thigh, in a nervous way.

And then, as I squeeze myself into a pew, the atmosphere imperceptibly changes. As if on a signal, people start craning their stiff-collared necks at the blaze of light that is the door behind us – and when I turn and look I see my ex-girlfriend, the bride-to-be, framed by the oblong of light. She looks stunning.

Why do all women look gorgeous at this point? Is it the white dress? If it is just the white dress, all girls in white dresses would look fab, and a week on the Costa del Sol on holiday shows that isn't true. No, I think it's because brides embody hope, the hope against hope, the hope of the world. When we smile at a blushing young bride we are smiling at our own deepest dreams.

That said, my ex does have fantastic breasts.

Visibly nervous, the bride approaches the flowery altar. The groom shares a sly, relieved and exhaling smile with her. And then, as the organ fades, the service kicks in.

Ah yes. The service. I'd forgotten how beautiful the marriage service is, the old one, from the *Book of Common Prayer*.

'*Dearly Beloved, we are gathered together here in the sight of God, and in the face of this congregation, to join together this Man and this Woman in holy Matrimony; which is an honourable estate, instituted of God in the time of man's innocency . . .*'

The flowers are yellow and blue in the streaming light. I stare dreamily at the stained-glass windows.

'*Wilt thou have this Woman to thy wedded Wife, to live together after God's ordinance in the holy estate of Matrimony? Wilt you love her, comfort her, honour and keep her in sickness and in health; and, forsaking all others, keep thee only unto her, so long as ye both shall live?*'

The groom is swallowing his nerves, as he replies. I wonder where he got his tie. A baby is softly crying behind me.

'*Wilt thou have this Man to thy wedded Husband, to live together after God's ordinance in the holy estate of Matrimony? Wilt thou obey him, and serve him, love, honour, and keep him in sickness and in health; and, forsaking all others, keep thee only unto him, so long as ye both shall live?*'

I can imagine my ex-girlfriend wryly giggling, as she chose this service. Someone less likely to 'obey' I can hardly imagine. But I know she likes the old stuff, the old words.

'*Thereto I plight thee my troth . . .*'

With that, we all stand up and lustily sing a hymn or two. Checking the pamphlet, I see that the hymn is from the 'Olney hymn book'. It's certainly moving, very moving; in fact, as I hold the book to my face the words become indescribably beautiful.

> Ye fearful saints, fresh courage take,
> The clouds ye so much dread
> Are big with mercy and shall break
> In blessing on your head . . .

Because that *is* what it suddenly feels like, here, in this church, in deepest England: like the clouds of my life have broken to shed their rain, the rain of mercy, of unexpected love.

Or maybe it's just the wedding; weddings always get to me.

But now we are near the end. The couple are doing the signing. We have all stooped to say some prayers. Then the organ surges in once more, and the choir sings, and slowly the bride departs down the aisle, escorted proudly by her new husband. And then on an unspoken signal everyone hurries from the church, women dabbing their eyes, men fingering their collars, everyone stepping out into the blazing summer light, to smoke hasty cigarettes or laugh at each other's hats.

The reception, it turns out, is agreeably drunken. So drunken, several happy young couples end up having sex in the bushes around the hotel. But I am alone – and I also have to get back to London, as Claire is returning.

Consequently, at about five p.m., I bid my goodbyes to the happy crowd, kiss my ex on the cheek, and cab it to the station again. And train it back to London. But when I get to my flat, I realise I've got an hour or two; I'm early. So I decide to amble towards the park, through the quiet Saturday streets of Fitzrovia.

As I go I start thinking about my own past. This could be because I have just seen my ex-girlfriend get married; equally it could be my nostalgic route through these sweet and sleepy streets. A lot of my history is bound up in this

neighbourhood; much of my life is threaded into the histor-
ical tapestry of this little corner of London. It's an
insignificant thread. But it's mine.

Here, for instance, is the university hall of residence where
I first had sex. With Briony. That room up there. A pretty
small room as I recall. The students have gone for the
summer so the building is now empty, yet it echoes with
laughter, our laughter, the girlish ghosts of happiness.

And here is where I first met Eleanor. A squat where we
lived amongst the pizza boxes, stealing electricity from the
council. The venerable Georgian house has been revamped,
it's now a lot posher, and smarter, and there are almost
certainly no kids inside playing guitars and smoking weed
and laughing uproariously until six in the morning.

And here is where I slept with the doctor. Teresa. I
remember making love with her when she was still in her
white coat; there was something sexy about that. But what
about the child we nearly had, but never had? That's less
sexy; it makes me feel piercingly sad. But perhaps it was
never meant to be; if I had taken that turning off the
motorway I would never have met Claire. And therefore I
wouldn't perhaps be happy the way I am now, happy, for
the very first time in my life, in a contented way, an anchored
way.

And now at last I am in the park. Regent's Park, heading
for Queen Mary's Garden. The flat green meadows are full
of people playing softball, young women pushing prams,
old people half asleep – with the creamy-whiteness of the
Nash Terraces looking perfect beyond them. It really is a

beautiful evening. One of those summer evenings when you feel like hitting atheists with a baguette.

Halfway across the park, I am struck with still another memory. Right here, by this bridge, Briony and I once buried a bottle. It was just after we had sex in the park, twenty years ago. A summer day like this. Briony and I were so in love, we decided we had to commemorate the moment: so we wrote a note, plighting our troth, and we put it in a bottle, and we buried it. Just here. And we did this because we thought our love would never die.

Standing here, looking at the grass, I could get melancholy about this memory. I could start to wonder what that means; whether it means all love is doomed, and if it does, why we bother. Not good thoughts when you are about to get married . . .

But I don't. Instead of spiralling into anxiety or sadness, I feel a surge of peace and optimism. Rather than dwelling on the impossibility of true love, I am thinking of that line from the Larkin poem: *What will survive of us is love.* I think that's maybe true. Whatever we do, however we fail, if we have loved then we have succeeded, even triumphed. Because that's what we are here for; that's what makes the world so hard to leave; love is what ennobles life. And besides, everyone I have ever loved is in my heart and my soul. And therefore everyone I have ever loved is here. In the park, this evening.

There's Trevor, for instance, by the ice-cream stall, waving to me. Perhaps he's in need of a beer. There's Briony, in her summer dress, pouting obscurely at a heron in the trees.

And coming around the corner is Min, the Thai hooker. She's pushing a pram – the boy that could have been mine. She seems happy. And now I turn and look left, and I see a blanket, spread beside the glittering lake. Tamara and Amelie are there, sharing some wine. Next to them, Joe is sorting out the sandwiches – he's in a lovely dress. Sally Long, my childhood sweetheart, is giggling away, as she chats across the blanket with Adrien Brody. And there behind a tree I can see Thomas Hardy. He's trying to stare up Amelie's skirt.

And beyond them – on the lake itself – I can just glimpse two figures, in a boat. They are young and they are laughing. It is, of course, my mother and father. They've hired a boat, and they've got a picnic basket. My dad can't row very well. As I watch, he nearly falls in the lake, making my mum laugh; finally the boat disappears, behind the golden willow trees.

And now I'm disappearing, too; now I'm gone. I'm heading back to the flat to meet Claire. I'm looking forward to seeing her; I'm also wondering, as I go, if Claire and I will be blessed with children. I hope we are; I'd like us to have a daughter, and then a son. Because, if we have a son, and he asks me about life, I know what I'll tell him.

I will tell him the truth: that it is a scary and brilliant world. A world full of sad and beautiful things. And then at the end, I'll say: Son, be still, be content, be happy. Because millions of women are waiting to meet you.

A NOTE ON THE AUTHOR

Sean Thomas was born in Devon in 1963. He writes
for the *Sunday Telegraph*, the *Guardian*, and the *Daily
Mail* and has published three novels.